THE SPAN OF MAINSTREAM
AND SCIENCE FICTION

THE SPAN OF MAINSTREAM AND SCIENCE FICTION

A Critical Study of a New Literary Genre

by Peter Brigg

McFarland & Company, Inc., Publishers
Jefferson, North Carolina, and London

Library of Congress Cataloguing-in-Publication Data

Brigg, Peter, 1942–
   The span of mainstream and science fiction : a critical study of a new literary genre / by Peter Brigg.
       p.   cm.
   Includes bibliographical references and index.

   ISBN 0-7864-1304-2 (softcover : 50# alkaline paper)

   1. English ficton—20th century—History and criticism.   2. Literature and science—Great Britain—History—20th century.   3. Literature and science—United States—History—20th century.   4. American fiction—20th century—History and criticism.   5. Lessing, Doris May, 1919-   —Knowledge—Science.   6. Science fiction—History and criticism.   7. Pynchon, Thomas—Knowledge—Science.   8. Science in literature.   I. Title.
   PR888.S34 B75   2002
   823'.08762090914—dc21   2002014130

British Library cataloguing data are available

©2002 Peter Brigg. All rights reserved

No part of this book may be reproduced or transmitted in any form or by any means, electronic or mechanical, including photocopying or recording, or by any information storage and retrieval system, without permission in writing from the publisher.

Cover art ©2002 Digital Vision

Manufactured in the United States of America

McFarland & Company, Inc., Publishers
   Box 611, Jefferson, North Carolina 28640
      www.mcfarlandpub.com

This book is for Andrea, Emma, Ian, and Doug,
who mark the center of the circle of my life,
and for Winston,
always the circumference of that circle.

Table of Contents

Preface   1

CHAPTER 1. Introduction to Span Fiction   5
CHAPTER 2. Doris Lessing: Experiments in Alternate Reality   25
CHAPTER 3. Thomas Pynchon: Science in Life   57
CHAPTER 4. A Bridge Takes Shape: Other Writers   99
CHAPTER 5. Border Skirmishes: Span and Science Fiction   172
CHAPTER 6. The New Alignment   188

Notes   193
Bibliography   199
Index   205

Preface

This book emerged from my own split of interests between contemporary fiction and science fiction, and from dissatisfaction running through the world of criticism about the confused edges between the two areas. It was meant to be a genre study, and Chapter 1 sets out my proposition for a new way of considering the field.

The body of the book is the examination of a wide range of writers and their relations with our "scientized" reality, as well as with science fiction. This was intended to illustrate the main proposal but seems to comprise a sort of second book within a book, because of the richness and variety of writers' approaches in an era so permeated with science. Some readers may prefer the rich tapestry of the imagination I hope to have illustrated in chapters 2 to 5.

Books are written in the midst of lives, and I want gratefully to acknowledge the support and assistance from those around me. During an exchange year in Christchurch, New Zealand, in 1989 my colleagues there, particularly Cassandra Fusco, Howard McNaughton, and my dear friend David Gunby, helped me to enjoy the southern paradise and get this book underway. In my own university, my colleagues in the School of Literatures and Performance Studies in English (formerly the English Department) have been a considerable support, particularly two department chairs, G. Douglas Killam and Constance Rooke, both of whom personally ground through the drafts and offered both suggestions and encouragement. Bruce Sterling sent me his "Slipstream" article when it seemed to have disappeared from the face of this Earth. The staffs of libraries at the Universities of Canterbury and Guelph brought forth what was needed, basted with helpful smiles. My colleagues in the Science Fiction Research Association engaged my mind in a myriad of ways.

Like all teachers I need to thank my students for sprinkling vinegar on the oversweet confections of my imagination. My men's group helped keep me sane; and Emma, daughter of daughters, took my mind off book troubles by growing up while I wrote. And finally there is my Andrea: partner, encourager, sustainer. Some debts can only ever be partially paid.

—Christchurch-Guelph-Toronto
1989–2001

If the labors of men and science should ever create any material revolution, direct or indirect, in our condition, and in the impressions which we habitually receive, the poet will sleep then no more than at present; he will be ready to follow the steps of the Man of science, not only in those general indirect effects, but he will be at his side, carrying sensation into the midst of the objects of the science itself. The remotest discoveries of the chemist, the botanist, or mineralogist will be as proper objects of the poet's art as any upon which it can be employed, if the time should ever come when these things shall be familiar to us, and the relations under which they are contemplated by the followers of these respective sciences shall be manifestly and palpably material to us as enjoying and suffering beings. If the time should ever come when what is now called science, thus familiarized to men, shall be ready to put on, as it were, a form of flesh and blood, the poet will lend his divine spirit to aid the transfiguration, and will welcome the being thus produced as a dear and genuine inmate of the household of man.

—William Wordsworth,
Preface to the Lyrical Ballads, 1800

CHAPTER 1

Introduction to Span Fiction

The change about which William Wordsworth speculated nearly two hundred years ago has come to pass. Science and its muscular sibling, technology, have transformed the world and the way human beings see it and behave in it. This change first spawned an entire branch of "poetry" (if one sees it, in the classical sense, as literature *in toto*) in the coming of science fiction and, in the later years of the twentieth century, has led to a growing recognition of Wordsworth's essential assertion that the mainstream of literature must embrace the precepts and influence of science and engender a vision of man that takes account of our science-laden times in both style and subject matter. Mainstream fiction writers have begun to make more and more frequent ventures towards the field formerly considered that of the science fictionist.

"Mainstream," "traditional," or "mundane"[1] fiction has been essentially an exclusionary term used by the science fiction community to describe work it sees as not being science fiction. It includes the movement in the eighteenth and nineteenth and early twentieth centuries to realism and naturalism (a movement which actually has never dissipated if one considers fiction in general rather than "high literature"), the romantic novelists such as Scott and Hawthorne, the swing to high modernist formalism in the experiments of writers as disparate as Woolf, Golding, Calvino, and Marquez, and genres such as romances, detective fiction, and the western. A number of mainstream writers have now turned to explore strange horizons and find opportunities to express parts of their vision that realms new to them (but the stock-in-trade of the science fiction writer) will permit.

These writers greatly extend the range of the "poets" prophesied by Wordsworth. One parent to this trend in the twentieth century was William F. Burroughs. Doris Lessing, Thomas Pynchon, John Fowles, Margaret Atwood, Anthony Burgess, Julian Barnes, Angela Carter, Paul Theroux, Kingsley Amis, P.D. James, Don DeLillo, and Lawrence Durrell are among those making such experiments.

Simultaneously an equally important movement has begun from the "other side." Some recent science fiction is reaching towards the mainstream of literature with steadily increasing subtlety of style, an active flirtation with postmodernist techniques, a growing attention to the complexities of character and situation, and an increasing complexity of attitude to both science and the form of traditional science fiction. This may be viewed as a loss or surrender by insular writers and theorists working in science fiction; it may be viewed as a wonderful expansion of the range of the genre; or it may, as I intend to demonstrate, help create a new genre. One father to the writers stretching the genre was Philip K. Dick, and the growing range of innovators includes Ursula K. LeGuin, J.G. Ballard, Christopher Priest, George Alex Effinger, Stanislaw Lem, and Ian Watson.

I want to investigate this confluence primarily from the direction of the mainstream authors, touching briefly in chapter 5 on the science fiction writing that is moving into this arena. I intend to propose the criteria applicable to separating traditional science fiction and this new genre, although space limitations will prevent extensive explorations. I shall keep in mind a series of questions intended to illuminate both the works and the theoretical questions raised by the movement of overlap and integration taking place. A study of this sort, centering on various works and authors, will not produce a coherent and final theoretical position, but will attempt to demonstrate the range and variety of the interplay of science and science fiction on writers of the mainstream and to map the paradigm of an emerging genre between them.

Genre Study

In order to propose a new genre category, it is important to consider the functions of genre in literary study and interpretation. In *Interpretation and Genre: The Role of Generic Perception in the Study of Narrative Texts* (1986), Thomas Kent offers an acute consideration of the problem. He speaks of a literary hermeneutic circle (9), a pattern of knowing in which the act of reading is dependent upon extra-text knowledge of genre and that extra-text is in turn modified by each new text read in the genre. Extra-text is all of the semiotic pattern for a text of a particular genre. What Tzvetan Todorov describes as the "literariness" (26) of a text is dependent upon the degree to which readers recognize a literary genre format as opposed to, say, journalism or political science. Kent quotes Derrida's maxim, "There is no genreless text" (150), as part of his much more extensive defense of the imperative need readers have to place any text with which they are confronted in a genre, in order to begin to perform the act of interpretation, to make the text "make sense" for them.

There are two approaches to extra-text: *synchronic* and *diachronic* (27); and Kent points to the need for both to be considered in the study of genre. The synchronic approach is an attempt to isolate the ideal signs for reading a particular genre, an archetypal vision of genre. The diachronic approach recognizes that the identities of genres are affected by cultural history and by the aspect of the hermeneutic circle, which dictates that each additional text created in a genre changes forever the overall pattern of signs that delineates the genre. In fact, the acts of transgression of the demands of genre make the zone where a great deal of the meaning of literary texts is generated. The transgressions, in turn, can be recognized only because the reader brings to the text an existing extra-text vision of the genre to be transgressed.

Genre study, then, is an act performed by every reader who ever picks up a text, for only by placing the text in the reader's personal extra-text—the sum of their reading in the genre and their cultural moment's understanding of it—can the reader interpret the text. Classification is only the first step in genre study. The act of understanding a text begins there, but is played out as readers implant the text in their extra-text, are assisted in grasping the text through their existing knowledge of the conventions of its genre(s), consider the transgressions against that extra-text as vital signposts in the meaning of the text, and come away from the reading with a forever slightly modified extra-text knowledge of the genre.

Genre "study" is also an act performed by every writer, for writers come to the page with their experience of other writing and the characteristics of existing genres, including their expected audiences, as a priori facts of creation. Since Chaucer (or the Greek tragedians, if one reaches backwards to antecedent cultures) first modeled the ironic overarching Preface, narrative writers of poetry, prose, and drama have been aware of the potentials of framing prefaces as tools to manipulate readers. Once a body of texts have defined a genre, the extra-text becomes vital to the writer, framing the formal conventions and presenting the possibilities of the fruitful act of transgression.

Background

The background to this investigation lies in the tangled jungles of genre study and is complicated by the important but indefinite term "postmodernism." A good deal has been written about postmodernism and science fiction,[2] but it is generally postmodern analysis of science fiction or the argument that postmodernism collapses genre boundaries.[3] Roger Luckhurst has examined various arguments that boundaries collapse and concludes that:

> In reviewing these cases where SF is explicitly invoked in the "effacement" of the border between the high and the low, however, I want to analyze how this border tends to be reinstated at crucial points in the argument.[4]

Cyberpunk science fiction has been the particular target of postmodern analysis. Postmodernism is not a genre in itself, but an historical term delineating important trends in the current era. It has been linked to late industrial capitalism (Frederic Jameson); to the radical modifications in the human situation of the late twentieth century brought about chiefly by nuclear angst; to substantial media developments including television and the computer; and to the influences of the theorists of literature, language, and culture who have pioneered Semiotics, Structuralism, Poststructuralism, and Deconstruction. Like Neo-Classicism, Romanticism, and Modernism, Postmodernism will, at some time in the reasonably near future, be a term describing a past literary and cultural era. Its attitude to genre will likewise be a past attitude, even though it may be one that offers a further evolutionary step in the concepts of genre.

My thesis has no argument with postmodernist analysis of texts or their identification as postmodern texts.[5] I do, however, side with Thomas Kent (who draws his support from E.D. Hirsch, Hans Robert Jauss, Wolfgang Iser, and Jacques Derrida[6]) and Frederic Jameson ("We need the specification of the individual 'genres' today more than ever, not in order to drop specimens into the box bearing those labels, but rather to map our coordinates on the basis of those fixed stars and to triangulate this specific given textual movement"[7]) in insisting that genres are necessary in the understanding of texts, even if that understanding may be complicated in postmodern interpretation by multigeneric texts and a predominance of parody, pastiche, irony, and satire. Moreover, the texts to be considered in this book range chronologically from the 1960s to the present, and not all of them take a postmodern approach.

There has been no absence of confusion over the definition of science fiction as a genre proper, and the materials applicable to the genre I am proposing to define have been an important part of such struggles. In the 1960s Judith Merril popularized "speculative fiction," a term originally coined by Robert Heinlein.[8] It was intended to be a recognition of the increasing use of the "soft" sciences such as psychology, anthropology, and sociology in science fiction; and as a recognition of the stylistic innovations of the New Wave, science fiction initially centered around the British magazine *New Worlds*, under the editorship of Ted Carnell and, later, Michael Moorcock.

Speculative fiction has found favor with such writers as Margaret Atwood who do not wish to take out membership in what they see as the old-fashioned science fiction community.[9] As a redefinition of science fiction, the term has gained credence in scholarly circles and embraces the wider range of activity that it was designed for. But it has clearly not accounted for a great deal of the work by mainstream writers, work that ventures into the uses of science fiction tropes, conventions, or methodology. It is, finally, an expansive term for a genre (science fiction) that was in transition at an historical moment.

In *Structural Fabulation* (1975), Robert Scholes proposed to redefine and broaden science fiction in a different fashion. He has a different use for the term "speculative fiction" than Merrill, seeing it as a description of antecedents:

> Considered generically, structural fabulation is simply a new mutation in the tradition of speculative fiction. It is the tradition of More, Bacon, and Swift, as modified by new input from the physical and human sciences. [39]

Scholes' explanation of the two-word term he is proposing has a firm clarity of purpose:

> Fabulation, then, is fiction that offers us a world clearly and radically discontinuous from the one we know, yet returns to confront that known world in some cognitive way. [29]

He attaches "structural" to "fabulation" not strictly based on his own work on literary structuralism, but on what he perceives to be the much larger general shift in human understanding:

> In works of structural fabulation the tradition of speculative fiction is modified by an awareness of the nature of the universe as

a system of systems, a structure of structures, and the insights of the past century of science are accepted as fictional points of departure. [41]

There is clearly a congruence of reasoning between Scholes' position and the one prophesied by Wordsworth in the epigraph to this chapter. Scholes also contends that Structural Fabulation will occupy an important part of the fiction landscape because it will offer the fixed forms, excitements and satisfactions of narrative[10] and closure that are no longer consistently offered by "serious" literature. To some extent this confuses the definitional issue, for Scholes opts for the conservative (if rewarding) in form, while he is expanding the range of fiction that SF (he points out that the initials of science fiction and speculative fabulation are deliberately congruent) might touch upon in terms of subject.

Scholes' description was extremely important as a legitimizer of science fiction/speculative fiction in its moment, but is finally flawed because its weight is on the side of a recognition of science fiction by a new name. Scholes' main exempla are Olaf Stapledon, Frank Herbert, Theodore Sturgeon, Daniel Keyes, and Ursula K. LeGuin. This selection confirms that his Structural Fabulation is another name, albeit one that informs and explicates, for the category previously known as science fiction. It does not effectively reach out to most of the texts that are my concern in this monograph, particularly since the conservative traditions of the serious treatment of science within the conventional popular fiction form are ill-equipped to handle irony, parody, satire, pastiche, and such contemporary formal acts as lack of closure or multiple closures.

Another attempt to cover the work of mainstream writers who venture into science fiction led to the coining of the term "Crossover" fiction. It is my contention that Crossover fiction is seriously misleading because it implies that mainstream writers are simply writing science fiction, whereas they are, in fact, usually working in the middle ground between mainstream and science fiction—which ground is to be the territory of this book.

In her 1980 *Poetics Today* article treating Samuel R. Delany, "The Convergence of Postmodern Innovative Fiction and Science Fiction," Teresa L. Ebert considers the relationship of genres in a fashion that exposes the clear space that I intend to fill with a genre name and its accompanying extra-text. Ebert's graphic representation is a useful summation:

1. Span Fiction

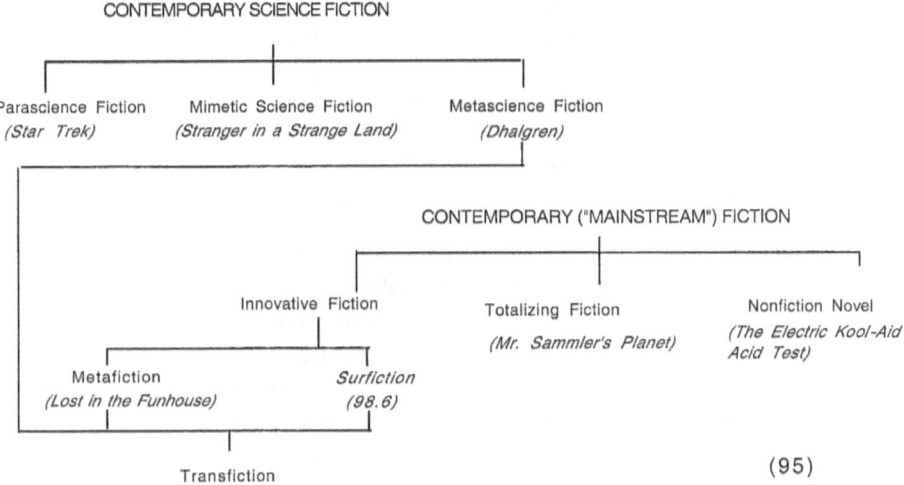

Ebert attributes the term "transfiction" to Mas'ud Zavarzadeh[11] and says of it: "Transfiction is a product of the post-novel synthesis: it is the narrative of the consciousness that has moved beyond the 'two cultures.'" (95)

She goes on to suggest that "metascience fiction" is a site distinguished by the way in which science and technology are backgrounded (rather than foregrounded as in "mimetic" science fiction). In transfiction, she argues, scientific and technological innovation are foregrounded within narratives distinguished by narrative and verbal experiment.

In Zavarzadeh's and Eberts' terms, the texts that this book will consider could be surfiction, transfiction, and possibly metascience fiction. Interestingly, although it was probably only a graphic necessity for Ebert, there is a long running line between transfiction and metascience fiction. It is the metaphorical "territory" of this line that offers the middle ground I wish to investigate, and while metascience fiction, redefined, might have been a suitable term for it (as might speculative fiction, redefined), the term has not caught on in seventeen years, and redefinitions of existing terms are, unfortunately, terminological disasters. From Ebert's diagram, however, can be seen the real genre challenges. A definition needs to claim and define that central space and contend at its edges for the texts which sit on the cusps of genres and whose bifurcated nature produces rich transgressions of textual variety.

A clear attempt to name this middle ground is Bruce Sterling's 1989 article "Slipstream."[12] In this short article, partly devoted to damning the bankruptcy of contemporary science fiction, Sterling attempts to create a genre name to cover texts near science fiction but not of it.

> These are books which SF readers recommend to friends: "This isn't SF, but it sure ain't mainstream, and I think you might like it, okay?" It's every man his own marketer, when it comes to slipstream. [78]

Sterling asserts that Slipstream, a term he coined with his friend Richard Dorsett, "is a parody of 'mainstream,' and nobody calls mainstream 'mainstream' except for us skiffy trolls [science fiction writers and readers]" (78). In trying to clarify the term, he asserts that the texts to which he is referring tend to tear at the structure of everyday life by narrative experiments such as pastiche and to play with the kind of clear respect for science that has identified science fiction.

Some of the promise of this genre identification is dissipated by the extensive list of suggested titles that Sterling provides. He himself admits, "Many of the books that *are* present probably don't belong there" (80). Moreover, such choices as *The Tin Drum*, *Perfume*, *Hawksmoor*, *Illywacker*, and *Water Music* are pretty clearly stretching any kind of definitional grouping for these texts. But one thing Sterling asserts, with which I am wholly in agreement, is that the attempt to name a new genre should not be confused with another attempt (like Merrill's speculative fiction) to stretch science fiction to include these new forms of work.

Sterling's term had some promise but he himself speculated that future critics would redefine it and perhaps rename it (78, 80). John Clute has pretty well necessitated the renaming when, in his entry in *The Encyclopedia of Science Fiction* (1993), he mines the dictionary meanings of the words in the term, something that Sterling apparently did not have in mind.

> The image is either nautical or aeronautical: a ship or an airplane (either of which stands for genre SF) can create a slipstream which may be strong enough to give non-paying passengers (Paul THEROUX, say) a ride. As a description of commercial piggybacking, the term seems apt; however, when used to designate the whole range of non-genre SF here called FABULATION, the term—which implies a relationship of dependency—can seem derogatory. [1116–1117]

The Encyclopedia of Science Fiction makes its own distinctive attempt to establish genre definitions and boundaries. It uses the term "genre

SF" to identify clearly fiction that follows the conventions of form and subject matter of golden-age science fiction and is readily identified as science fiction (483–484). This is a surprisingly elegant definition that neatly accords with Kent's description of the extra-text. The *Encyclopedia* uses Fabulation to cover the middle ground with which this book is concerned, but there are problems with its redefinition of Robert Scholes' term:

> We can now say what we mean in this encyclopedia by a "fabulation": *a fabulation is any story which challenges the two main assumptions of genre SF: that the world can be seen; and that it can be told.* We have chosen to use the term "fabulation" because it seems to us the best blanket description of the techniques employed by those writers who use SF devices to underline that double challenge, and whose work is thus at heart profoundly antipathetic to genre SF. [400]

The italicized core definition opens the door to most modern fiction, metafiction, and most postmodern fiction. Had "using SF devices" been worked into the core, it might have come closer to a "middle genre" definition. Even then it would not have embraced the category of texts that do show respect for and acceptance of the scientific method and scientific descriptions of reality, and do engage in exploring the effects of this knowledge on the human condition, while not drawing on genre SF conventions. While for *The Encyclopedia of Science Fiction's* purposes the distinction between genre SF and fabulation may be effective as a near boundary between genres, it lacks a far boundary to other fictional forms and does not provide for an adequate extra-text definition of genre to allow full understanding of texts in the territory between genre SF and the mainstream.

The Thesis: Span Fiction

It is the need to establish a genre center and describe the extra-text basis for the consideration of such texts that caused me to attempt this book. My "thesis" is that a new genre is emerging that fulfills Wordsworth's prophecy, in a world where science is increasingly a household commodity. Most of the discussion of "What is science fiction?" has centered on establishing a line dividing it from mainstream fiction (and another, less-difficult-to-establish line setting it off from fantasy), producing this graphic representation:

EXISTING MODEL

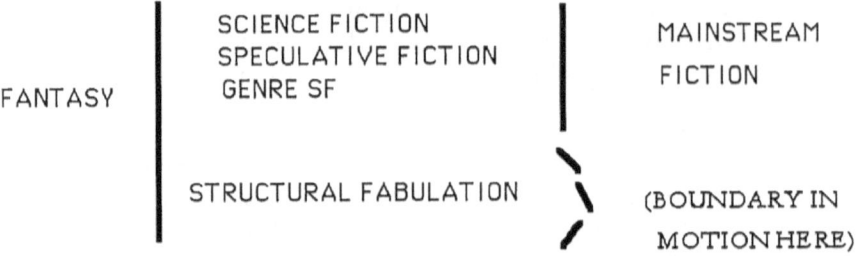

I want to replace this visualization with a set diagram that creates a space in which the new blended form can exist. I intend to name this new genre nexus "span fiction." In diagrammatic form the thesis is:

SPAN FICTION MODEL

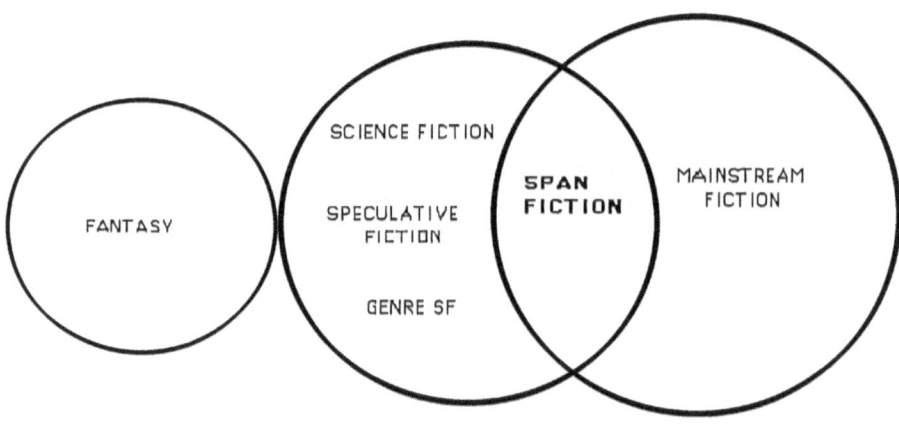

STRUCTURAL FABULATION OR POSTMODERN FICTION WOULD, IF ADDED TO THIS MODEL, OVERLAP THE DIVISIONS

Span fiction was selected for a number of reasons.[13] The most common modern use of the word is for the span of a bridge, a structure that joins two land masses but, I would stress, *is neither*[14]: it is a structure unto itself, blending physics, metallurgy (in modern structures), engineering, and the aesthetics of the architect. It is a thing to be described in different terms from the masses at either end of it. This clearly marks my central argument, that span fiction has it own distinct genre nature and characteristics.

Span is also a verb meaning to reach across, which effectively describes the nature of the area covered by the proposed genre. Span's original use in Old English was as a measure, the space between thumb and fifth finger of an outstretched hand.[15] Derived from that is its verbal meaning "to enclose or confine,"[16] suitable for the idea of a separate genre by this name. Its obsolete meaning, as a past tense of spin,[17] stands nicely for the complex blending of elements which characterize the genre.

The introduction of the term span fiction is intended to realign the interpretation of genres in this disputed territory; to change, therefore, how texts in the area are seen; and to propose new ways of describing the newly created genre borders. It is not intended to denigrate genre SF, which this writer takes to be a powerful conventional form that has been and continues to be a forum for soaring imagination, social, scientific and political debate (as at this moment, for example, in the hands of David Brin, Nancy Kress, Gregory Benford, Linda Nagata, Larry Niven, and Joan Slonczewski). As a boundary is defined, span fiction will appropriate some texts previously perceived as genre SF, but the wealth left behind (along with, admittedly, some dreck from hasty commercial writing) is not the poverty of a ghetto but the wealth of a kingdom sovereign unto itself.

The advantage of placing span fiction in its distinct place between mainstream and genre SF lies in the opportunity thus provided to define the genre, establish generalizations about its extra-text (precise extra-text lies in the experience of individual readers), and to consider the borderlines to its surrounding genres through study of contested texts, where the act of contestation is itself vital to the hermeneutic circle of genre definition. In touring the circle it will become possible to see the texts within it anew, judged by the emerging extra-text so that the reader can conquer the puzzles of texts that stand partly exiled from genres, as refugee claimants without states. Some texts that have been sharply criticized as genre SF may actually be span texts and need to be judged accordingly. Some texts that move towards the use of scientific world vision (e.g., Thomas Pynchon's *Gravity's Rainbow*) or borrow from the tropes and methods of the genre (e.g., Joseph McElroy's *Plus*) need to be considered as span texts rather than mainstream texts.

A Caveat: Genres and the Publishing Industry

"Some people think it's great to have a genre which has no inner identity, merely a locale where it's sold."[18]

One important question about genre interplay is beyond the reach of this book. The publishing and book-selling industries face a constant conundrum in dealing with the authors who work along the borderlines between mainstream fiction and science fiction. Marketing strategists will often list and dress books as science fiction because an author's previous titles have been packaged in this fashion and booksellers will often follow the indications on the books' covers. A search for the works of authors considered in this study will soon reveal that different booksellers keep the same title in different bookstore sections. There are several important outcomes of this situation. Writers like Kurt Vonnegut Jr. rail against science fiction because they feel themselves packed into a ghetto and lose both sales and prestige in the process. Moreover, they may feel an aesthetic indignation that their works are sold in the company of some very poor writing which passes for science fiction. Writers of traditional fiction may find their science fictional works appropriately shelved, only to realize later that their regular readers are not finding them.

While only extensive market surveying could accurately assess the impacts of these difficulties and while it borders on impossibility to assess accurately the effects this situation has on the writers themselves, a rearrangement of markets such as this is undoubtedly important in the creative process. One of the most tantalizing possibilities it raises is the detachment of the "upper end" of science fiction from the mediocre and ultraconventional portion of the genre. If this separation occurs (it may already be taking place because of the increased academic attention to science fiction, and the growing interest in it by the intellectual media), it can only increase the importance of the territory with which I am concerned here and further open the roads out of the wasteland of ultraconventional Grade C science fiction. There appears to be no way in to a close study of this aspect of the situation. Sales figures alone would not serve to determine the nature of the readership and only detailed studies of individual reading histories of a large number of readers would begin to yield a basis for determining the movements within the readership.

The approach that I can take to the works of span fiction is, first, to establish and examine the ways in which traditional fiction is changing through its considerations of science and the traditions of science fiction and, conversely, to examine what aspects of works of science fiction mark a movement towards the mainstream and into the realm of span. This leads to a mixture of ways of studying the forms of discourse, including: questions of the depth of characterization, complexity of narrative techniques and relation of works to the established mythic and archetypal patterns underlying fiction; consideration of the differing ways in which underlying patterns relate to narrative surfaces in terms of realism, stylized presentation, or devices such as parody and irony; and language forms.[19]

And, of course, the role of science as subject matter or setting or theme will be crucial in my considerations. If each age clothes the great patterns of action according to its times, then Wordsworth and Jung would both expect the fiction of our times to wear the outer garments of the scientific world view.

Modernist Ventures

In the realm of mainstream fiction it would appear that a strange conflict of intentions has dominated twentieth-century writing. In Joseph Conrad, Henry James, D.H. Lawrence, and even Virginia Woolf there was a pressing need to record what would at least appear to be the "real" world. This desire to apprehend and report accurately on the world (including the depths of the individual's consciousness) was founded on the scientific realism that had gradually superseded the romantic imagination in nineteenth-century public thinking, even if the methods became increasingly more formal and abstract as the complexity of the task came home to writers such as Woolf.

Yet against this desire for realism, evident in the clothing of even such philosophically and psychologically shaped novels as John Fowles' *The Magus* (1978), there was a curious general refusal to go into the realms of the modern science and technology that actually dominate the texture of contemporary life. This amounts to a strange form of tunnel vision. For while the twentieth-century English novel has been dominated by realism or a coating of realism founded in the observational style of physical science,[20] the attention of authors has been focused upon an ever-increasing solipsism presented in studies of families or small domestic groups or, eventually, in novelists as varied as Joseph Heller, Iris Murdoch, or Samuel Beckett, in the novel focused almost entirely on the mystery or dilemma of modern man, the singular individual.

While man is, no doubt, the fit subject for the study of man, the strange thing about this focus is that it has tended to exclude the science-induced trends of the century, the ways in which the frame of human life is affected by the impact of the understanding of various aspects of the physical universe and, moreover, the impact of the actual changes in the ways in which people live their lives. The effects of technology, which have certainly influenced graphic artists ranging from Picasso to Warhol and music from Stravinsky to synthesizer rock, are pushed into the background of much modern fiction. The possible exception to this is the influence of modern war, the technological dragon that has overshadowed our time. But with a few exceptions such as Joseph Heller's *Catch-22* (1961) the implications of technology have not been at the center of war fiction.

The chief historical exceptions to this situation of a modern fiction without essential aspects of the modern world are also the earliest twentieth-century examples of writers who crossed the line between conventional fiction and science fiction. H.G. Wells and Aldous Huxley were both concerned with the impacts of science on human lives.

Wells' style was essentially that of an Edwardian popular novelist, as witness *The History of Mr. Polly* (1910) or his satire on capitalist enthusiasms, patent medicines, and advertising in *Tono-Bungay* (1909). Thus when he turned his often pessimistic eye in the direction of science he tended to produce powerful, straightforward stories like *The Island of Dr. Moreau* (1896) or *The War in the Air* (1908). His theme in these works is clearly the danger of scientific progress but the framing, the narrative method, remains that of the Edwardian popular novel.

In novels like *Antic Hay* (1923), *Point Counter Point* (1928), and *After Many a Summer* (1939) Aldous Huxley created the clear precursors of the middle ground novel that this study will examine. At the epicenter of *Antic Hay* is Gumbrill's frivolous invention of the patent smallclothes and the demon image of Shearwater pedaling a stationary bicycle in a scientific experiment that literally gets him nowhere. In *Point Counter Point* Lord Tantamount is presented as an elegant amateur biologist who has surrendered his social and domestic roles to pursue his scientific obsession. Huxley chose the analogy of the precise and mathematical fugal musical composition as the structural model for the novel. His attitude to science is ambiguous because he clearly sees that scientific pursuit is detached from human social and domestic life as an activity, yet affects its practitioners.

There is no doubt that he does see science is deeply embedded in modern reality. *Brave New World* (1932) is both dominated and run by science, from the decantation of the fetus to orderly euthanasia. The New Worlders are conditioned to happiness and order in the cause of world peace. Although technology dominates the foreground, Huxley makes a considerable effort to focus simultaneously on the moving human stories of Bernard Marx and John the Savage, who both come to despise the scientific utopia stripped of unnecessary emotion and freedom of choice. Like Wells, Huxley sees that science must affect the way we live our lives and view our reality.

From Suvin to Span

Darko Suvin has offered what fast became the categorical definition of science fiction:

> SF is, then, a literary genre whose necessary and sufficient conditions are the presence and interaction of estrangement and cognition, and whose main formal device is an imaginative framework alternative to the author's empirical environment. [7–8]

In explaining his definition he makes clear that estrangement is a characteristic science fiction shares with fantasy and other literary forms (and was partly inspired by Bertolt Brecht's famous distancing effect). Estrangement is a deliberate distancing from reality which, in turn, by perspective gained, makes the reality clearer. Cognition—the ability of writers to know their times and through this to formulate the possibilities of other times (or places)—is the characteristic that qualifies the act of the imagination so that a work of fiction so created is science fiction. Estrangement's senses of separation and withdrawal are achieved by projections in space or time or social custom or technology.

Suvin further establishes the idea of the *novum*, the novelty or innovation that dominates the narrative and that must be "validated by cognitive logic" (63). Cognitive logic, in turn, means that the narrative must present a *novum* and support its presence with a scientific explanation. This explanation will naturally be a fabricated one, in that the *novum* does not presently exist within the known realm of science, but it must appear to emerge from the cognitive logic of science (taking science in its broadest sense to include the social sciences). It will, finally, be pseudo-scientific and it will need to be logically complete only insofar as it is required to support the fictional narrative. The idea of the *novum* (which creates the estrangement in Suvin's basic definition) supported by cognitive logic provides both a working definition of science fiction and a useful insight into the border areas of the genre.

Past one border, not relevant to this study, the *novum* is not justified by the cognitive logic of an effective scientific or pseudo-scientific explanation. This is the realm of fantasy: the home of fairies, sorcerers, and talking rocks. (It should be pointed out that some science fiction, such as Anne McCaffrey's *Dragonriders of Pern* (1971–1978) series or Clifford Simak's marvelous *The Goblin Reservation* (1968), actually pivot on pseudo-scientific *novums* that "explain" dragons and fairies.) It is also the realm of myth. Myth implies a metaphysical underpinning, an eternal verity, whereas cognitive logic is based on the known scientifically observed reality of historical and material circumstance which will change over time. The fact that, for Suvin, cognition is heavily influenced by his Marxist position has been a chief objection to his definition of the genre, but if the cognition is seen as placing weight on scientific and technological reality as well as the social and political, then the definition broadens into a far more generally acceptable one.

The other direction, the borderline area between science fiction and mainstream fiction, is the territory of this study. Here the *novum* is present but so, to varying degrees, are the methods and devices of mainstream fiction. These may include experimental contemporary prose narrative techniques (ranging from stream of consciousness to pastiche), a special attention to prose style often including symbolic or metaphorical patterning, and a high degree of moral and ethical complexity. Suvin calls such works "modern parables" and says of them:

> Departing from the older rationalism, a modern parable must be open-ended by analogy to modern cosmology, epistemology, and philosophy of science. [30]

Another frequent indicator is subtlety of characterization. Within the vast body of science fiction writing there has been a general tendency to treat characters as ciphers, using the hero, villain, mad scientist, military mind, and many other stereotypes drawn from the well of popular literatures ranging from science fiction's own tradition to the western to the detective story to the romance. The presentation of the *novum* was frequently the reason for this abdication of character development because the complexity of that task often absorbed so much of a novel or story that simplified characterization resulted.

The science fiction writers whom this study will mention—such as Philip K. Dick, Ursula K. LeGuin, J.G. Ballard, etc.—have, in various ways, moved towards additional complexity of characterization, mythic evocation, satiric or parodic intent, and towards other characteristics of mainstream fiction. These criteria also can be stated in Wordsworth's terms of the degree to which the mainstream writer succeeds in making the *novum* a real factor in the human condition, affecting characters' feelings and behaviors in the subtle and complex ways that are associated with the sensibility of the humanist: concerns with identity, soul, morality, and social reality.

For writers of mainstream fiction the movement into the middle ground of span fiction has, as its chief new challenge, the management of the *novum*. Writers moving towards science fiction may not entirely be guided by the cognitive logic element of Professor Suvin's definition, so that their fiction may not closely adhere to a narrow prescription of science fiction. Thus the position of these writers and their work on the middle ground of span will not solely depend upon their previous histories as writers but rather will be tested by the degree of cognitive logic, whether they bring science and scientific attitudes into play effectively.

The quality of the estrangement in the work of such writers also may be decreased, particularly if their treatment moves towards irony, parody or pastiche, traits regularly found in mainstream writing in the twentieth century. Writers such as Thomas Pynchon, Doris Lessing, Margaret Atwood, Lawrence Durrell, Angela Carter, and Anthony Burgess do not see themselves under any of the specific obligations that have strictly bound genre science fiction writers to plan the physics and societies of their estranged universes with coherent exactness. Rather, they feel free to liberate their imaginations by edging into non-naturalistic universes. Mainstream writers and their readers have generally had more finely tuned sensibilities for the nuances of tone, irony, and satire that have important effects upon the degree to which the *novum* needs to have a cognitive logic within the work. To partly believe in the world presented has not been a characteristic response to most works of science fiction (which, incidentally, accounts for the anomalous positions of Stanislaw Lem and Kurt Vonnegut Jr.). Generally science fiction has departed from the known world so aggressively that writers have struggled to maintain a tight and integrated world built on cognitive logic, forcing belief on readers.

But it is clearly a characteristic of much span fiction to challenge and undercut its own embellished *novum*. This playing with doubt, the creation of a deliberate tension within the work as opposed to the traditional tension involved in making a future or distorted present wholly believable, will be frequently a clearest distinguishing mark of span fiction and an examination of its purposes and methods will be grounds for understanding individual works. Novels such as John Fowles' *A Maggot* (1985) or Julian Barnes' *Staring at the Sun* (1986) positively feature discordance and stray far from Suvin's demand for cognitive logic. Span fiction writers are often willing to depart from Suvin's demand for "an imaginative framework alternative to the author's empirical environment," which features a "tight" adherence to cognitive logic, by sketching estranging circumstances. They are willing to leave their worlds up in the air, not providing every detail or dovetailing every aspect of their *novum*.

In the Introduction to the Ace Edition of *The Left Hand of Darkness* (1976) and elsewhere, Ursula K. LeGuin has posited the idea that science fiction writers engage in "thought experiments" similar to those performed in theoretical physics, in that the attempt to understand the complexity of reality can be made by creating an abstract, non-physical model. She argues that the science fiction writer creates a world or a universe that is no more physically real than Schrödinger's famous cat in the box or Einstein's parallel trains.

If we extend the idea of the thought experiment to the consideration that all writers of mainstream fiction are presenting their understanding of reality by the shaping and selection process involving the non-existent characters, locales and events present in their work (for even real locales are made fiction by the act of verbal selection), then another way of looking at the movement into span fiction by mainstream fiction writers emerges. It may be that their means of expressing a vision of contemporary reality must, for various reasons, involve elements of a projective *novum*, a casting outward to include aspects of the future or of a markedly alternate reality. What writers of mainstream fiction may feel is necessary to express their sense of our world may involve technology or prevalent scientific paradigms as central elements of telling or subject. The pressure of the complexity of our historical present may demand such innovation and span fiction may be where writers feeling such pressure find their metier.

On the other hand, for these writers the essential romantic forging of literary worlds by acts of the imagination may not willingly yield itself to the sort of single and simple vision of things that a rigidly extrapolated *novum* would demand. Such writers may have been unwilling to take up with science until science in turn was willing to accept the essential position that there are no single and simple answers to the complexity of man living in a complex universe. The developments through which contemporary science has begun to accept multiplicity and limitations on its competence (such as Heisenberg's articulation of the Uncertainty Principle) may make the employment of an open-ended and flexible scientific view a far more comfortable option for writers whose world view is unwilling to submit to the iron grip of an absolute, logical, and rigidly reasoned universe.

Wordsworth's moment when "what is now called science, thus familiarized to men, shall be ready to put on, as it were, a form of flesh and blood," has come to pass, and span writers are the among the "Poets" active in expressing this vital intersection.

Structure of this Text

It is, then, the aim of this book to attempt to illustrate one side of the double movement or trend that is producing the middle ground of span fiction. Length will not permit detailed exploration of the borders between span and SF, although chapter 5 will outline the terrain. There is no assumption that the specialized genre of science fiction will disappear because of this development. It will always be important as a playground for "hard" ideas, an articulation in fiction of the excitement of explorations in science and the projective evaluation of their implications, a place for thought experiments But span fiction is an important trend and one whose characteristics, variety, and causes deserve detailed study.

Chapters 2 and 3 will consider two writers from mainstream fiction whose work models differing versions of the movement towards span fiction. Doris Lessing's fiction illustrates the pattern of a writer who reaches out from a base of personal and political fiction to undertake expression in the new mode. Thomas Pynchon, on the other hand, is a writer who has always acknowledged the presence of science in the world of his work and who often turns to it for the approaches to reality that direct his thinking and his writing.

Chapter 4 will touch on works by a wide variety of writers usually considered mainstream who have engaged in experiments in span fiction. It will point to the characteristics of these fictions and emphasize the dizzying variety of possibilities for the genre.

Chapter 5 will offer the briefest of summaries of some of the writers who are eliding from genre science fiction to span.

Chapter 6 will attempt to sum up the characteristics of span and suggest the effects of its existence on the reading of texts.

In Sum

I repeat that what I undertake here will not produce hard and clear edges for span. As with most attempts to categorize works of literature, the real benefits will lie in the study of individual works and the combinations of the various elements that each holds in balance to produce a coherent work of literary art. The study of genre is, in large part, a study of transgressions of the semiotic code at the boundaries of a particular genre. What is needed is an outline of the code for the new genre of span fiction.

This book also will provide a portrait to the moment, a snapshot of the change as it has taken place to 2001. It will concern itself with what kind of critical yardsticks may be profitably applied to this hybrid form, for there has undoubtedly been a good deal of approbation leveled at examples of such work by critical observers from either science fiction or mainstream fiction whose expectations are not fulfilled by works they are considering. The intention of this book is not to oversimplify the complex situation of the development of a blend of two types of writing, but rather to offer a first mapping of this emerging terrain—span fiction.

CHAPTER 2

Doris Lessing: Experiments in Alternate Reality

> *What Doris Lessing has discovered, and I honor her for it, is that we must use the future in precisely the same way, as a probe into the truth of the present.*
>
> —Robert Scholes[1]

There are polar models of approach in the spectrum of the work created by writers associated with conventional fiction who move into the new middle ground. The purpose of this chapter and chapter 3 is to examine in detail the work of one writer chosen as an example of each of these models, before proceeding in chapter 4 to survey the large number of novels which illustrate the trend to span from the mainstream of fiction writing.

The first model, represented here by Doris Lessing, is that of a writer who chooses to incorporate science fiction motifs or to write fiction in which science has a featured place as a development from her former working methods. In such instances a writer who has an established pattern in realistic or fantastic or another mode of fiction moves on to create in a new mode incorporating the elements which characterize the new middle ground.

There are a number of questions raised when this happens. A very important issue is the reason for the development. Given the relative rarity of direct statements from authors it is usually necessary to infer cause from the texts themselves. It must also be granted that a writer may attempt a new mode out of sheer whim or for reasons related to the publishing industry. But the most obvious aesthetic generalization for the change will almost certainly be that authors may come to feel that there is something they very much wish to express which cannot be expressed within the framework of their previous methods of working.

Our chief concerns with writers who fall within this model will be to consider what matters or problems have led them to work in the new middle ground and how they have met the challenges by moving into what, for them, is unfamiliar territory. Consideration of the texts they have created will begin the assembly of the body of examples of the middle ground which in turn will provide a base for any conclusions and generalizations about the form. Of secondary interest will be the question of whether these writers set out to solve their dilemmas by attempting to write conventional science fiction but varied the genre in ways that make the resulting works fall into span.

The second model, represented in chapter 3 by the work of Thomas Pynchon, is fiction that sees the world through the eyes of the science and technology that dominate modern culture. This vision may actually be a subject for fiction. Writers may make extensive use of imagery or aspects of formal design drawn from science, such as the experimental search. They are working in various ways to come to terms with the fact that the world about which fiction is to be written, in modes ranging from realism to satire, parody, and surrealism, is now permeated with science and technology.

This raises questions about the ways in which fiction can embrace this new reality. How writers are experimenting, how they present human responses to science and technology, and how the old patterns of the quest, love, and search for meaning are re-enacted in this "new" world are among the issues raised by the second model. In these works the *novum* may be less the basis for a projection of a coherent future and more the sudden shock of a particular scientifically-based perspective on the "real" world.

From 1950 to 1968 Doris Lessing published nine novels (including four volumes of the *Children of Violence* quintet and *The Golden Notebook*), several volumes of short stories, plays, and two fragments of memoir. A reader who had followed her writing to this point and then stopped would be justifiably surprised to find her work featured in this chapter. For Lessing's career to 1968 was as a realistic writer dwelling particularly upon fictionalizing her early life in Rhodesia and London from a perspective increasingly dominated by social analysis reflecting Marxist ideology.

A Proper Marriage (1954) may be taken as an example of the work of this period. It begins five days after Martha Quest's casual and quixotic marriage to Douglas Knowell and follows that marriage through the birth of Caroline, Martha's daughter, and Martha's growing involvement with the Communist movement in a fictionalized Salisbury, Rhodesia, to her abandonment of her husband. It is characteristic of Lessing's work at the time in a number of ways. It has omniscient narration but places a good deal of stress on Martha's often dispassionate view of her own predicament and the predicaments of those around her.

Thus, towards the close of the novel, it is with bemused irritation that she responds to her husband Douglas as he performs a childish emotional pavane, trying to hold his marriage together to preserve his public image as a successful young civil servant. Martha and the reader see the melodramatic futility of devices such as his carrying Caroline in to remind Martha of her maternal duties or waving a loaded revolver about, threatening first Martha and then himself. The novel and, indeed, Martha have a very strong sense of perspective overview, so that Martha's personal life is seen within the context of the color problem, the power structure of the colony, the long historical perspective of Marxist thought, and the impending clouds of World War II.

This puts to full use the distancing, the godlike quality, of omniscient narration, so that even at emotional crises Lessing holds the reader at bay by the frequency of sentences beginning "Martha felt" and "Martha saw." Lessing is choosing to keep the reader from intimacy with her characters, but not necessarily from the development of a deep sympathy. While it is possible to consider this distance as an artistic flaw, a failure to bring the novels to life, that was clearly not Joyce Carol Oates' judgment of the fifth volume of the *Children of Violence*, *The Four-Gated City* (1969).

> For all the ups and downs, the domestic and international crises, this is a strangely undramatic novel, and it is certainly Miss Lessing's intention that it be so. [48]

Ms. Oates' comment could serve to describe most of Lessing's fiction and it places a focus on what Lessing intends to achieve. By the time she begins to move into the middle ground of *The Four-Gated City* she had already advanced into a form of fiction which deliberately stresses objective distance in order to let the reader both experience individual human travail and simultaneously perceive each character's destiny in terms of a much larger historical reality. The way in which the method conveys private struggle is analogous to Professor Elaine Scarry's description of Francis Bacon's painting.

> The solitary figure in the typical canvas of Francis Bacon is made emphatically alone by his position on a dais, by an arbitrary geometric box inserted over him, and by his naked presence against a uniform (in its uniformity, almost absolute) orange-red

background; yet while he is intensely separate from the viewer (a separation Bacon wanted to heighten further by having the canvasses covered with glass) he is simultaneously mercilessly exposed to us.... [53]

As the reader follows Martha Quest in *Children of Violence* or Anna Wulf of *The Golden Notebook*, it is like looking in on them trapped in the arbitrary glass box of their social and historical realities, not made less intensely private by the all-embracing presence of their worlds and relationships, but framed and displayed all the more effectively by them.

By 1969 Lessing was under the pressure of her own motives to undertake more experimental approaches to fiction. Her existing intention, to demonstrate the interplay between private lives and the larger society, had deeply strained the bounds of realistic fiction, as the "longer" views kept threatening to break into polemic, and the treatment of individuals trapped in the glass cages of their worlds drew some critical approbation by its failure to realize the intimate suffering of naturalistic characters in the tradition of nineteenth- and twentieth-century realism in fiction. What Lessing needed was a form which could better encompass her characters' private lives and individual experience in a frame that stressed the interplay with Lessing's ideologically inflected "long view" of the contemporary human situation.

The sense of critical discomfort with Lessing's position in the tradition was probably exacerbated by her position as an outsider, someone born outside the British-American publishing axis and iconoclastically self-educated outside the conventional patterns of understanding fiction in the academies. Her fiction has always been dominated by a powerful and often inchoate vision of the human situation and that vision has always been flexible, incorporating her youthful experience for examination, then embracing and later rejecting the rigid prescriptions of Communist thought, and coming to terms with a feminism rooted in experience rather than theory. In the 1960s a number of new and disturbing elements came into focus for Lessing: the world-interpreting positions of psychotherapy, the wisdom of the Sufis, the possibility of nuclear Armageddon in a world approaching political inertia, and a growing awareness of the potential for ecological disaster.

The work of Freud and Jung served to open alternate perspectives on human behavior and society and Lessing easily absorbed yet another objective vision to go with her colonial and Marxist-influenced positions. In particular the work of R.D. Laing opened the way to seeing states of "insanity," in particular schizophrenia, as possible entrances to other realities which might be equal in validity to those generally considered "real" and normal.

Sufism, which is often mistakenly described as Islamic mysticism (it has mystical elements but its proponents assert that it predates Mohammad), is a system of inner development and expansion through which humans can seek both a true sense of their place in the universe and an inner evolutionary development. Writing in *The Elephant in the Dark* (1976), an introduction to Sufism, Lessing quotes her own teacher, Idries Shah:

> Man must develop by his own effort toward growth of an evolutionary nature, stabilizing his consciousness. He has within him an essence, initially tiny, shining, precious. Development depends upon man but must start through a teacher. [75]

While Sufism is an extraordinarily worldly form of mysticism, stressing presence in the world rather than reclusive isolation, it clearly suggests that humans can move forward into a new evolutionary form, not primarily by bodily change but by mental evolution. While not a religion (although its practice is presently dominated by Muslims), it certainly asserts the possibility of some overarching universal consciousness and structure for the universe. Lessing's consideration of Sufi ideas in conjunction with Laing's intuitions about madness suggested the possibility that the radical consciousness of some forms of insanity might in fact be advanced stages in human mental evolution that were unacceptable to the shared standards of our time.

The expression of these new and radical possibilities in fiction ran the immediate risk that they would be dismissed as part of the misty and murky cult rubbish of the late 1960s. Moreover, Lessing's interest in Laingian psycho-politics and Sufism did not mean that she in any way lessened her interest in the framework of social and political realities upon which her work had previously rested. On the contrary, her writing now needed to include the new ideas along with consideration of the worsening international picture (with its nuclear standoff) and a new awareness of ecology (specifically, the recognition of humanity's unfair dealings with the natural world).

In fact, for Lessing it was not possible to simply stuff these various elements into a sprawling, multifaceted potpourri of fictional form. They were, of necessity, integral parts of the complex nature of the world, and the fiction Doris Lessing now turned to writing had to include the elements from the head of political, psychological, and ecological science, plus those from the heart of humanity represented in the Sufi holistic vision of human evolution. She needed to find a way to establish the unity of a grand and complex design. In addition, the novel she was in the process of writing was the be the fifth and last volume of the *Children of Violence* series, which she had conceived[2] within the existing novelistic category of Bildungsroman.[3] She would have an enormous advantage if she could maintain the mixture of objective realism and political perspicacity upon which her reputation was grounded and incorporate the Laingian and Sufi elements in such a way as to give them an increased realistic "hardness" which would guide her readers to take them seriously rather than to view them as flights of fancy.

The presentation of alternate realities and unexpected developments was already the familiar territory of science fiction writing (the *novum*), as was the perception articulated by Suvin that the science fiction writer applies her "cognitive logic" to the real world in order to assess the directions in which projections should go to reflect important trends in the present. It is this intellectually driven analysis of the present as a basis for projection which differentiates science fiction from fantasy. The evidence is clear enough that Lessing had been considering science fiction as a possible model. In a conversation with Florence Howe in 1966, she mentioned an early effort:

> We've got a series here [Britain] called "Blackmail" which anything fits into. So I've written two for this program and also a space fiction one. I postulated a situation where Britain was a colony of Africa, about X-thousand years from now. ["Conversation" 18–19]

In May 1969, Jonah Raskin interviewed Lessing:

> Raskin: How do you view the future?
> Lessing: I'm very much concerned about the future. I've been reading a lot of science fiction, and I think that science fiction writers have captured our culture's sense of the future. ["Stony," 175]

One science fiction writer she was definitely interested in was Kurt Vonnegut Jr., for she wrote " Vonnegut's Responsibility," a consideration of the moral position of his work:

> There is another way he is an original; for most of his career he has been in the category "space fiction" or "science fiction," where, for the most part, the chilliness of space derives from the writers' insistence that we do without the comforts of our own patterns of ethic, where we can see whole galaxies crumble with less emotion than we feel pouring boiling water into an ant's nest.
> Usually, in the center of Jex 132 (male) or Janni X56 (female) there is an emptiness which some claim is the proper imaginative

> response to the possibilities of all-space, but which in Vonnegut's people is filled with the emotions you and I would feel if we knew a molecule was loose that will freeze our world solid in a breath. [*A Small Personal Voice*, 141]

The precise attraction of Vonnegut for Lessing is the humanizing of science fiction, the imposition of "the emotions you and I would feel" which leads Vonnegut himself to demand release from the category "science fiction writer." So Lessing's admiration for science fiction is qualified by this demand for emotional realism.

An important aspect of the science fiction she was reading which must have attracted Lessing was its objective approach, its tendency to develop radical fantastic futures which are nonetheless based on the approach which Suvin defines as "cognitive" in "cognitive estrangement." Lessing had always seen herself as a critic and objective observer of the world around her. The "cognitive" approach fits in admirably with her objective realism and her method of holding her characters 'behind glass.' She found another analogue for this method outside of science fiction in the work of Eugène Neilen Marais, whose *The Soul of the White Ant* she perceptively reviewed.

> He studied animals, and was preoccupied with the nature of the human soul, or psyche, or mind.... His comparison of a termitary with a human being was a worm's—or ant's—eye view, most easily compared to the S.F. stories where shrunken people go voyaging along veins and arteries, through valves, and among hearts, livers, and lights like great animals or like countries, in a continent or an orchestra of individually working units all held together by an invisible force "like electricity." [*A Small Personal Voice*, 144–145][4]

In a short story "The Antheap" (1951) Lessing paid an indirect tribute to Marais both in the title and when she described a vast open pit gold mine where black workers have dug their way so far below the surface that they are like ants when viewed from the lip of the great crater. This story was a first venture in guiding readers to attitudes of sympathy towards tiny human figures seen at vast perspective distance. Her own experiment with the television script, her science fiction reading, and the perspective method of Marais all came together in Lessing's first venture in the middle ground form, *The Four-Gated City* (1969). The novel can be divided roughly into a progress of three parts for the purpose of describing it, although it should be stressed that in reading only the Appendix (62 pages of 710 in the MacGibbon & Kee edition) is formally demarcated in this scheme of division. Prior to the Appendix the novel has moved over a vast canvas of London in the 1950s and 60s, at first following Martha Quest's discovery of London and later her long and multifaceted relationships in the house of Mark Coldridge, where she went initially as a sort of private secretary and stayed to be mistress, intellectual companion, foster mother to the children of others, and observer of cultural and political shifts of the remarkable decade of the 1960s.

The second major movement of the book grows out of the first as Martha helps Lynda Coldridge, Mark's wife, in what initially appears to be her struggle against madness. But as Martha gains a more complex understanding of Lynda's situation she becomes involved in a self-analysis so deep that she experiences many of Lynda's horrors. Martha begins to realize that some people who "hear voices" may in fact be developing human potential in ways not yet acceptable to society and therefore adjudged madness. Martha, who chooses to go into the inner darkness and return, becomes Lynda's collaborator, and together they explore various ancient and modern attempts to make useful sense of the inner voices of this "madness." The Appendix presents scattered letters and reports which, pieced together, offer an historical sketch of the latter part of the twentieth century as viewed from the end of the century.

> The Appendix section [of *The Four-Gated City*], whose archives span the years 1968 to 1997, represents Lessing's first attempt at future fiction; its graft on the realism of the novel proper creates a new kind of disjunction and another kind of plural text. [Tiger, Sprague 12, 13]

This speculative picture is of a world deeply scarred by human foolishness in which, for example, the British Isles have been depopulated by a catastrophe rumored to have been either a vast poison gas leak or a radiation leak. The world centers of power have shifted to the Mongolian National Area, Mexico, Brazil, and Kenya, and vast changes in populations have taken place, leading to strict dictatorial management of the remaining resources. Martha and some of the others with the mental second sight and communication powers which had been developing out of Lynda Coldridge and Martha's work have survived until nearly the end of the century on the island of Faris off the coast of Scotland. Among the children of those who escaped there are a number who may well be supernormal, developing along diverse paths to strange new skills and knowledge. Elsewhere in the Appendix emerge mentions of the Memories, possibly people with special minds whose talents have now been recognized as being other than madness, and references to the ways that the new mental skills permit prescience and telepathy.

Of interest to this study is the way in which Lessing bonds the disparate elements of this novel. There are many science fiction novels which begin briefly in the "real" world and then move away from this familiar base to leap into space or propose entire alternate universes or unsuspected futures. But in "pure" science fiction there are no examples of novels whose vast bulk is a complex social and political realistic presentation, followed by a sudden leap into the scientific fantastic. While there have certainly been critical attacks on this choice,[5] the juxtaposition makes one great gain for the novel over its science fiction relatives: it offers an immense weight of realism in order to convince the reader of the genuine possibility of the content of the projected future of the Appendix. Lessing is switching the science fiction paradigm so that the *novum* is much more solidly grounded in the complex society and individual lives pictured in the bulk of the work.

Another more complicated link is forged between the bulk of the novel and the Appendix in the form of Martha's growing understanding of her own psyche and the powers which are eventually released as a result. Martha first goes to Lynda's psychiatrist, Dr. Lamb, in order to cope with an approaching breakdown brought on by the prospect of a visit from her mother. While he is helpful in certain ways (he finally meets Martha's mother once and after her resulting discharge of loathing Mrs. Quest immediately returns to Africa), Martha decides that he costs too much in emotional energy and begins an ongoing daily self-analysis. Later this is augmented by her sharing of the intense bouts of Lynda's madness and an eventual partial sharing of Lynda's special gifts of prescience and thought reading.

These Laingian elements, which coincide with the Sufi ideas of individual mental evolution, continue to be interspersed with the political movements of the 1960s and Martha's social life, but they provide an important bridging to the Appendix, where the powers Lynda, Martha, and others they have contacted are shown to have played a vital role in the thirty or so years being reported upon. The retrospective nature of the Appendix strongly emphasizes the "truth" of these personal powers, particularly as they are integrated with a complex and possible political "future history." In their letter and report forms, with Martha's last testament as the central document, the elements of the Appendix do not differ from the naturalistic style in which the rest of the novel has been written. Yet as Sprague and Tiger have pointed out, the Appendix is "grafted" onto the novel, with all of the strangeness that a graft implies. Lessing's more approving critics clearly view the new hybrid strain as a positive step:

> Moreover, the way that Lessing's philosophical quest leads her to break novelistic forms as soon as she has created them has left even the most devoted readers breathless in pursuit. Similarly, her elision of political realism into the worlds of insanity and science fiction has left those unable to make as graceful a leap between realism and fantasy puzzled and confused. [Pratt viii][6]

> This is a first in Lessing's oeuvre, and probably the most crucial step in the development of her vision away from individual-bound realism and toward holistic fantasies. [Knapp 13]

For Enright and others it is not successful, but one must consider that those who looked to Lessing for strict socialist-realistic assessments would probably bulk large among the dissatisfied.

Lessing's real difficulty has to do with the multiple focuses of the book and the resulting problems of style. In the Author's Notes she says; "I would be the first to grant that I'm not the smoothest of writers" (*Four-Gated* 711), and although she is saying this to preface a remark about publisher's misprints, it must be seen on a broader level. In a novel such as *The Four-Gated City* Lessing is ranging from political debate to social description to analyses of family structures to the ravings of the nearly insane to her reportage from the future, and it is little wonder that at times the method does not rise to the matter. This is particularly true of the periods of Martha's near insanity, for describing them from the position of Lessing's external and objective narrator considerably lessens their potential impact.

The epigraph of *The Four-Gated City* is the Sufi teaching story about a fool sent with a dish to get flour and salt for his master. In his effort to keep them separate he turns over the plate after he has been given the flour, thus dumping it on the floor. On his return to his master with the salt he is asked where the flour is and inverts the dish to show it to him, thus losing the salt as well. Lessing has chosen this epigraph because it so aptly illustrates the difficulty of capturing the different realities clearly ("separately") without losing everything in the effort. Seen another way, the epigraph expresses the difficulty of enclosing the coexistence of the inner and outer person in a narrative—concern with the psychological and Sufi development on one hand and with political, social and ecological issues on the other.

In *The Four-Gated City* this duality is not only a major theme but it is also a formal matter which Lessing answers in the transitions from external realism to psychological study to the Appendix. Even if this major undertaking is not entirely successful it has, like many of Lessing's other novels, that special energy bred from deep personal belief and the courage to take artistic risks on behalf of important ideas. *The Four-Gated*

City is a first strong step into a new form of writing by Doris Lessing. The methodological break marked by *The Four-Gated City* led to a series of experimental stories and novels in the years that followed and to the *Canopus in Argos* series beginning with *Shikasta* in 1979. Nineteen seventy-one saw the publication of the important short story, "Report on the Threatened City," and *Briefing for a Descent into Hell*. These were followed by *The Summer before the Dark* (1973) and *The Memoirs of a Survivor* (1974), the latter being her last novel until *Shikasta*. In varying degrees each of these works considered and experimented with some of the concepts pioneered in *The Four-Gated City*, thus preparing the way for the "space fiction" which was to follow.

"Report on the Threatened City" is Lessing's first work of fiction principally presented from a viewpoint outside the human. The "report" is being made by six aliens who have landed in the inland of California for the purpose of communicating to the inhabitants of a city (San Francisco?) that a vast natural disaster is imminent. After trying numerous methods they fail in their mission and retreat, leaving the "creatures" to their fate. In this story Lessing discovers the powers that the distancing effect can have and experiments with the range of shock, surprise, and revelation that the language of extreme objectivity can produce.

One of the central premises of the situation is the observers' deep confusion as they gradually deduce that the inhabitants are fully aware of the risk. There has even been a similar disaster in earlier times (the 1906 San Francisco Earthquake is not specified but the description of the accompanying fire strongly suggests it), yet the inhabitants refuse to act on the obvious facts. The observers also note this extreme dislocation of logic in the armaments race:

> Everyone in the System knows that this species is in the process of self-destruction, or part destruction. This is endemic. The largest and most powerful groupings—based on geographical position—are totally governed by their war-making functions. Rather, each grouping *is* a war-making function, since its economies, its individual lives, its movements, are all subservient to the need to prepare for or wage war. [154]

This outside perspective, with its ability to put the human way under a logical microscope, no doubt owes something to Swift, a debt which Lessing pays quite directly later in the story:

> As for helplessness, this is tragic anywhere, even among these murderous *brutes*, but there is no apparent need for them to be helpless, since they have every means to evacuate the city altogether and to....

>...THE NEW SUBURB PLANNED TO THE WEST. THIS WILL HOUSE 100,000 PEOPLE AND WILL BE OPEN IN THE AUTUMN OF NEXT YEAR.... (italics added for emphasis) [165–166]

Not only does the reference to brutes pay homage to Swift, but the accompanying juxtaposition of a human news report has the shock value of interjecting a telling example of the course of human stupidity. Out of their own mouths comes the proof of human idiocy in the building of yet another suburb in an earthquake zone.

This valuable perspective, new to Lessing's work, can also be used at a lighter level to describe structures and behaviors in the society. The visitors land near a teenagers' party in the desert:

> We knew at once that we were visible, because a herd of their young was near, some 50 or 60 of them, engaged in a mating ritual that involved fire, food and strong sound.... [153]

In the course of the story she is able to comment extensively on the power structure, the function of discussion to defuse desire for effective action, and upon the mental blockages which prevent the humans from effectively receiving the warning the aliens are trying to transmit. Interestingly she also pictures the aliens as flawed, for they too assume that reality should be as they see it:

> ...our Commissioners for External Affairs decided these people could have no idea at all of what threatened, that their technology, while so advanced in some ways, had a vast gap in it, a gap that could be defined, in fact, precisely by that area of ignorance—not knowing what was to befall them. [149]

Nor, of course, are the aliens able to triumph in the end or even grasp the reasoning behind the human choice to stay in danger. This choice comes as the greatest shock to the aliens. It is prepared for by a long dramatic build-up in the story to an amazing discovery the envoys have made about the humans and which they fear will not be believed by those to whom they are reporting:

> This is incredible, we know. Of course, you will find it so.
> INDIFFERENCE TO LOSS OF LIFE
> We can only report what we find—that at no point have the inhabitants of this city even considered the possibility of abandoning it and moving to an area that is not absolutely certain to be destroyed. Their attitude towards life is that it is unimportant. [172]

Lessing here discovers a powerful two-handed weapon long familiar to writers of science fiction. She is able to make a telling observation about human behavior from an objective perspective, something no human narrator can ever do, and she can have it voiced by someone (or something) with exceptional powers who must therefore engender respect from the reader. Additional strength also comes from the fact that the comment is a report from alien to alien, which allows a shared surprise at the strange behavior of these oddities, the humans.

It can only be offered as a speculation but it seems that Lessing discovered new approaches in this story which she found conducive to several aspects of her state of mind. Her sense of being an outside observer of her own world and of Western society, the historical perspective of her Marxist period, and the long view of human personal mental evolution derived from the Sufis: all find satisfaction and expression in the calculated distance of the alien perspective. Lessing must often have felt very outside of the societies she was experiencing, whether they were those of urban Salisbury after a girlhood spent on an isolated farm or London after a colonial youth. Support for this vision came from the Marxist long perspective on human political and social history, and from the deep philosophy of the Sufis, emphatic believers in a doctrine which urges humans to a longer view of their development and perspectives. "Report on the Threatened City" took the large step forward from the report from the future humans which comprised the Appendix to *The Four-Gated City* into territory which Lessing found most productive in terms of suggesting the possibility of higher powers and a perspective on the human animal.

The novel *Briefing for a Descent Into Hell* appeared in the same year as "Report on the Threatened City" and marked a number of different experimental approaches. Betsy Draine offers an extensive analysis of the techniques in play in the novel, at the center of which is a deliberate disorienting of the reader so that none of the five "realities" offered in the novel can be determined to be the base or true one (90–110). A man (later identified as Charles Watkins, professor of classics) is found wandering and disoriented in London. The novel presents a mixture of external and clinical descriptions of his progress and several situations that may be hallucinatory. By the end of the novel the reader may have had a glimpse through the curtain of "madness" at a man being trained, in images which he can understand in the same way as we understand dream images, to descend into the hell of our world bearing a message of sanity.

The extraterrestrials who "train" him are presented as personifications of the ancient gods in a rendition which begins with semi-mystical speculations about the planets and moves to parody involving

Minne Erve and Merk Ury. While the reader knows conclusively that Lessing is not seeking acceptance of this as realistic fiction, on the other hand it must be accepted on some level if the experiences of Charles Watkins are to have any meaning beyond the delusions of temporary insanity. There is also a crystal vehicle, half object and half force field, in which Watkins is taken off the Earth for his strange meetings with the gods, and there is a birth sequence of sorts in which one of the "gods" is born in a human form to convey the news of imminent planetary disaster to the Earth.

As these brief glimpses of the novel suggest, it is a potpourri of experimental techniques attempting to express the reality of levels of consciousness beyond normal human recognition by a mixture of scientific projection, mythical reference, and mystical description. It is heavily dominated by the Laingian assertion that insanity is not agreeing with one's therapists, as for example considering what they describe as solid reality less important than the meaning and complexities of a series of paradoxical experiences that may have happened in or out of physical reality.

Certain elements of the novel carry on with some of the ideas first tested in *The Four-Gated City*, such as the possibility of states of mind which are superior to the normal but are defined as insanity, and the imminence of planetary collapse. From "Report on the Threatened City" comes the idea of extraterrestrials attempting to intervene in human lives and the surprise and dejection of objective observers looking at the Earth. *Briefing for a Descent Into Hell* marked a further attempt to break away from conventional fiction in order to incorporate the new possibilities in the author's thought into her fiction. And while it has its own disturbing power, at least partly due to its quite deliberate multiplicity of conflicting styles, it is clearly a stage on the way to the *Canopus in Argos* novels.

The Summer Before the Dark is a different sort of fictional experiment, a study in the distances which exist within the "normal" world. Its central figure, Kate Brown, is a middle-aged woman who arrives at the moment when her family have grown and gone and her husband is teaching in America for a summer and pursuing one of his many affairs. Kate chooses to close up the house, take work with an international relief agency, and plunge into a minor romantic affair which collapses when the man becomes dangerously ill. Then she returns to England where she tries life near the bottom, wearing old clothing and living anonymously with a group of uncertain young people. Lessing is at least partly interested here in the process of what could be described as "domestic consciousness raising," a process by which one learns to recognize the social net in which one is enclosed and to consciously decide, rather like an outsider, whether to take one's expected place or to challenge all that life has been before. Without the element of insanity present this is another novel about the human being alien to her own kind, moving through the world and seeing it anew. As such it is clearly another step on the way to the writing of *Shikasta*.

The Memoirs of a Survivor is a novel which splits its experimental intentions down the middle. From a psychological perspective, it is a novel about a mature woman who suddenly discovers a strange world reached by passing through the wall of her apartment. She discovers a realm full of someone's experiences of childhood which she can watch and a lot of enigmatic empty rooms and deserted courtyards. The haunting tone of these sections is achieved through the recapitulation of many of the principal psychological events and archetypes of a human life, and it could have served as the sole subject matter for a novel. What makes the book considerably more interesting is that the woman having these mental experiences is living her "conscious" life in an urban society (presumably the outskirts of London) which is undergoing the later stages of a collapse into barbarism as public utilities cease to function and raw power takes over from civil order. To complicate this world of the near future, an enigmatic young girl and her strange, almost mythical dog are arbitrarily left in her care, and it appears that it may be the childhood of the girl which is glimpsed "through the wall."

The incidents seen through the wall clearly function at the level of a mixture of psychology and mysticism, and while the narrator appears to have survived the vortex of the hard times to write retrospectively about them, Lessing assigns a special approval to the visionary portion by having all of the principal characters escape from the troubles in the book's unsettling conclusion by passing through the wall.

Of real interest in terms of span is Lessing's vision of the collapse of social order. As a reader of *The Four-Gated City* would have predicted, she has a special and quite precise sense of what might happen as society collapses, based largely upon her acute and practiced objectivity in examining the social world about her. She writes of the way people avoid recognition of change, subduing the brief flurries of violence or other unusual events beneath everyday routine. She writes of the Talkers, those in distant places of power who devote themselves to controlling the changes but are only able to secure preferment for themselves and their families. She writes effectively of the slow changes as people choose to do without sporadic supplies of electricity and trade all their appliances for a few of the newly useful items such as an enamel jug or a scrubbing brush. Or she pictures the slow decline into violence as the strongest and smartest and those accustomed to live off the land come to the fore. In Lessing's hands all of these are blended into a coherent vision of the imminent future.

In *The Memoirs of a Survivor* there is a much easier and less forced control over the blending of these images of the grimy apocalypse than in *The Four-Gated City*, where the view is retrospective and lacks the sense of participation. It is also far less immediately science fictional than "Report on the Threatened City," and it is probable that Lessing observed the value of at least some narration from involved human narrators as a result of this novel.

The chronicle of development of Lessing's experiments to this point has been a preparation for a discussion of her major concentrated effort in span fiction, *Canopus in Argos*, beginning with *Shikasta* published in 1979. Through the 1970s she had been experimenting to meet needs dictated by what she wished to write about,[7] and the difficulty of enclosing her social and political visions with her Sufi metaphysics and Laingian perspectives had led to several partial solutions. The five volumes of *Canopus in Argos: Archives* show that she has found a way to loosely bind together a series of varied experiments into a kaleidoscopic montage which can adequately present her varied yet interpenetrating approaches to the state of the human race in our times. The paths through the jungles of genre definition concerning these novels have been turned into a maze, both by Lessing and by her critics. In "Some Remarks" preceding *Shikasta*, she begins with a statement which could stand as the epigraph for the entire trend towards span from the mainstream:

> *Shikasta* was started in the belief that it would be a single self-contained book, and that when it was finished I would be done with the subject. But as I wrote I was invaded with ideas for other books, other stories, and the exhilaration that comes from being set free into a large scope, with more capacious possibilities and themes.... I feel as if I have been set free both to be as experimental as I like, and as traditional.... [10]

She goes on to offer her assessment of science fiction:

> What a phenomenon it has been—science fiction, space fiction—exploding out of nowhere, unexpectedly of course, as always happens when the human mind is being forced to expand: this time starwards, galaxy-wise, and who knows where next. These dazzlers have mapped our world, or worlds, for us, have told us what is going on in ways no one else has done, have described our nasty present long ago, when it was still the future and the official scientific spokesmen were saying that all manner of things now

happening were impossible—who have played the indispensable and (at least at the start) thankless role of the despised illegitimate son who can afford to tell truths the respectable siblings either do not dare, or, more likely, do not notice because of their respectability. They have also explored the sacred literatures of the world in the same bold way they take scientific and social possibilities to their logical conclusions so that we may examine them. How very much we do all owe them! [11]

These sentences in praise of science fiction reveal several aspects of Lessing's understanding of the situation. First, she uses science fiction and space fiction interchangeably. Second, her vision of the genre is a very wide one, including the consideration of sacred traditions. In the paragraphs before and after the passage quoted above Lessing specifically mentions Olaf Stapledon's seminal *First and Last Men* (1930) and H.G. Wells. So when she says that she is going to write space fiction she clearly has in mind a broader perspective than that offered by the "hard science" science fiction of the American Golden Age, particularly with regard to her approach to metaphysics. In fact, she is clearly planning to work within the scope of what I am defining as span.

After the existing five volumes of *Canopus in Argos* had appeared, Lessing gave a speech in New York in which she complicated the genre question:

> "Literature of the Fantastic," the brief lecture which followed, not only gave the clue, but amounted to an apologia for her *Canopus* series. Born in magic and religion, fantastic literature has a long tradition, she argued; fables and parables have always run beside the realistic novel and now that stream is growing stronger and stronger, since technology has laid the basis for "a rebirth of fantastic literature." [Tiger "Candid" 5–6]

She is describing her *Canopus* novels in terms very close to Todorov's definition of science fiction as "fantasy in the scientific mode." She has found the liberation of new ground on which to work. This liberation is, after all, the reasonable and necessary activity for the creator, as opposed to the function of the critic. For Lessing there is an important sense of continuity between what she now begins to do and what she had formerly been doing: "I see inner and outer space as reflections of each other. I don't see them as in opposition" ("Feminism" 28).

When the critics enter the debate, matters do not become immediately more simple. Betsy Draine asserts that "...Lessing violates utterly some of the essential elements of the science fiction code" (143), as though such a rigid code existed like a ruled border between contending states. She goes on to say:

> Nonetheless, the reader continually feels a sense of scandal at the incursion of religious imperatives onto essentially agnostic ground, the territory of science fiction. [144]

She later expresses disapproval at Lessing's assertions that she is writing in the mainstream of science fiction. I do not think that Lessing has been treating the definitional terms with any particular rigor. Draine, on the other hand, has read several of the principal theorists of science fiction[8] and is seriously disturbed by the implications of a science fiction containing elements of allegory, metaphysics and the fantastic. Had she read widely in science fiction itself, considering writers as diverse as James Blish (*A Case of Conscience*), Roger Zelazny (*Lord of Light*), Arthur C. Clarke (*Childhood's End*), Michael Moorcock (*Ecce Homo*), Stanislaw Lem (*Solaris*), and Mary Doria Russell (*The Sparrow*), she would have realized that the genre has always wrestled enthusiastically against the bands of critical criteria set to enclose it. This is, in fact, the core of Mona Knapp's assessment of the same situation in her consideration of *Canopus*:

> Science fiction eludes compartmentalized definition—it shares common ground with detective stories, fairy tales, scientific and historical documents, as well as many other genres—and thus appears well-suited to an author who progressively disdains the conventional demarcation lines between literary genres, between truth and fiction, the sane and the mad, the objective and the subjective. [131]

Professor Knapp does not really pursue the definitional question further, moving instead to seek to disassociate Lessing from the taint of Communism in a manner reminiscent of Eric Bentley's defenses of Bertolt Brecht in the United States of America in a previous generation.

Where Knapp has respected the definitional difficulties and let the matter lie, Draine has captured the essential differences between Lessing and conventional science fiction but has, from the point of view of this study, made a negative out of a positive of the utmost importance. Where she objects to the damage Lessing does to the definition of science fiction, it is clear that what is really happening is the establishment of the new middle ground in Lessing's work. What now must be done is to consider that new ground and how it serves the author's needs better than either conventional fiction or science fiction.

Critics and audiences who dislike Lessing's work often point to what they take to be its heavy-handed, didactic, and "preaching" tone. In fact it is far more the case that Lessing as a person has always had a flexible and probing imagination, a desire to find new and rewarding ways of understanding the world and a strong moral commitment to function in the global society. She has been engaged in her fiction in an indirect reportage on her own development, but this has not been the classic process of shedding one theory or approach for another. Rather, she has come gradually to a complex vision and, insofar as her fiction is a sincere expression of her vision of the world, she requires a fictional form which can express her mature understanding.

One essential element of the form must be its ability to cope with both the macrocosm and microcosm. Working as a Zolaesque social realist buttressed by the Marxist-Communist worldview of vast changes in society and government, Lessing had until 1969 produced fiction governed by a cool, objective eye, using the authorial distance to heighten her readers' sense of outrage at social injustice. While she has evidently pulled away from the Party, she nonetheless remains an advocate of a long historical perspective. This vision must coexist with her more recent absorption in Freud, Jung, R.D. Laing, and Sufi thought, other systems of both cosmology and microcosmology.

Neither realism nor science fiction nor fantasy could encompass all of these demands. Science fiction has not usually been a field where individual characters have stood aside from the types they were representing, and its relations with metaphysics, while not as inimical as Draine suggests, have been uneasy and have particularly floundered when the metaphysics have lacked systematic articulation. The Laingian approach clearly ran into grave difficulties when juxtaposed with realistic fiction, particularly with regard to the acceptance of the world(s) envisioned as real rather than delusional. Because the "mad" are so profoundly distrusted in Western society, it was a dead end for Lessing to articulate through them her coherent contemporary vision of reality and its meaning. And as the madness sections of *The Four-Gated City* testify, Lessing discovered the loss of immediacy involved in attempting to describe insanity from the outside.

The need for a realistic fiction capable of embodying a metaphysic, and at once responsive to psychologized images of character and those communicated through Sufi insights or the Laingian commentary on the relative qualities of kinds of consciousness, prompted the development of *Canopus in Argos*. Clearly Lessing saw this format as literary rather than as a didactic articulation of systematic belief: "If I have created a cosmology, then it is only for literary purposes!" (*Sirian*, "Preface"). She also wished that the books be seen as a grouping:

> I would so like it if reviewers and readers could see this series, *Canopus in Argos: Archives,* as a framework that enables me to tell (I hope) a beguiling tale or two; to put questions, both to myself and to others; to explore ideas and sociological possibilities. [*Sirian,* "Preface"]

The matter of "a framework" is important to understanding what she has achieved, for it is arguable that the five volumes are very unlike in style and tone and that this is a serious flaw. The alternative way to look at this is to see the varying styles and tones of the novels like the substances changing in a chemical reaction. Something new is created which did not previously exist and the individual substances, in this case the science fiction epic or fable or satire, are transmuted by their indivisible integration into the resulting form.

Shikasta begins as a conventional large-scale science fiction novel comprised of reports, directives, and fragments of history concerning Canopus' activities on a planet called Rohanda (later renamed Shikasta after a disaster) which readers soon realize is Earth. Over many millennia, Canopus has watched and assisted in the development of this planet, opposing the agents of a planet called Shammat who seek to introduce evil and greed and who drain off the spiritual energy Canopus is supplying. At this point the science fictional elements distinctly begin to overlap with theological ones, a version of the struggle between good and evil.

Johor, the principal Canopean agent, relates much of the history of the planet in a semi-mythical fashion often linked to the Old Testament, but draws in such things as an ancient and extinct race of giants from other mythologies. He is also directly involved on Shikasta on several occasions, during which the narrative becomes a relatively conventional description of sequential events with a first person narrator. Then, after a leap over most of human civilized history followed by an excerpt from a Canopean history book which sums up the last two centuries of imperial greed, domination, and rapine on Earth, Johor offers a series of specific vignettes of people in the late twentieth century whose lives were adversely affected due to the temporary falling away of a Canopean agent. There follows a long series of "portraits" of people in our times ranging from the poor to terrorists and from contemporary Britain and America to a picture of African colonialism. In addition there are general "essays" from the historical documents on topics ranging from drug use to pollution and nuclear threat.

At this point, when the narration has lost a good deal of momentum in the detailed depiction and criticism of our contemporary reality, Johor is incarnated as George Sherban to play a major role in adjusting the direction of civilization. His story, which is a narrative of growth and development in the near future, is told not by himself, although he has contributed a great deal of the novel up to this point, but is instead a diary kept by his sister Rachel. After her death, a sacrifice to save her brother, it is narrated in snatches by agents of the Chinese empire which gains power on the Earth in the latter days until major pollution, starvation, nuclear events, and epidemic catastrophes overthrow all governments. The narration is completed by letters among the survivors who found a new world community, which begins to regain contact with Canopus.

This vast and varied banquet of events and styles permits Lessing to achieve a large number of things, some of which coexist in most unusual fashion. Draine refers to this range of methods in uncomfortable conjunction in terms of Roland Barthes' "readerly text," stressing the importance of readers' generating their own overall meanings for a text (143–144). But given Lessing's mixture of didacticism and the constant reconsideration of her own thinking which she tends to work out in her fiction, it is more easily seen as an extension of the objective method she has been accustomed to use.

In *Shikasta,* Lessing is sometimes writing a conventional science fiction epic and she can, for long stretches, keep to the principal constructions of the form. Her powerful imperial Canopeans with right on their side (identified as the Necessity), space vehicles, very long lives with the accompanying superhuman temporal perspectives, and the mysterious Lock which carries "energy" from Canopus to Rohanda/Shikasta, are all appropriate to science fiction epics. So are the parallels to various elements of mythical history, such the legends of the ancient giants and the little people, and to the ancient history of the Old Testament. Science fiction writers have long used such parallels to generate verisimilitude though the readers' sense of "That explains the ancient writing, or the myths of the giants, or...." Nor does Draine's complaint that Lessing "downplays the scientific and technological aspects of her story" (143) really affect the novel's status, for such things as space vehicles and energy beams have become so conventionalized in science fiction that they need only be mentioned, not explained.

The real test of the need for scientific explanation in a science fiction text is similar to the tests usually applied to character or incident in other forms of fiction: Is the fiction believable to the reader at the level of detail or explanation given? This aesthetic, rather than logical-scientific judgment has come, in the world of contemporary science fiction with its emphasis on sociological and psychological themes, to mean that a great deal of the engineering science aspects of works are left unexplained. Also at work here, of course, is the observation that in a person's daily interaction with their kitchen they do not pause to consider the intricacies of the thermocouples in their refrigerator. Fiction which tries to live by technological explanation soon degenerates into a popularized scientific paper.

What does make *Shikasta* unlike most epic science fiction novels is its quality of self-parody. While novels like Kilgore Trout's *Venus on the Half-Shell* (1974) are whole-hearted parodies of the form (in this case written by Philip José Farmer after the manner of Kurt Vonnegut Jr., himself interested in parodying the Asimov-Heinlein space story), it is most unusual for a serious novel to undermine itself. Yet Lessing definitely does this, as, for example, when she presents an agent's report to Shammat as evil in an exaggerated fashion:

> Day and night, planet that is the lowest of the Low, you shake and shiver beneath our Rule, Shammat the Glorious, the all-glorious son of Puttiora the Glorious, offering your fat and your substance, the perfumes of your anguish, the aromas of your cruelties, your disgustingness. [430]

So melodramatic is this (and it is only a fragment of the message) and the descriptions of Shammat and its agents in the series, that the question must be asked as to whether it is simply an example of deeply bad writing. But Lessing makes clear that her presentation of them is self-conscious and controlled in the Preface to *The Sirian Experiments*: "No, no, I do not 'believe' that there is a planet called Shammat full of low-grade space pirates...."

In *Shikasta*, Lessing also names several things in such deliberately awkward ways that they undercut "belief" in the central science fiction. For example, the energy transmitted in the Lock is called SOWF, an awkward acronym (but one actually drawn from Sufi principles[9]) for an awkward term, "substance-of-we-feeling." Likewise, some of the reporting, even by the Canopean agents, has an awkward hauteur, a coy and unconvincing omniscience:

> For instance again: Shammat's preoccupation was always to weaken and soften the moral fiber of the inhabitants. Ours was always the opposite effort. But Shammat was not always—and increasingly less so, towards the end—able to control her own efforts or to observe and understand ours." [425]

The stylistic variety of the novel includes satire on the jargon of Marxism and Maoism. Lessing, who spent a considerable portion of her adult life in contact with the practitioners of these philosophies, is able to caricature the jargon and make it additionally suspect because the reader has other narrative access to the Canopeans.

> *Benjamin Sherban. No. 24.* What can we say about this decadent philistine whose filth pollutes the glorious struggle transforming the ownership of the means of production for the benefit of all the toilers of mankind. The lesson of such degenerates is that we have far to go to achieve total victory on the political and ideological fronts. We have to gird ourselves to wage a protracted and ever-hawk-eyed struggle against the reactionaries enslaved to the undertow of capitalist influences from the filthy past in order to mount the heights of true socialist achievement. [327]

(The reader knows that from the long Canopean viewpoint "the benefit of all the toilers of mankind" is slightly limited by the fact that the Chinese Overlords who are writing this are starving out the white races of Europe.) Lessing is also able to parody the distanced observations of the social worker or psychologist, and she does this most effectively in George Sherban's reports on the people he is observing in twentieth-century society.

> This man, after a hard struggle in childhood and youth against poverty and lack of education, became a journalist. For many years he was a dubious figure in the eyes of the authorities, for he was one of those—sharing a critical and analytical capacity not dissimilar from that of 1(5)—who were continually attempting to present a factual picture of events and processes to the public very different from that of the majority view. This from a nonpolitical viewpoint, though he was branded as a socialist at a time when it was unfashionable and ill regarded. [229]

The play on the style here does not prevent some of these accounts from being movingly typical of the dilemmas facing individuals in the late twentieth century.

There is also the major tone, particularly in the early sections of the book, of the tired, slightly jaded, yet deeply concerned colonial administrator, Johor. As he relates the early history of Rohanda/Shikasta, Lessing uses him to focus the long view of history characteristic of the science fiction epic, but he injects it with a sense of personal involvement unusual for the style:

> And now I will describe Rohanda as I found it on my first visit.
> But it was Shikasta now: Shikasta the hurt, the damaged, the wounded one. The name had already been changed.
> Can I say that it is "with pleasure" that I write of it? It is a retrospective emotion, going back before the bad news I carried. [38]

And, of course, some sections of the book amount to rhetorically powerful generalizations on the contemporary human condition, made all the more effective because they are in the form of objective observers' reports, slightly dry yet capable of harshly exposing human futility.

> Science, the most recent of the religions, as bigoted and as inflexible as any, has created a way of life, a technology, attitudes of mind, increasingly loathed and distrusted. Not long ago, a "scientist" knew he was the great culminator and crown of all human thinking, knowledge, progress—and behaved with according arrogance. But now they begin to know their own smallness, and the fouled and spoiled earth itself rises up against them in witness. [248–49]

Finally, as a counterweight to all of these distanced and absolute forms of narration and the nagging authoritarianism of Communist rhetoric, there is Rachel Sherban's journal. At the beginning she is a child of fourteen, critical of her brother George, whom the reader already knows is the incarnated Johor. Her account is consistently quite emotional and it is cleverly laden with dramatic irony, for the reader can see what George is preparing for but Rachel cannot. This deeply human account of a strange older brother has a vaguely biblical tone; it is myth in the making in a fashion faintly reminiscent of Mary, the Mother of Jesus, who " kept all these things, and pondered them in her heart" (Luke 2:19). It is enormously effective in at once humanizing and dramatizing the major narrative events of the last portion of the novel.

The other four novels in the series have their own stylistic and tonal qualities which contribute to the span character of the whole. These range from the satiric through polemic and include mythic and fantastic sections. Portions of *Shikasta* have made mention of the unearthly setting for *The Marriages Between Zones Three, Four, and Five.* Zones Two through Six are a curious amalgam of the Ptolemaic crystal spheres, a purgatory for those awaiting reincarnation (Zone Six), and the scientific speculations about alternate universes which may "share" Earth's physical space. ("Adjust yourself to the various levels of being which lie in concentric shells about the planet, six of them in all...." (16).) Lessing tells us that: "*The Marriages Between Zones Three, Four, and Five* has turned out to be a fable, or myth. Also, oddly enough, to be more realistic [than *Shikasta*]" (*Shikasta* 10).

The Marriages Between Zones Three, Four, and Five mythologizes the human interaction of marriage by making the event the amalgamation of two distinctive kingdoms (one containing the virtues of nurturing and closeness to nature, and the other the military and mechanical) which in turn brings about permanent changes in the partners and a spiritual growth arrived at through great tribulation. Its place in relation to *Shikasta* is secured by the presence of the Providers, who essentially direct the history and lives of these Zones and who clearly are or are closely analogous to the Canopeans, if only because the overlap of the ideas about the Zones themselves places the novels in the same universe.

There is, moreover, an implication of an overall cosmography for the two novels, for there is a sequence in *Shikasta* in which Johor roams Zone Six on his way to be reincarnated, which establishes that Zone as the one closest to the grossness of Shikasta. In *The Marriages Between Zones Three, Four, and Five* there is a hierarchy of Zones, in which Two is the most spiritual and ethereal, and there is increasing physicality, violence, and crudeness in the progression towards Six. Beyond or beneath Zone Six lies even worse, as Ben Ata, the ruler of Zone Four, tells his bride, Al·Ith:

> "They talked of a place where they had weapons we hadn't even imagined. They can use the air itself to make weapons of."
> "But if they can use air to make weapons, they can use it to make things that are useful?"
> "He said nothing about that. It is a place somewhere. A planet. It is an evil race. They kill and torture each other all the time, for the sake of it...." [97]

The identity of that planet is clearly Shikasta, for it is "beyond" Zone Six and there they create weapons out of air, which implies nuclear fission and fusion.

Thus Lessing binds the psycho-myth of human interaction, which is *The Marriages Between Zones Three, Four, and Five*, to the universe of *Shikasta*. She continues from the first novel to the second to explore the relationship between freedom and the Necessity, the will of the Providers. The behavior of the two very realistic and sensitively portrayed central characters in *The Marriages Between Zones Three, Four, and Five* absorbs us for some time in a passionate love story, but the narration once again is drawn back as one of the parties is instructed to marry someone else. The other suffers as an outcast when she retires to her homeland, only to finally reap the benefit of her spiritual maturation by being permitted to advance into the ethereal realm of Zone Two.

The Sirian Experiments returns to the physical planet of Shikasta and is, on the surface, the story of the genetic and social experiments performed by Sirius, a former enemy of Canopus which was given the use of parts of Shikasta (particularly an area like South America) for its work. The narrator is Ambien II, one of the Five who administer the vast Sirian Empire. Sirius emerges as an empire hungry for acquisitions and power, moving and developing races for its own aggrandizement. Some of the details of its activities, such as using part of Shikasta to grow crops for export to a planet which exists to "Think" about the "existential problem," are reflections of British colonial rule. But as this novel (ostensibly dealing with the conflict between galactic empires) unfolds, it becomes increasingly clear that it is really the story of Ambien II, the narrator, awakening to the true nature of both Sirius and Canopus.

Against a background of maneuvering against Canopus, including interventions in Babylon, Peru, Persepolis, and the American Southwest, Ambien II gradually becomes aware that she is being taught in subtle ways about the nature of Canopus and Sirius. The novel really centers on the enlightenment of this single individual, who slowly becomes aware that Canopus is taking care of its colonial peoples rather than using them, and that Canopus has a sophisticated maturity which accounts for its particular kind of success.

The novel draws on the idea of superior and nearly invisible knowledge depending upon inner recognition and growth—the Sufi way. Quite early in the story, Ambien II goes away from Adalantaland (clearly Atlantis) pondering the Canopean-inspired policies of that state:

> I was thinking, as I went, about their third precept, that they must not take more than they could *use*, for it seemed to me to go to the heart of the Sirian dilemma ... *who* should use *what* and *how much* and *when* and *what for*? Above all what for! [81]

Through all of her subsequent visits to Shikasta and through her extremely frustrating "indirect education" from Klorathy of Canopus—a training loaded with experiences and vague questions like those a Sufi master poses to his pupils–Ambien II grows slowly in an understanding that Canopus' way is to serve the Need, which can be roughly equated to a caring and universal evocation of love. The novel is cast as a retrospective narrative, which means that Ambien II is leading the reader along the same course of discovery which she has already followed, and at its conclusion she discovers that Canopus' influence upon her has affected the rest of the Five (her group of managers), so that they are ready to turn Sirius' empire from its self-aggrandizement to serve the Need. Thus the novel combines a science fiction world with the lines of development of the self drawn from Sufism or from a description of psychological maturation.

In the Afterward to *The Making of the Representative for Planet 8*, Lessing asserts that the Scott Expeditions to the Antarctic were the source of *The Sirian Experiments* and explains it thus:

> It seems that everything they did has to be seen in this other light: they were engaged, or the key people were, particularly Wilson, and some consciously, in an attempt to transcend themselves....
> This need to break out of our ordinary possibilities—the cage we live in that is made of our habits, upbringing, circumstances, and which shows itself so small and tight and tyrannical when we do try to break out—this need may well be the deepest one we have? [134]

So *The Sirian Experiments* is, in effect, an extremely complex tale of human inner development which is mirrored in the external realm of intergalactic colonialism through the hinge-figure of Ambien II, seen as individual and as colonial overlord.

In some respects *The Making of the Representative for Planet 8* is a return to archetypal-fabulisitic method of *The Marriages Between Zones Three, Four, and Five*. It has a formal storyteller or Memory Maker, Doeg, and it becomes clear that the characters are named with a rigid formality, so that when a young woman begins to tell a story she is "Alsi, who was being Doeg" (98).

The story is starkly linear, telling how Johor comes to a planet whose million inhabitants must freeze to death in a climate change because they cannot be taken off to the newly degraded Rohanda-Shikasta. It simply relates their gradual dying until, in a strange and haunting conclusion, they go on beyond the lives of their bodies to "a different world, or zone, or reality" (118) where they join to become the Representative:

> The Representative swept on and up, like a shoal of fishes or a flock of birds; one, but a conglomerate of individuals—each with its little thoughts and feelings, but these shared with the others, tides of thought, of feeling, moving in and out and around, making the several one. [119]

This sort of a conclusion has been tried before in Arthur C. Clarke's *Childhood's End,* although Clarke's individuals sacrificed all remnants of selfhood in joining together. Lessing's version opens the doors for a number of things to happen in terms of the Canopus series. It comes as a severe shock that the Canopeans, so close to omniscience in *Shikasta,* absolute in authority in *The Marriages Between Zones Three, Four, and Five,* and observed as the overwhelming secret power of right in *The Sirian Experiments,* should in this novel be unable or unwilling to save this race on the planet where they, Canopus, originally placed them. In fact the novel is used to call into question a good deal of the readers' previous impressions about Canopus. Doeg points sharply to Canopus' limitations:

> "We have always thought of you as all-powerful, able to do what you like. We have never imagined you as limited. Limited by what, Johor?" And I answered myself: "You are the creation and creatures of something, some Being, to whom you stand in the same relation as we stand to you...? Yes, that must be so. But I have not thought on those lines before.... And you cannot transcend your boundaries, as we may not transcend ours...." [56]

Johor in effect admits that Canopus is inflexible, using a description which leads the reader to compare Sirius (from *The Sirian Experiments*) with Canopus, thus lowering the latter:

> "There is nowhere to take you. Our economy is a very finely tuned one. Our Empire isn't random, or made by the decisions of self-seeking rulers or by the unplanned developments of our technologies. No, we have a very long time ago grown out of that barbarism. Our growth, our existence, what we are is a unit, a unity, a whole—in a way that, as far as we know, does not exist anywhere else in our galaxy."
> "So we are victims of your perfection!"
> "Perfection is not a word we have ever used of ourselves—and not in thought either ... that word belongs only—to something higher." [57]

In *The Making of the Representative for Planet 8*, Johor suffers and dies with Doeg's civilization, but Lessing casts his experience aside and concentrates on the slow agony of the dying race. This novel of transformation combines the movement towards unity of *The Marriages Between Zones Three, Four, and Five* with a much greater engagement between the suffering narrator and the reader. The Chroniclers of Zone Three in *The Marriages Between Zones Three, Four, and Five* were not its emotional Center. Doeg is a sensitive and suffering representative of his race. Lessing slides easily between a quality of archetypal event and the realism of arctic suffering (drawn from her interest in Scott), sustaining a tone of awful and irrevocable loss which can be quite overwhelming if this short novel is read without pause. The escape to a different plane certainly fits with the Canopus framework of higher knowledge and deeper purpose, but both Doeg in his anguish, and Johor in his silent suffering and frustrated inability to justify the genocide he must oversee, bear witness to the reader that there is an implacability to the Need or Necessity which puts it beyond the reach of explanations based on galactic imperialism. The novel is a triumph of tone—stark and sere and monumental although only 121 pages long in the Cape edition.

As if the four volumes of *Canopus in Argos* to this point did not demonstrate their absolute novelty by dint of their range of tones, methods and motifs, *The Sentimental Agents in the Volyen Empire* further varies the framework. It is essentially a satire directed against the verbal excesses of political language and debate, with particular parallels to the excesses in emergent Third World states. Its narrator is Klorathy, who speaks about directing the affairs of several planets while attempting to "cure" Incent, a young Canopean agent, of a severe case of "undulant rhetoric." The disease, whose sufferers tend to leap at slogans and spout theories, is treated by a comic series of silences and reason but relapses are frequent, requiring incarceration in a Hospital for Rhetorical Diseases. Meanwhile Klorathy is rearranging demagogic societies, playing politics with fragments of the collapsing Sirian Empire, and offering "Rocknosh", a handy food which will grow on rocks, to a race who need a food supply in order to liberate their planet.

The novel is laden with tongue-in-cheek portraits of various types of political leaders and spies. The satire is so overt that an early outburst from Incent begins; "We shall fight them on the beaches" (18). The spy sections of the novel suggest that the "sentimental agents" of the title are closely parallel to the British intellectual spies such as Philby, Blunt, Burgess, and McLean who surrendered to the "undulant rhetoric" of their time. Lessing puts the essential point of the satire directly into Klorathy's mouth in a trial scene quite early in the book:

> "Calder," I said, "there are those who exist on words. Words are their fuel and their food. They live by words. They make groups of people, armies of people, nations, countries, *planets* their subjects, through words. And when all the shouting is done, nothing has changed. You may 'rise' if you like, you may drag Grice or some other puppet to the bar of history or geography or 'revolutionary inevitability,' and you can make yourselves and your entire people drunk on shouting, and at the end of it all, nothing will have changed." [47]

The Sentimental Agents in the Volyen Empire brings into focus the wholly original aspect of *Canopus in Argos,* which separates it from science fiction even as it is partaking of the freedom which Lessing finds in the methods of that genre. In terms of style and tone these novels are so different that only their Canopean frame of reference can hold them together, a galactic space which has room for everything. Lessing trusts to the moment-by-moment quality of the novels to interest the reader, and what eventually emerges is complex in the extreme. Without launching into the critical language of deconstruction, it is clearly fair to assert that the reader who has accepted the cosmic dominance portrayed in *Shikasta* and the omniscience of the Providers in *The Marriages Between Zones Three, Four, and Five* must ponder deeply the implications of a stumbling and limited Canopus in *The Making of the Representative for Planet 8* and the frankly scurrilous and satirical entanglements of Klorathy of Canopus in *The Sentimental Agents in the Volyen Empire*.

From above and below and from within and without, Lessing is observing this imperial conundrum which is Canopus, and in the process is able to find the space to work on a vast variety of the matters which she wishes to consider in her fiction. The objective distance which has long been a part of her method can come and go in a work with this variety, allowing the intimacy of the lovers in *The Marriages Between Zones Three, Four, and Five*, the satiric mix of coldness and buffoonery in *The Sentimental Agents in the Volyen Empire*, the suffering of *The Making of the Representative for Planet 8*, and the cool cosmic overview of *Shikasta* and parts of *The Sirian Experiments*.

Through this range of approaches, enclosed in a common and liberating galactic empire framework, Lessing is able to deal with an enormous number of subjects and personalities, always equipped with the kaleidoscopic capability to rotate the perspective to deepen the effect. In fact, there seem to be certain common themes and patterns which are repeated on different levels and in different tones in the five novels. All of the novels deal with worlds (technically parts of the empires of Canopus and Sirius, but so varied in their styles, approaches, and tones that the novels cannot be seen as a chronological series) in which very serious things are going wrong, both at inner and outer levels of experience. But the difficulties of Canopus' agents with Shammat can be presented as essentially comic in Incent's plight, or as mortal and terrifying in the situation of Nasar in *The Sirian Experiments*. And in *The Making of the Representative for Planet 8*, Shammat, the cause of the race's plight, is not even really present to be fought.

Moreover, with the exception of *Shikasta*, which is dominated by the need to demonstrate the possibility of an external and objective view of the human experience, all of the novels essentially continue Lessing's preoccupation with forms of the Bildungsroman. Ambien II in *The Sirian Experiments* gradually comes to the fore as she undergoes an enlightenment in cosmic realities and her own nature patterned after Sufi experience. In *The Marriages Between Zones Three, Four, and Five*, each principal character undergoes a personal struggle, is initially reluctant to change and break out of the structure of their own vision, but finally, after the prompting of the hard authority of the Providers, is transformed and expanded.

In *The Making of the Representative for Planet 8*, Doeg's race undergoes the most exotic growth of all, the transformation of transcending the physical body. Individuals are pictured in all the agony of an extended cooling like the cells of a vast corpse. And in *The Sentimental Agents in the Volyen Empire*, Lessing turns on her own preoccupation with the Bildungsroman development and prods at that stuttering stage, usually in the world of the young but all too unfortunately also in the world of public life, where words obscure genuine growth.

It is as if this great theme of human growth and development, with Lessing's accompanying sense, derived partly from Sufism, that there must be masters and a greater knowledge for which a great price must be paid, is the central axis of *Canopus*. But the forms she chooses and holds together with "galactic paste" permit her to vary and deepen her expression of this essential action of the human experience.

Indeed, through the linking figure of Lynda Coldridge, who is brought from *The Four-Gated City* into an important place in *Shikasta*, Lessing may be asserting that the Bildungsroman so thoroughly explored in an essentially realistic way in the five volumes of *Children of Violence* is to continue in the five volumes of *Canopus in Argos*. The fictional borrowing of Lynda and the essentials of her situation may be of the utmost importance in two directions. If the reader "accepts" (as fiction, of course) the *Canopus* series, this in effect explains and places Lynda's experiences in a much larger context and adds weight to the difficult assertions which come as such a shock at the end of *The Four-Gated City*.

Much more importantly, connecting the two series makes clear that *Canopus* provides a series of parallels to human experience, particularly the Bildungsroman, in the different registers of the new genre. "Parallels" must be used here, for given the level of complexity of the *Canopus* series as a whole, it would be nigh unto absurd to suggest the regularity of allegory. It is span fiction because, on a page-by-page basis, a great deal of *Canopus* has the flavor and intensity of realistic fiction, even when it may be embodied within a larger structure of myth or the outlines of science fiction.

There are undoubtedly some awkwardnesses in the *Canopus in Argos* novels, but then it would have been surprising if such an intricate and committed experiment, which attempts to range so far and include so much, could have succeeded in every way. Moreover, it is hard to imagine any writer taking the out-and-out risk of deliberately connecting a series of books in the only context she felt was broad enough, and then *choosing* to make the volumes differ in style and tone in order to open up a variety of approaches to the same situation. There is no doubt whatsoever that Lessing has surrendered both the traditional verisimilitude of the realistic novel and the large, evenly painted but lurid canvas of the galactic-scale science fiction novel in *Canopus in Argos*. On the new fictional middle ground she can speak about humanity at large in numerous different ways, ranging from extreme objectivity, which she can treat both as distance and as a device to attract sympathy, to intimate personal portraits of the intricacy of love. If the temptation of the philosophical novelist is always to model figures, to make them typify something, she is certainly able to do this in *Canopus*, protected on occasion by the polar morality common to science fiction. But she can also work in great detail with the intimacy of human experience, which accounts for the fact that *The Marriages Between Zones Three, Four, and Five, The Making of the Representative for Planet 8,* and portions of the other novels move their plotting much more slowly than science fiction action plots would dictate.

To establish *Canopus in Argos* in this new place in the realms of fiction, Lessing has had to bring from her extensive experience in realistic fiction her abilities to create complex and vital characters who live within entirely realistic microcosmic situations of love, power, ambition, and betrayal. And she has had to take advantage of the broad realms of the imagination native to science fiction, which allow her to exercise in a new way her talents for the constructive use of distanced viewpoints, both as philosophical model-makers and as the creators of the special sympathy of seeing the suffering "behind a wall of glass." The resulting shifts in perspective achieve a status of metafiction in that they keep attacking the readers' conventional expectations of consistency of approach. This shifting of perspectives within *Canopus* is central to its speculative quality.

What moves a writer like Lessing to the new fictional middle ground is the possibility of domesticating the *novum*, of placing realistically portrayed human behavior in larger contexts created from the whole cloth of the free imagination characteristic of science fiction. She does not feel bound by the "laws" of science or the strict accounting for scientific innovation which are characteristic of classical science fiction. This (and the fact that she is playing with metaphysics and personal development) is why her later work is not simply science fiction. So it is the depth, level, and complexity of her treatment of human character and relationships which shows more sensibility and subtlety than that of all but a few science fiction writers.

On the other side, her semi-scientific universe, created in the grand tradition of science fiction cosmology-making, moves her fiction out of naturalism but not into the realm of pure fantasy. She ends up standing on the new middle ground of span fiction.

CHAPTER 3

Thomas Pynchon: Science in Life

Thomas Pynchon has never been as concerned as Doris Lessing with the liberation which variations in genre could permit, because he has always written as a comic-ironic-intellectual-fantasist, little bound by any rules of realistic psychological-historical fiction. Up to *Vineland* (1990), his fiction has been, in major part, a recognition that the world of the later twentieth century is shaped by and permeated with science, technology and the scientific cast of mind.

In most of the short stories from 1958–1964 collected in *Slow Learner* (1984), in *V* (1961), in *The Crying of Lot 49* (1965), and in *Gravity's Rainbow* (1973), he treats science and technology as sources not only of subject matter and a lens through which to view the human condition, but as the basis of a style involving narrative position, language, imagery, and structural metaphors for vital elements of modern experience. His is the model of a new fiction written absolutely "within" the world of science, at a moment in history when, with the bomb, technology's dubious triumph, looming over us, and the explosion in information cascading into our lives and demanding organization, we turn and turn again seeking meaning, often using the new instruments of the "wizard" science without full awareness of what this may imply. Pynchon certainly suggests on occasion that what we may come to know might well be something that we would prefer not to know at all.

Many of Pynchon's critics have pointed to the fact that he began university in the most theoretical branch of engineering before switching to the study of literature.

At Cornell University, where Thomas Pynchon first won a

scholarship to study engineering physics and later took a degree in English, one of his professors "wonderingly remembers his apparently voracious appetite for the complexities of elementary particle theory." [Nadeau, 454]

In his fiction Pynchon goes far beyond simply indicating a knowledge of modern science. What distinguishes his work is his acceptance of the challenge to understand, explain, and make fiction about the world in terms of a coherent integration of science and other branches of modern knowledge, a *Weltanschauung* or worldview which breaks down the barrier between science and humanism. Pynchon's combination of Engineering Physics and English at Cornell peculiarly fitted him for unpredictable non-literary references and his scholastic imagination has made even his short stories dense and complex (Seed, 11).

The outcomes of this approach are most strongly felt in the overwhelming presence of things in Pynchon's fiction (and, as a result, in the considerable length of *V, Gravity's Rainbow,* and *Vineland*). David Cowart ranks Pynchon alongside Joyce as a twentieth-century encyclopedic novelist, at home ranging through music, painting, philosophy, and theology, as well as science. To this list could be added Pynchon's familiarity with the detailed history of the Second World War and a sensitivity to the social currents and style of America, both historically and in his own lifetime.

David Cowart's assertion that "Thomas Pynchon impresses his readers as that rarity, the literary artist undaunted by science and technology" (1) comes as an opening remark to his book devoted to showing Pynchon's non-scientific interests and, as such, may even be seen to understate the case. What really absorbs Pynchon is the desire to achieve a truly holistic, integrated, interpenetrating fiction which represents the world in all the ways that can be seen, including, at its center, the mentally disorienting discoveries of twentieth-century science. Cowart aptly expresses this challenge: "Science becomes fictive to the extent that an artist succeeds in dramatizing human participation in and response to its revelations" (3) (It sounds as though Cowart is echoing the Wordsworth quotation at the head of this study in this observation.)

Pynchon does just that: brings together the human element, life as lived in the fictive universe, with the predominant contemporary ways of knowing, including science. In so doing he moves to the middle ground of span, away from the intense psychological introspection and "realism" of much of the modern novel (from Woolf to Beckett to Murdoch to Heller) that seems often to exist in a closed social reality impermeable to

3. Thomas Pynchon

the explosions of modern technology and scientific knowing. Yet in doing so he does not arrive on the territory of science fiction, for his writing remains in a comic and fantastic tradition clearly indebted to Sterne and Joyce, and he does not, as science fiction does, extrapolate from some aspect of scientific knowledge but rather applies both scientific knowledge and scientific perspective to attempts to describe and understand the worlds his fiction delineates. Pynchon is interested in themes and subjects such as preterition, the collapse of the hero myth, human identity, the impending holocaust, the massive and oppressive aspects of international finance and manufacturing cartels, and above all with concepts of order and disorder in the world and the individual—but none of these are exempt from being seen through and in relation to science.

To Catherine Hume, setting about to establish that behind what she sees as Pynchon's scientifically based "deconstruction" of ways of seeing the world, there lies a mythology his overruling concern with science cannot be allowed to overwhelm. While Hume's presentation of a mythology is strongly put in her book, I think that she mistakenly argues herself wide of the mark in attempting to justify her right to read Pynchon in this fashion.

> In making his world so uncertain, Pynchon has not created a postnewtonian cosmos, but rather a fictional analogue to that world, one in which characters and readers must deal with uncertainties as radical as those of physics. His creation remains an analogue, however, not a scientific reality. Hence, I would argue, Pynchon's scientific concerns do not form a valid barrier to his using various kinds of ordering structure. Science is one of Pynchon's metaphors, not his starting point for examining reality. [190–191]

It is difficult to see what Hume is asserting about a work of fiction when she says that it remains an analogue, not a scientific reality. All fiction is, in the end, analogous to reality. While Pynchon's concern with science probably does not form a barrier to an "ordering structure," there is every possibility that modern science is that essential ordering structure, providing metaphors at a number of levels but also providing the overarching coherence of Pynchon's worldview, a worldview which in our century is slotted in with the corresponding views of philosophy and other vital paradigms of human understanding. There is every indication that he does see science as "his starting point for examining reality" or, at the very least, as a coequal starting point with other contemporary patterns of thought. The matter is further complicated because twentieth-century science has become highly self-conscious about the fact that scientific descriptions of the universe themselves now tend powerfully towards metonymy.

The first stage in considering Pynchon's interface with science is to consider the extent to which it figures as the subject matter of his fiction. This is complicated by the fact that science is often subject, structural analogy, narrative arbiter, and metaphor at the same instant; and it is intended that after considering science as subject, this section will proceed to a consideration of science as style in Pynchon, looking at its effect on structure, narrative position, language, and imagery.

The preeminence of science as it contacts human lives places it in Pynchon's foreground. A consideration of Pynchon's uses of science as subject is very much a survey of Pynchon's critics who have done a great deal of work on this matter. Robert Nadeau has looked at the new physics in *Gravity's Rainbow*, David Seed has looked at thermodynamics and other aspects, and both William Plater and Molly Hite have dealt with science although they have incorporated their considerations in larger theses. I will select a sampling of issues from Pynchon's fiction to illustrate his commitment.

Of the five stories collected in *Slow Learner*, "Entropy" (1960) offers the most direct example of science as a theme in Pynchon's early work. Its title refers to that complex and multifaceted concept whose primary applications are in thermodynamics and communications theory, and whose implications are the heat death of the universe and the total failure of communication.

In a third-floor apartment in Washington, a lease-breaking party is moving towards its third day, and in the course of the story it accelerates to a frenzy and then dies away again, having used up some of the energy of the participants. Upstairs, in a sealed apartment, Callisto, an aging intellectual, is dictating memoirs of his intellectual life which parody *The Education of Henry Adams* and cradling a tiny sick bird against his chest, while his lover, Aubade, takes dictation and maintains the hothouse plants in the miniature cultivated jungle of their sealed apartment. Outside the building the temperature remains a stable 37° Fahrenheit, as it has for the past three days.

Pynchon deals with entropy in a wide range of fashions in the story. Meatball Mulligan is breaking his lease so that when the motion of his party has ceased completely, as all parties must eventually, he will cease to exist in the "system" of the building. Meanwhile, the swirl of drinkers, flirters, listeners, card players, musicians, and fighters are the model of active atoms, the differentiated energies in motion whose eventual increase in entropy will signal their cessation.

Upstairs, in the other part of the system of the building, the process is much further advanced. Callisto actually contemplates the Laws of Thermodynamics in his memoirs:

> It was not, however, until Gibbs and Boltzmann brought to this principle the methods of statistical mechanics that the horrible significance of it [entropy] all dawned on him: only then did he realize that the isolated system—galaxy, engine, human being, culture, whatever—must evolve spontaneously toward the Condition of the More Probable. [87]

Callisto is trying to transfer heat (according to the Second Law) to the bird, but when it dies he has evidence that heat transfer has stopped, the law has failed. He is also deeply afraid of the stable temperature in the external environment, for the heat death of the universe, the point of maximum entropy, will occur when all heat is evenly distributed, when form surrenders entirely to chaos. So while Mulligan's corybantic party defies entropy though action (but of course fails as energy is dissipating), Callisto is trying hopelessly to freeze change while temperature differentiation still exists. When, at the close of the story Aubade dramatically breaks the window with her bare hands, she signals the surrender to the inevitable.

> ...[She] turned to face the man on the bed and wait with him until the moment of equilibrium was reached, when 37 degrees Fahrenheit should prevail both outside and inside, and forever, and the hovering, curious dominant of their separate lives should resolve into a tonic of darkness and the final absence of all motion. [98]

Thus there are two closed model "engines" in the story. The Mulligan party has fluctuations, but it is gradually running down. They have run out of champagne and will run out of tequila. But their model is not perfect, because three coeds and later five sailors arrive from outside, bringing further energy and supplies. Theirs is the model of a traditional "engine' running at less than 100 percent efficiency and being fueled from without. But there is no without outside "without." The system which is fuelling the party is the known universe, and when it runs out of supply the machine will stop, and entropy will triumph.

Upstairs, Callisto and Aubade are maintaining a constant temperature that it is supporting their lives and a profusion of plant life, and Callisto hopes the transfer of heat to the sick bird will save its life. But the temperature outside has stabilized and the conclusion of the story is that they must join it. If the apartment building is the world, both representations of it move, as everything must, towards the More Probable Condition.

Within the Mulligan section of the story there is also the application of entropy to communication. Saul, who climbs in off the fire escape, has just had his wife walk out on him during an argument about communications theory in which he took the position that better human communication would be more machinelike. Effective communication depends upon differences, the way in which elements of a signal differ from other elements and from the background "noise," which is presumably a constant. This relates to the More Probable Condition because of course all signals, just like all matter, tend towards sameness. Saul describes this in a model that contains the crux of his collapsing marriage:

> Tell a girl: "I love you." No trouble with two-thirds of that, it's a closed circuit. Just you and she. But that nasty four-letter word in the middle, that's the one you have to look out for. Ambiguity. Redundance. Irrelevance, even. Leakage. All this is noise. [90–91]

There are other smaller models of communications beginning to fail as the "noise" begins to overcome the signal. The Duke di Angelis jazz quartet at the party express awe that Gerry Mulligan had the audacity to leave out the piano and hence the root chords in a piece, and hence must have "thought" the roots. They experiment with carrying this to its obvious outcome by going through the motions of a piece with *no* instruments, miming the sounds without making them. This revolutionary advance in jazz playing has one obvious weakness to anyone but the quartet: it fails to communicate the music because there is no signal at all. In fact, only the quartet itself can "hear" the music and express dissatisfaction that they were not "playing" the same piece or that one of them had begun in the wrong key. Droll this may be, but Pynchon is on a serious subject here, the explanation that entropy in communication spells an end to communication, and the less signal there is above the background noise, the less clearly anyone will be understood, to an infinity which will be reached by stages.

> The final hiss [of the phonograph recording of *The Heroes' Gate at Kiev*] remained for an instant in the room, then melted into the whisper of rain outside. [85]

Presumably outside the hiss of the rain is the hiss of the background noise of the universe, which, when it has become Condition of the More Probable, will by definition communicate nothing. Upstairs meanwhile, Callisto is remembering how there were fewer and fewer instruments playing in the tangos after the Great War, falling away to the tango in *L'Histoire du Soldat* with only seven instruments. Of course seven instruments cannot communicate the same information as a full orchestra, so Callisto is also mourning the gradual loss of signal and the impending onrush of undifferentiated silence.

"Entropy" is very much a characteristic Pynchon evocation of a scientific theme. With approaches varying from the amusing touch of the soundless jazz quartet to the stomach-wrenching implications of all systems—including human beings—moving to the Condition of the More Probable, to dissolution, Pynchon applies the concept of entropy to the lives and destinies of his characters and makes us see their lives through aspects of science. In his detailed exposition of "Entropy," David Seed accurately observes: "Already then it should be obvious that Pynchon is not using the term 'entropy' loosely" (37). The characters in his fiction are not exempt from descriptions of the universe or physical systems. All human stories take place in the realms of science. That is Pynchon's premise and, to a large extent, his point. [1]

It follows that Pynchon cannot let go of entropy in his later fiction, any more than one can choose to "forget" the laws of science at will. It is true that the degree of focus may vary, and in *Vineland* the concept is only indirectly present in the losses in humanity of the Reagan years and the final collapse of Brock Vond, but in *V, The Crying of Lot 49,* and *Gravity's Rainbow,* Pynchon offers further investigations of entropy.

In *V* the world is clearly unraveling, running down, falling apart on both the private and public levels. Pynchon constructs the novel so that an extremely chaotic present, primarily New York's bohemian life of the 1950s with the Whole Sick Crew at its center, alternates with an historical panorama running from the end of the nineteenth century to the Second World War on Malta. By switching eras and class ethos Pynchon creates an immense sense of a gap, which illustrates that disorder is increasing. Sidney Stencil, the spy trapped in changing eras and styles at the turn of the century (his floreat in the novel is from 1897 to 1919), is a conscious echo of Henry Adams, whose education wrenched him from the past into the twentieth century, from the Virgin to the dynamo.

The Situation, the term used by spies and diplomats in the nineteenth century to describe political reality, becomes hopelessly confused in the course of the novel, its only apparently consistent element being V, an enigmatic woman (or women, so enigmatic that it cannot be determined) whom Stencil pursues around the Mediterranean in her "declining" guises from the apparently innocent Victoria Wren in Egypt to Veronica Manganese on Malta, a spy with a glass-clock eye and a mutilated face who is passing through "her own progression toward inanimateness" (410). To be certain that the direction she is moving will be clear to the reader,

Pynchon has Herbert Stencil, Sydney's son who is seeking the meaning of the V his father pursued, fantasize on her eventual state:

> Perhaps—Stencil on occasion could have as vile a mind as any of the Crew—even a complex system of pressure transducers located in a marvelous vagina of polyethylene; the variable arms of their Wheatstone bridges all leading to a single silver cable which fed pleasure-voltages direct to the correct register of the digital machine in her skull. [410-411]

Herbert sees her turning from person into machine, becoming inanimate. The Bad Priest, whose nearly mechanical body (the clock-eye, removable feet, wig, star sapphire in navel, false teeth) is crushed in the Second World War air raid on Malta, is presumably the last living form of V. Fausto Maijstral, who chronicles her/his/its death, fantasizes on the composition of the figure:

> ...the skin of her legs peeled away to reveal some intricate understructure of silver openwork. [343]

As a model of the movement towards entropy, V becomes unalive in gradual stages and finally disappears into component parts. But for Herbert Stencil, who stands near the center of the novel's action (Pynchon constructs it so that, like reality, it has no absolute center, V her/itself self-destructing as the "V-symbol is chronically overdetermined" [Hite 48]), it is arguable that the remaining idea of V is the purpose of his existence, that her/its influence continues unabated without physical form. In *V*, the first of Pynchon's novels about unachieved and perhaps unachievable quests, the Condition of the More Probable is accelerating. Pynchon sets half the novel in a past that seemed to have more solidity but which was coming unraveled. Attempts to get at the past dominate *The Crying of Lot 49* and *Gravity's Rainbow,* both novels which also stress the entropic drift. Some of their characters express a knowledge of entropy and others do not, but Pynchon correctly maintains that ignorance is no excuse under the laws of science.

The *Crying of Lot 49* begins with dissolution, the death of Pierce Inverarity (whose name suggests piercing the truth), which happens offstage but dominates Oedipa Maas' odyssey through the craziness of California, and by detours into the history of Europe since the Renaissance and America since its European settlement. Oedipa, Pierce's executor and former lover, finds her world disintegrating around her as she pries into a number of mysteries which surround his estate. She flings herself around California, meeting a galaxy of unusual types, most of whom seem to possess information or evidence for her hunt. But the facts are elusive and the people go mad, disappear, commit suicide or stop helping before anything is certain.

Oedipa's reality unravels around the death of Pierce, who as far as Oedipa and the reader are concerned, seems to have disappeared without trace. It is as though the entropic dissolution that comes to all humans has come to him. Nor does he leave Oedipa any material thing, only the mystery of Tristero, which may be a conspiracy of underground information transmission that has functioned since the Middle Ages. Here Pynchon turns from the entropy that affects matter, such as Oedipa's friends and Pierce himself, to the entropy which affects information theory, to a foreground of "noise" which increasingly masks the "signal" of the truth about Tristero. Tristero itself, however dark its designs, at least represents a force for order in the universe, but Oedipa never finds it and her quest ends a moment before she will perhaps meet an agent of Tristero. The reader rightfully places little confidence in the possibility, having been frequently disappointed earlier in the story.

Gravity's Rainbow, the novel above all his others which typifies Pynchon's commitment to science, deals with entropy as one concept interlocked with many others. Entropy is one aspect of the speculation about order and disorder in the modern world which is carried on congruently on a number of other levels.

The novel begins in the seeming chaos of the V2 rocket attacks upon London but its entire first section is laced with the conundrum that in the face of such chaos, humans seem to feel that they are closer than ever to understanding and fixing the order of events. People like Edward Pointsman, the Pavlovian, Roger Mexico, the statistician, and Brigadier Pudding, the rational historian, are all on the track of "meaningful structures." While London is becoming progressively more fragmented and thousands of people are attaining the Condition of the More Probable, it is the opinion of these practitioners of science that they will soon have answers. The primary aim of Pointsman, Rollo Groat, Edwin Treacle, and an uncounted shadowy group of supporters in high places is to discover why Tyrone Slothrop, an American stationed in London, makes love to a woman (never the same one) at every location where the V2 rockets will fall within ten days.

They expect to solve this problem in terms of cause and effect, but in fact *Gravity's Rainbow* never does offer an answer. From these high hopes of recognizing order, an order also reflected on the inorganic scale by the fascination with the benzine ring and the inevitable destructive action of the rockets, the novel moves to progressive disorder on all levels. Its long third section, "In the Zone," pictures the chaos which has come to Europe after the Nazis, slaves to logic and order, have been displaced and the last section, The Counterforce, actually features the movement of Slothrop, who has been the questing figure throughout most of the novel, towards the Condition of the More Probable. According to various reports he is becoming transparent:

> He's [Pig Bodine] looking straight at Slothrop (being one of the few who can still see Slothrop as any sort of integral creature any more). [740]

or scattering, coming apart in random entropic distribution:

> ...Tyrone Slothrop, who was sent into the Zone to be present at his own assembly—.... The plan went wrong. He is being broken down instead, and scattered. [738]

Slothrop is surrendered to chaos and as central character simply fades away at the end of novel. In this and in ending the novel with a series of loosely linked fragments and scenes, Pynchon thus makes the structure of the novel conform with entropy, showing a world moving to confusion and dissolution.

The rocket is the other major force of entropic movement in the novel. Slothrop, in his meandering quest for the secret of his connection to it, provides what sense of plot there is early in this encyclopedic work. It turns out that Slothrop had been conditioned as a baby by the diabolical Pavlovian, Dr. Laszlo Jamf, to get an erection in the presence of the polymer Imipolex G, and that the polymer is somehow connected to the rocket. It may be that Slothrop's erections and seductions in London are outcomes of this (crazily inverted since the response precedes the stimulus) and the rocket certainly becomes the central goal of the novel. Yet in the end Pynchon allows no clear solution to the mystery, no attainment of the goal. Slothrop does not find the answer and the reader is given a most unsatisfactory one. It emerges that one rocket fitted with an Imipolex G window has been fired by the mad Blicero and contained his catamite Gottfried, whose sacrificial death is to somehow balance Blicero's own.

The firing of that rocket is virtually the last element of the novel. Yet the rocket ending is deliberately truncated, for the *Schwarzkommando*, the survivors of the Southwest African black Herero people who, in an immense irony of racist reversal, are depicted as forming part of Hitler's rocket-firing groups, have decided that the V2 has religious significance as part of their conscious drift to racial extinction (which the German attempts at genocide in the Sudwest in 1904 and 1919 originally began).

They are covertly attempting to assemble a last symbolic rocket which they will fire. Thus there are *two* climactic rockets being organized in the Zone, which deliberately weakens the centrality of any possible solution.

The rocket is a most concrete model of entropy. At the beginning of its flight it is a model of maximum organization, the complex product of a highly developed science in a highly organized political state. But even on the way up to its sixty-mile-high peak, its dissolution begins. At the *Brennschluss*, or burnout, it ceases to be driven or steered by man and enters the inevitable realm of the ballistic arc, a slave to momentum and gravity. Its destruction and the destruction it will bring are implicit from the start and, once past the apex of its flight, dissolution and death come at a constantly accelerating pace, the elegant laws of the calculus describing the movement towards chaos but in no way influencing it. The rocket is death on all sides. It is death in London, death in the Zone even to those who work on it, death to Gottfried imprisoned in it, and the vision of death for the Herero. It draws Slothrop up the ballistic arc towards knowledge and then down towards his scattering. Just before the closing moment of the novel, when the rocket hangs poised to destruct over the Orpheus Theatre in Los Angeles (apparently in the early 1970s), it is tentatively related to Slothrop as a physical stimulus but not the one he has been seeking through the novel:

> ...what he [Slothrop] felt so terribly, so immediately in his genitals for those rockets exploding in the sky ... to help him deny what he could not possibly admit; that he might be in love, in sexual love, with his, and his race's, death. [738]

Noah's rainbow was a promise of life, but gravity's rainbow is the promise of death, dissolution and the Condition of the More Probable.

The matter of entropy is central to Pynchon because it is so central to several schemes of modern thought about the "meaning" of nature. Its thermodynamic implications are particularly tied to the question of closed systems and the rules and descriptions that govern them. In philosophy, which in the twentieth century seeks to emulate science in precision and also acts as a constant commentator on the language and methods used in describing the world, Ludwig Wittgenstein is a vital contributor, and his influence on Pynchon is most thoroughly investigated by William Plater in *The Grim Phoenix*. But the bridge between philosophy and science proper, particularly on the matter of the closed system, is Kurt Gödel, who worked both in mathematics and philosophy. Gödel's Theorem (1931) asserts that no logical system can be complete because all such systems depend upon external axioms, givens which are brought to the system from the outside.

As Molly Hite extensively explains in her study of order in Pynchon, this bears directly upon what Pynchon writes fiction about. Many of Pynchon's characters are engaged in searches for meaning and order and they seem doomed to always fall short of "tying up" comprehensive meaning. The systems and explanations, such as V in *V*, the Tristero in *The Crying of Lot 49*, the "Theys" (presumably the vast modern industrial cartels which run governments and wars) or the ballistic arc in *Gravity's Rainbow* are never proven to be complete or comprehensible, so that readers have their expectations in the quest for structure roundly defeated. Not even authorial authority steps in, for Pynchon dissipates the narratives, offering alternatives and deliberately inconclusive closure.

In the realm of physics—more specifically thermodynamics—Gödel's Theorem is both the entropic deathknell for the universe and raises questions which border on the theological. It is the former because the universe, as a closed system or engine (the thermodynamic term), must run down unless there are inputs of organizing energy from the outside and, given our definition that the universe is the system encompassing all of physical reality, there is no possible source of external energy. It may be the latter because Gödel's Theorem suggests by definition that there must be some factor outside of the closed system we call the universe, and Pynchon coyly hints at this with mention of the Angel of Lübeck[2] and the Brocken-specter[3] in *Gravity's Rainbow*. He suggests in the novel that Murphy's Law, which asserts that the unexpected will always occur, is a popular form of Gödel's Theorem[4], implying that there is always the surprise of something outside of the realm of knowing which we thought was complete.

There is some confusion in the above observations because they move from questions of logical systems to the 'system' that is the physical universe to the "system" of thermodynamics. It is not, however, any accident or error which overlaps these conceptual perspectives. We are at the very root of Pynchon's treatment of science when we recognize that the scientific perspectives are integrated with other visions of reality. To fully encompass life in the modern scientific world involves a fictionalized consideration of the overlap between science, the humanities, physics, and theology. In his consideration of entropy Pynchon is doing just that.

Entropy is, of course, only one aspect of science that forms Pynchon's subject matter, although it is an overarching one. While no catalogue of reasonable length could be exhaustive, the point of his variety does need to be established to illustrate the depth of penetration of science as subject matter. He ranges from chemistry to medicine to electronics to rocketry to robotics to physics to aerodynamics to biology.

Chemistry, particularly the benzine ring, is central to *Gravity's Rainbow*. Laszlo Jamf has told his students that there is a National Socialist chemistry, preaching the distorted values of death over life, of inorganic permanency over the carbon-hydrogen bonds:

> "move beyond life, toward the inorganic. Here is no frailty, no mortality—here is Strength, and the Timeless." Then his well-known finale, as he wiped away the scrawled C–H on his chalkboard and wrote, in enormous letters, Si–N. [580]

This inorganic icon, in the form of the polymer Imipolex G, is central to the novel, for it has been used by Jamf as Slothrop's Pavlovian key and it is what Slothrop is sent to track down in the Zone. It is death in the rocket for Gottfried, whom Blicero will send to his death in the V2 with a window of the plastic so the catamite can see "The first star hangs beneath his feet" (760) as he begins the descent to his death. The fallacy of Jamf's assertion, of course, is that of the narrator in Yeat's "Sailing to Byzantium," who would choose to be the artificial golden bird in the emperor's garden, a creature that will never die because it will never live. The facts of organic chemistry lie at the heart of the fact of death, and death is at the heart of *Gravity's Rainbow*.

Modern medicine is also integrated into the novels. Pynchon offers a lovingly detailed description of Esther's nose job in *V*, prefacing it with a history of plastic surgery which he ties in to her surgeon Schoenmaker's early and traumatic experience with the discipline:

> Thus Godolphin received a nose bridge of ivory, a cheekbone of silver and a paraffin and celluloid chin. [100]

The horror emerges a few lines later when it is revealed that this reconstruction will be rejected and Godolphin's face will collapse within six months, killing him in agony. This ties tightly to the basic themes of transformation and the desire to attain form with meaning that underlie *V*. It is Pynchon's method to present the sciences, in this case plastic surgery, which are used to "shape" us to comment on the human desire to attain meaningful shape and to comprehend it.

In *Gravity's Rainbow*, Pavlovian psychology is a central idea, for Jamf has conditioned Slothrop, and Pointsman (the man who controls the switches) realizes that he has a rare chance to study a conditioned human. Pavlov's ideas are the scientific form of the argument against human free will, and in *Gravity's Rainbow* they tie into the larger context of the closed system and the "Theys" of the cartels who may even be dictating the events of history such as the Second World War. But, in *Gravity's Rainbow*,

Pynchon also touches on other medical matters in detail, including the logical reasons why the Herero may be facing extinction and the precise procedure through which Major Duane Marvy, because he is mistaken for Slothrop, is castrated so that Slothrop's very special gonads (presumably in some way responsive to Imipolex G) can be returned to Pointsman.

Electronics also permeate the novels, whether it is the precisely observed sign at the Scope bar in *The Crying of Lot 49,* where electronic music reigns:

> The green neon sign ingeniously depicted the face of an oscilloscope tube, over which flowed an everchanging dance of Lissajous figures. [31]

or in the complex and fascinating concept of "sferics" which Kurt Mondaugen studies in the Sud-West in *V.* Sferics (atmospheric radio disturbances) are the background signals on radio frequencies and serve Pynchon as a prime illustration of man's desire for understanding and ordering of things when Weissmann, the tireless proto–Nazi who will later appear as Blicero in *Gravity's Rainbow,* "decodes" some of the pops and whistles after weeks of trying. The message he receives is DIEWELTISTALLESWASDERFALLIST ("The world is all that the case is"), which is Wittgenstein's opening statement in the *Tractatus.* It is also, Weissman asserts, an anagram for Kurt Mondaugen (attained by extracting every third letter). The message, presumably from a non-human source, a source outside the system, is immensely ironic as it asserts that there is nothing outside the world and at the same time implies that attempts to deduce order must flounder on "finding" something which is already inside the order. (Wittgenstein published the *Tractatus Logico-Philosophicus* in 1921 and so it was "in the air" when Weissmann decoded it from interference noises in the Sud-West in 1922.) This piece of complex paradox is characteristic of Pynchon's use of science as subject. It is not metaphor, for there are real signals and a real act of decoding, but Weissmann's involved system for decoding the message smacks of an emotional desperation to get meaning and throws what he has discovered into real doubt. On the larger stage of *V* this reflects on Herbert Stencil's struggle to assemble a meaning for his own world through an understanding of V.

The concept of the robot or cyborg gets attention from Pynchon. Bongo-Shaftsbury, who in 1899 tells the child Mildred and her sister Victoria Wren he is a clockwork driven by electricity and proceeds to show them the switch sewn into his arm, is the first such creature. Victoria, as she moves into the twentieth century as V, becomes progressively more mechanical. Her direction is made clear in chapter 14, "V in Love," where her real fascination is with the fetish, the inanimate love object. Here Pynchon asserts that she was resisting automation but offers the image of its implications:

> ...that she became—to Freudian, behaviorist, man of religion, no matter—a purely determined organism, an automaton, constructed, only quaintly, of human flesh. [411]

V advances from the glass eye with the clock in it to the creature with all of the prosthetic parts who is disassembled on Malta in 1942. In *V*, Benny Profane becomes the nightwatchman at Anthroresearch, where he takes care of SHROUD and SHOCK, the former a human skeleton with plastic organs and skin used to measure the effects of radiation and the latter a humanoid manikin used to simulate automobile injuries. Oley Bergomask, their owner, introduces them to Profane in terms which sum up science's rational views of humanity. He states that man was viewed as a clockwork automaton in the eighteenth century, as a thermodynamic heat engine in the nineteenth century, and is viewed as an absorber of X-rays, gamma rays and neutrons in the twentieth-century world of nuclear physics.

In *Gravity's Rainbow* synthetic automatons do not play a major role, although the rocket with Gottfried as a component, receiving but not sending signals, can be seen as a composite being. In *Gravity's Rainbow* the emphasis shifts from the machines made in the image of humanity to humanity seen through the eyes of science as Pavlovian puppet or as cog in the vast machines of the system.

The rules and practices of physics are also central to Pynchon's subject. The physics of the rocket dominate *Gravity's Rainbow*. Pynchon presents its development in great detail, constantly linking it to the human experience. Franz Pökler, one of the engineers, watches the distortion of the windtunnel model:

> and see[s] how his own face might be plotted, not in light but in net forces acting upon it from the flow of Reich and coercion and love it moved through.... [422–433]

The way in which the lives of those concerned with the Rocket are linked with the control of the Rocket itself is suggested in the way the yaw equation is presented:

> ...preserving, possessing, steering between Scylla and Charybdis the whole way to Brennschluss. If any of the young engineers saw correspondences between the deep conservatism of Feedback

and the kinds of lives they were coming to lead in the very process of embracing it.... [239]

Physics is even being employed outside the Rocket world after the War in the aerodynamic design of the perfect hashpipe, which turns out surprisingly to be an already available item:

> ...and guess what, in terms of flow rate, heat-transfer, control of air-to-smoke ratio, the perfect shape turns out to be that of the classical kazoo! [745]

Not surprisingly, in fiction that brings man and science together, Pynchon also implants elements of biology. These range from young Gavin of the White Visitation in *Gravity's Rainbow*, who can change his skin color at will through a complex enzyme and pigment control, to Slothrop's final "scattering" which may leave parts or replicas of him drifting around the Zone.

Besides all of the scientific subjects brought into the fiction, there is a great deal of attention paid to modern technology. Its use as imagery will be considered later but it forms a great deal of the content of the fiction. This is a primary way in which Pynchon shows how science is involved in contemporary reality and separates his work from that of writers who focus on social or solipsistic realities, such as Iris Murdoch or Samuel Beckett. Pynchon is assuming that the changes in our physical circumstances and the changes in our activities have real meaning in terms of how the world is and how we see it, and he most emphatically chooses to create worlds which are immersed in contemporary technology. Where "pure" science fiction is often about science more than it is about people (a point that would certainly be challenged by many of its better practitioners but which is nevertheless often the case), Pynchon's span fiction is about people in a world surrounded by the physical presence of science (technology) and holding a worldview frequently expressed in the language or metaphors of science.

In his first story, "The Small Rain," Pynchon begins to include details about such things as army radio gear and the treatment of dead bodies after a hurricane. In *V*, McClintic Sphere, alto sax player, tumbles on the basic functioning of computers, which he turns into a song:

> Out of the conversation had come Set/Reset, which was getting to be a signature for the group. [193]

Also in *V* there is such detail as the manufacture and nature of false teeth and fillings:

> The upper right canine was pure titanium and for Eigenvalue the focal point of the set. He had seen the original sponge at a foundry.... [152]

In *The Crying of Lot 49* there is detail about electronic music ("We got a whole back room full of your audio oscillators, gunshot machines, contact mikes, everything man" [31–32]) and the implications of the loss of information when a sweaty mattress in a flophouse is burnt:

> So when this mattress flared up around the sailor, in his Viking's funeral: the stored coded years of uselessness, early death, self-harrowing, the sure decay of hope, the set of all men who had slept on it, whatever their lives had been, would truly cease to be, forever, when the mattress burned. She stared at it in wonder. It was as if she had just discovered the irreversible process. [88]

But it is in *Gravity's Rainbow* that technology is most emphatically part of the subject matter. Large portions of the novel are given to the details of rocket manufacture, firing, and such problems as control. Pynchon pays the same sort of attention to the makes of guns and cars that Ian Fleming did. There are chemical details of drugs, of invisible writing fluid, of such statistical methods as Poisson Distribution, the technical details of Pavlovian experimentation. This list could easily go on for a page. It extends into everything, even the nature of the souvenirs made from the Rocket, such as key rings.

Pynchon's presentation of science and technology as subject matter in his fiction is a reflection of the world in which it occurs and the effect that living in that world has on human beings. He grasps that science and its practical offspring provide much of our environment and many of our activities, and he deliberately and intensively makes them a part of his writing. His expansiveness in this direction is a major contributor to the "feel" of his fiction, to the particular sense of crowding and confusion that is characteristic of living in the modern world.

Plater, Hite, and Nadeau are among the critics who have taken up the question of the structure of Pynchon's novels. Some of their considerations are not germane to this examination, but what is of interest is the degree to which Pynchon's structures and his implicit comments about structure in the fictions have their origins in or are parallel to the thinking of science. It can be said of *V*, for example, that it tends towards the chaotic, moving from The Situation which, even for Sydney Stencil, was becoming less a coherent view of the world than an agreement by several minds working on it, through the increasing activity of the twentieth century to the Whole Sick Crew with their nearly meaningless peregrinations around New York City. Against this trend to disorder Herbert Stencil struggles to impress (to "stencil") a meaning upon the chaos, to set an anchor in the V symbols whose interconnection he seeks. But although a great deal of V information is forthcoming in various forms, it does not cohere. In this Pynchon has found an expression of entropy, the process leading to chaos which brooks no alternate vision. In both Stencils, Pynchon has represented the type of Henry Adams seeking to preserve and form the world upon some elegant humanist basis. But man is moving out of the center of the meaning of things, being replaced by the automaton and the entropic universe. (See Hite, 104)

The Crying of Lot 49 presents another world where meaning seems to be taking some shape but does not do so by the end of the novel. Maxwell's Demon, the molecular information sorter who is supposed to exist in the Nefastis Machine, is a close parallel to Oedipa Maas (Plater 57), who is trying to sort out whether the Tristero System exists to offer historical continuity that would embrace a number of events. But the Demon is only a thought experiment model and so does not exist, which in effect reduces Oedipa to an ordinary human rushing about accumulating data that shifts, changes, and disappears faster than she can tie any of it firmly together. Oedipa actually speeds up in the novel as the flow of information increases until, in her all-night wandering through San Francisco, she is being bombarded with possible clues, but unlike the imaginary Demon she finds it all too much work and is left faced with a binary choice and no answer. The hot and cold molecules which faced the Demon represent for Oedipa the choice of Tristero or not-Tristero, but for Oedipa the work of sorting is overwhelming.

In *Gravity's Rainbow* there is no question that the ballistic arc of the title is the central structural principle, and it is worked into the narrative in a myriad of ways. Katje tells Slothrop that each of them was at one end of the Rocket's parabolic arc and that the Rocket lived its entire life in one flight. Pynchon then observes:

> They must have guessed, once or twice—guessed and refused to believe—that everything, always, collectively, had been moving toward that purified shape latent in the sky.... Yet they do move forever under it, reserved for its own black-and-white bad news certainly as if it were the Rainbow, and they its children. [209]

The arc is the shape of the book, as Slothrop is launched on his quest (in reverse direction to the rocket) from the organized command post in the chaos of London, reaches his Brennschluss either on Katje's disappearance or after reading Laszlo Jamf's file (which makes things as clear to him as they will ever be), and then descends into the Zone, obeying the arc of his destiny. At the close of the novel he can be seen either as the product of an airburst (scattered) or hovering, like the Rocket over the Orpheus cinema in Los Angeles, in the final delta-t of the calculus before impact and destruction.

This shape has all sorts of implications, some of which Robert Nadeau investigates. He stresses that the Rocket does not reach the Absolute Zero of impact, which implies that the system it represents is not finally closed, although closure would seem inevitable. But Nadeau goes on to explain that:

> What the rocket worshippers in the novel fail to understand is the nature of the force of gravity. If the resistance of any object to acceleration is a measure of its interaction with the rest of the cosmos, then the rocket at rest in its gravitational field is just as close to absolute zero as the rocket at its highest point of trajectory in flight. What Pynchon implies here in his treatment of the rocket worshippers is that irreconcilable polarities and oppositions are fictions of the mind which have no real existence in nature. Our efforts to transcend them to reach the absolute is [sic] simply a product of our failure to realize we are at absolute zero without making any effort at all in the sense that our participation in the life of the "entire" cosmos is a given. [464]

(This question of human centrality will recur shortly in a consideration of the narrative positions in the novel.) The promise of gravity's rainbow is not transcendence, as Nadeau's "absolutists" would seek outside the system, but participation in the ballistic process, the attainment of order and direction as a prelude to physical dissolution. Molly Hite puts this in the context of concepts of the promises, the first of which was made to Noah in the rainbow, upon which the Calvinists and later the American Puritans (such as William Slothrop) constructed their doctrine of predestination (105). She draws her reader's attention to the irony that the Rocket is about to destroy by fire rather than water.

The arc of the Rocket is measured by the calculus, as Pynchon explains in a passage where Slothrop remembers it while looking at the stairstep gables on the houses at Cuxhaven.

> Three hundred years ago mathematicians were learning to break the cannonball's rise and fall into stairsteps of range and height, x and y, allowing them to grow smaller and smaller, approaching zero.... This analytic legacy has been handed down intact—it brought the technicians at Peenemünde to peer at the Askania films of Rocket flights, frame by frame, x by y, flightless

> themselves ... film and calculus, both pornographies of flight. Reminders of impotence and abstraction.... [567]

This literate rendering of the way in which calculus divides time and distance represents the shape of the novel, for it is filled with random incident and intense activity at the start, slows to Slothrop's "trajectory" in the middle, and then accelerates, breaking into tiny segments in the closing pages. Equally importantly, the passage comments on the vital relationship between the action and its observers. The film and the calculus are pornographies of flight because they watch and analyze without direct participation. Man can only watch and intellectualize the Rocket's flight with the impotence and abstraction of the scientist watching nature. The overpowering domination of nature, as represented by the ballistic arc, conditions the shape of the narrative and the roles of the characters, narrators, and possibly the readers.

The principles of narrative voice and position are, then, for Pynchon questions of how the closed system of each of the fictions and its implicit comment on the closed system of the real world are to be understood and represented. William Plater gives this problem its most brilliant analysis in *The Grim Phoenix* and, while he has other approaches to the matter, he places a high priority on the way in which Pynchon's scientific interests condition choices of voice and position:

> With his scientific background, Pynchon is particularly conscious of the role of the observer. [10]

One major shift in twentieth-century science, that Pynchon is well aware of, is from the vision of objectivity to the vision of relativity. Put crudely, science used to believe that the observer of a system, be it of pulleys, chemicals in reaction, or astronomical phenomena, stood outside and observed the behavior of the system and so came to understand it. Humanity observed the universe, and, it was often assumed, God observed humanity. In fiction this produced external narrations that made stories "true" or "factual" seeming, sometimes with morals being explained by godlike narrators.

The transition brought about by relativity rests upon the fact that the experimenter is always involved in the experiment, that, in fact, observers in differing positions will not observe the same phenomena and observers affect the results. In quantum mechanics results cannot occur without the observer which leads to a widely held proposition that experimenters create the meaning of events in the act of describing them. Henry Adams had foreseen this:

3. Thomas Pynchon

> In plain words, Chaos was the law of nature; Order was the dream of man. [451]

Its implication is clearly that no one in a system can ever "know" anything because all patterns of understanding are part of the "dream of man."

The implication for Pynchon's fiction is his refusal to be a godlike author, his rejection of the overwhelming narrator of the first person narration prominent in the early twentieth-century novel, and an intent to draw the readers into the closed system of the fiction where, along with many of the characters, they will try to compose their "dream of order." The other implication is that the chaos of nature, including the observing characters, will resist the dream and the reader will be quite deliberately prevented from removing some reducible central meaning from the work.

In practice Pynchon's position has meant that in all of his fiction he has used omniscient narrators who do not tamper with events openly or spell out meanings, keeping rather to a distanced stance. *V* is offered in 17 discrete sections that do not keep to chronological order, and the combination of this, with the sort of authorial descriptions which could as well come from other characters ("How tired her face looked, in the scatter from the brow lights" [443]), and the overwhelming profusion of events and details makes the novel simply "come at" the reader without any strong sense of control. This makes readers sympathetic to Herbert Stencil's attempt to impose meaning on the V symbol and to other characters' usually futile attempts to get their lives in order. As Plater observes, it is arguable that to understand any constructed system that proposes to describe the world, we would have to stand outside both to compare them, and it is Pynchon's method to draw us into the narrative where we share with certain of the characters the struggle to know if we know reality through the systems we perceive (13ff).

This struggle the reader shares with the characters to make sense of the world in the narratives is brought into finer focus in the compressed narrative of *The Crying of Lot 49*. Here Oedipa is the searcher and she is much more intent and direct than Stencil in *V*, whom the reader realizes is very unsure of whether he ever wants to reach a goal. Oedipa is not certain either, for the existence of the Tristero would make several deaths murders and might endanger her personally, but these are much clearer objections than Stencil's, which are constituted of fears of identity and a hidden desire to keep the chase in motion. Oedipa's experiences range widely, but this is chiefly done through historical reportage by other characters so that a tight time line is sustained in the novel. Again Pynchon refrains from any direct guidance to the reader about the understanding of the story so that he cannot be seen as standing outside the fictional system verifying anything. He reinforces the position that we live in the world and that that is the only perspective from which we can ever attempt to comprehend it.

In *Gravity's Rainbow* there is a far wider range of information about scientific and technical processes, political realities, histories of individuals and races, and many other "factual" informations that are presented with the apparent solidity of omniscient narration. There are also a lot more characters attempting to impose system on the vast chaos they are laboring inside of, but Pynchon goes further in this matter by having them range from the absurd in Brigadier Pudding to the seemingly rational Roger Mexico. A full list of those seeking pattern and meaning would also include Dr. Laszlo Jamf the chemist, Edward Pointsman the Pavlovian, Captain Blicero the Rocket commander, and all those who get hints of the "They" of the cartels behind the War, the Rocket, and History. Somewhere in the middle is Slothrop, whose search is more desperately personal and thus typifies any human's real and desperate attempt to find meaning in life.

But Pynchon tries something new in *Gravity's Rainbow* as part of his method of dealing with the closed system. To further draw the reader into the novel, the text will shift to direct address, a tactic that erases time and distance between the events and the reader. The method is characteristically ambiguous, so that what is being said may apply to the character in the action but also reaches out at the reader:

> ...just now, waiting in this broken moonlight, camouflage paint from fins to point crazed into jigsaw ... is it, then, really never to find you again? Not even in your worst times of night, with pencil words on your page only Δ+ from the things they stand for? And inside the victim is twitching, fingering beads, touching wood, avoiding any operational Word. Will it really come to take you, now? [510]

This technique reaches its climax at the close of the novel when the Rocket is poised over the theater (which presumably—"theatrum mundi"—represents the world) and Pynchon writes:

> There is time, if you need the comfort, to touch the person next to you, or to reach between your own cold legs ... or, if song must find you, here's the one They never taught anyone to sing, a hymn by William Slothrop.... [760]

Pynchon has also brought himself into his own narrative earlier by referring to on a number of occasions to "us" and "we":

> The rest of us, not chosen for enlightenment, left on the outside of Earth, at the mercy of a Gravity we have only begun to learn.... [590]

There are even occasions when "you" and "we" are used together, creating the impression that the narrator is in the narration with the reader, that there is, in effect, *nowhere* outside the narration at all:

> About the only one not participating here, aside from the two prowling surgeons, is Seaman Bodine, who we left, you recall.... [594]

This goes beyond standard assertions about fiction being a conventional artifact which creates a world. It pulls the reader into a fiction whose characters are clearly concentrating on this very question of the closed system, the thermodynamic engine, where we find to our surprise that we are sharing the world with the narrator. Like the modern scientific observer the narrator admits that he is inside the system, affecting it, and this helps to stress that the readers are there too. Everyone—characters, narrator, and readers—is free to apply patterns of meaning to the system but no one can prove the precise correspondence between their system and THE system. Relativity rules.

In addition to the involvement of science as subject matter, in the underlying structural principles, and as a governing agent in the selection of the narrative method, it is clearly a major aspect of the actual texture of the language in Pynchon's fiction. This matter of the use of the language of science can be suitably divided into two categories; general use and metaphorical language. The former is Pynchon's reflection on the way in which science permeates people's daily lives and is most likely a reflection of his own milieu as well. It is obviously not going to be present very strongly in his historical sections such as Egypt in the 1890's in *V* or Renaissance Italy in *The Crying of Lot 49*, but its general prevalence is of major importance to my demonstration of how science is "entering" literature as part of the verbal "household of man." As early as "Low-Lands," Pynchon brings in technical detail when he has the crazy psychiatrist Geronimo Diaz:

> ...spend whole sessions reading aloud to himself out of random-number tables or the Ebbinghaus nonsense-syllable lists, ignoring everything that Flange would be trying to tell him. [58]

"Entropy," constructed as it is around scientific ideas, is heavy with the language of science. Beyond the subject matter proper there are details of language such as love makes "the nebula precess" or this description of Aubade's response to the distant sound of a jazz trumpet:

> The architectonic purity of her world was constantly threatened by such hints of anarchy: gaps and excrescences and skew lines, and a shifting or tilting of planes to which she had continually to readjust lest the whole structure shiver into a disarray of discrete and meaningless signals. [88]

This complex verbal construction is an example of a sensual transformation (synaesthesia) in which the effect of sound is rendered as geometry. Then it switches to describe the possible outcome of Aubade's concept of the universe in terms of information theory, "a disarray of discrete and meaningless signals." What is notable about Pynchon's method here is the use of the register of scientific language in such a way that persons not particularly familiar with its basis will still be able to take its meaning. He supports this by having brought up the ideas behind the language elsewhere in the story, in this case in the discussions of information theory and ecosystems.

Even "Under the Rose," set in 1898, and "The Secret Integration," a story about children and race relations, illustrate Pynchon's use of a scientific register. Porpentine, the aging spy in "Under the Rose," suddenly realizes that his enemy is no longer human but some sort of system:

> But they—no, it—had not been playing those rules. Only statistical odds. When had he stopped facing an adversary and taken on a Force, a Quantity?
> The bell curve is the curve for a normal or Gaussian distribution. An invisible clapper hangs beneath it. Porpentine (though only half-suspecting) was being tolled down. (134–135)

Here the language precisely represents the change from a humanistic world to a mechanical one because it is presented in mechanical terms. It is also, of course, an image, for a bell curve is not a bell and does not have a clapper. That same curve recurs in "The Secret Integration" where the "boy genius," Grover, explains how the school authorities have discovered that he has a racket doing homework for other students.

> They knew somehow (they had a "curve," according to Grover, that told them how well everybody was supposed to do) that it was him behind all the 90s and 100s kids started getting. "You can't fight the law of averages," Grover said, "you can't fight the curve." [142]

In this story the boys are full of enthusiasm for science, building sodium grenades, discussing the properties of nitrogen and playing with a model of a protein molecule. The story centers around the fact that Grover initially mistakes the problem of racial integration in the neighborhood for the sure and elegant integration of the calculus, with its cool promise of a permanent freedom which Pynchon brilliantly illustrates through Grover's description.

> ...drawing straight vertical lines from the curve down to the x-axis, like the bars of a jail cell—"you can have as many of these as you want, see, as close together as you want."
> "Till it's all solid," Tim said.
> "No, it never gets solid. If this was a jail cell, and those lines were bars, and whoever was behind it could make himself any size he wanted to be, he could always make himself skinny enough to get free." [186–187]

But the jail bars close around the Negro jazz musician in the story and the pressure of the anger of the adults and the confusion over the other, irrational human responses to the integration of race leads the boys to fantasize a black playmate. In this story Pynchon establishes the attractions of the cool sense of science to the young and describes how the boys discover that it cannot fill in the vast swamp of human irrationality.

There are a number of examples of the common uses of the language of science in *V*, even in the sections of the novel which are set in the early twentieth century. V in Paris speaks to Mélanie of the chemistry which will make Mélanie exciting to her:

> "What are you like unclothed? A chaos of flesh. But as Su Feng, lit by hydrogen, oxygen, a cylinder of lime, moving doll-like in the confines of your costume.... [379]

Pynchon offers a terrifying medical rendering of the eerie laughter of the hyena:

> It was a product of alien secretions, boiling over into blood already choked and heady; causing ganglia to twitch, ... an unbalance, a general sensation of error that could only be nulled by those hideous paroxysms.... [268]

The nature of this last description stands as a model of a great deal of what Pynchon aims for in his use of scientific language. It plants the reader in an alienating yet real world, made mechanical by the description of biological processes yet containing the key ideas that the beast is threatened and that in its cry it releases a sensation of terror. The world of *V* is becoming progressively more inhumane, more mechanical, yet nonetheless more horrifying for all that. Even love gains this mechanical quality:

> Ready at the slightest pressure surge in the blood lines, endocrine imbalance, quickening of nerves at the lovebreeding zones to pivot into some covenant with Profane the schlemiel. [358]

When Profane and Rachael reach intimacy, the world hovers horribly behind them in the happy popping sound of champagne:

> "Yes." What percentage was there in telling her what it really sounded like? At Anthroresearch Associates there'd been radiation counters—and radiation—enough to make the place sound like a locust-season gone mad. [422]

Here the scientific language occurs in a novel whose chief concerns are the interpretation of history on all levels from intimate to global. But Pynchon is integrating the attempt to see these humanistic issues with the way in which we now perceive the world. He is refusing to stay in the tradition of the language of the older humanism, when we live in a world made more complex through widely disseminated scientific attitudes and the language of these attitudes has become part of the common currency of thought and understanding.

The Crying of Lot 49 has a central scientific metaphor which will be considered later in this section, but in addition this short novel continues the natural integration of the language of science. Examples of this range from the detail of the statistically inclined poker player:

> ...whose steady loser entered each loss neat and conscientious in a little balance-book decorated inside with scrawled post horns. "I'm averaging a 99.375 per cent return, fellas," she heard him say. The others, strangers, looked at him, some blank, some annoyed. "That's averaging it out, over twenty-three years. I'll never get ahead of it. Why don't I quit?" [84]

through the "linear obstinacy" as approaching police sirens grow louder to Mucho's LSD certainty that he can precisely analyze one of seventeen violins on a muzak tune:

> "His E string," Mucho said, "It's a few cycles sharp. He can't be a studio musician. Do you think someone could do the dinosaur bone bit with that one string, Oed? With just his set of notes on that cut. Figure out what his ear is like, and then the musculature of his hands and arms, and eventually the entire man." [98]

In this short novel, so deeply permeated with historical detail such as that of Tristero and with the zany Southern California of the sixties, Pynchon still speaks even of the dead with scientific precision.

> She tried to reach out, to whatever coded tenacity of protein might improbably have held on six feet below.... [121]

In the very special blending of scientific and traditional language which he has developed, such cold terms as "coded" and "protein" are juxtaposed with "tenacity" and "held on," placing the readers where Pynchon wants them in a world where science is no longer divorced from immediate human experience.

Of all of Pynchon's fiction, *Gravity's Rainbow* is obviously the book in which the language of the sciences is most pervasive, partly, of course, because the Rocket is one of its main subjects. But the novel travels over almost every area of reality, establishing science in the world of human experience and rendering human experience into the language of science. So pervasive is the method that, in conjunction with the intense use of metaphoric language involving science, it gives the novel a flavor which no grouping of examples can fully demonstrate. Incorporation, the putting of something into the body of, is perhaps the best word to describe the power and flexibility of Pynchon's insertions and their deep integration into the text. While only a full reading of the novel can convey this, examples can demonstrate its presence and effect.

When Slothrop first meets Katje on the Riviera, she has been put there to meet him by their managers, but she points out that they have the prior connection of the rocket, she having been where it was launched and he "on the other end" where it came down. It is a circle of which they are both a part:

> He understands that it's something back in Holland, before Arnhem—an impedance permanently wired into the circuit of themselves. [208]

The language of electricity captures the sense of invisible reciprocating exchange between them, of a power over which they, as the wired hardware, have no control. Characteristic of this mature handling of the language of science is the way in which it uses a word ("impedance" in this instance) which is technically correct in terms of its science (electrical physics) but which also carries correct overtones for someone who is reading without the technical knowledge. The idea that the connecting force is impeding Slothrop and Katje, permanently interfering with their freedom of action, is contained in the word as a reflection of the larger idea of an electrical circuit that is fixed in its intricate and circular design by its engineers and can only convey current as it is wired to do so. Thus there is a subtle layering of ideas in this single example and an accessibility for those who do not grasp the implications of the electric circuit.

Sometimes the scientific language can achieve a poetic depth of sensibility which really makes the reader stop short at what it implies and reveals. Franz Pökler is cruelly managed by Weissman in order to secure his vital aid on the rocket. He is given a visit with his "daughter," (actually different children to service his pedophelia) annually:

> The only continuity has been her name, and Zwölfkinder, and Pökler's love—love something like the persistence of vision, for They have used it to create for him the moving image of a daughter, flashing him only these summertime frames of her, leaving him to build the illusion of a single child.... [422]

Here the suggestions are extremely varied and wonderfully rich. The psycho-physiological phenomenon of the persistence of vision, which permits the perceived effect of motion in cinema and television, involves the way that the brain continues momentarily to perceive light after the source has been removed, so that rapidly succeeding images appear to be continuous, a sequential action. It is a lie, of course, but a lovely lie which permits illusions of continuity.

That the power of love can cause Pökler to occlude the various "daughters" into a "continuous" Ilse is an immense (and, in its relation to the mixed quality of the love with its incestuous outcomes, monstrous) tribute to love and at the same time a severe criticism of the lengths to which human beings will go to preserve the illusion of love and the loved one. At one and the same time it has about it the strange, almost stoic triumph of human desire and the overriding pessimism of the human animal as a pawn to biology and the forces of control which menace the characters in the novel. And, passingly, it reminds the reader of Salvador Dali's "Persistence of Memory" (1931), whose soft watches and desolation, the weaving of scientific "realistic" precision and the confusion of dreams are so much the mark of the twentieth century, of surrealism, and of Pynchon's method.

The same sort of extremely suggestive use of scientific language is seen in the philosophical speculations on the meaning of the rocket. After considering the possibility of the existence of good and bad rockets, the narrator turns to a chilling vision of the Rocket as the bringer of private and specific death.

> Stored in its [the Rocket's] target-seeker will be the heretic's EEG, the spikes and susurrations of heartbeat, the ghost-blossomings of personal infrared, each Rocket will know its intended and hunt him, ride him a green-doped and silent hound, through our World, shining and pointed in the sky at his back, his guardian executioner rushing in, *rushing closer*.... [727]

The intensity of the personal threat in this description comes from our shared sense of reverence for the precision of modern medical technology, the acceptance that we can be known, precisely and clinically, in ways which brook no argument or evasion. Thus the EEG, a modern equivalent of the Lord knowing our innermost thoughts, the graphically presented fine details of the movements of our hearts (usually seen only when someone dear is hooked to a monitor in an intensive care ward), and the infrared imprint of our body, the picture of the energy which confirms our mortal existence, all serve to place an inescapable absoluteness on the way in which the rocket will hunt and find us. When Pynchon combines this with the image of the rocket "shining and pointed in the sky at his back," a detail so visually clear [5] and immediately physical that it sets the shock frame for the wonderful "guardian executioner," he has once again made masterful use of the language of science.

Pynchon's denotative use of the language of science, then, carries with it the general aura of the modern world and our complex emotions towards this apparently most precise and rational language, which in fact, because of the linguistic overlap in which so many of the terms of science (such as impedance) have been drawn from earlier words with non-scientific language, is enormously evocative and bonds the two realities. Beyond these uses lies the vast country of metaphor, which offers images chosen from the world of science and technology, and in revealing complexity places them inside and beside the lives of the characters. The quality of the object in metaphor to be both suggestive in its equivalence and itself present in the text helps to overwhelm the reader with science and provide stunning, original and often intellectually shocking new ways of seeing the world. What follows here are a few selected examples of this vital anchoring practice of Pynchon's integration of modern science in the fabric of his work.

In his early short fiction Pynchon was already adept at the suggestive mixing of the actions of science and human lives. "The Secret Integration" begins with boyhood innocence about racial conflict:

> "What's integration mean?" Tim asked Grover.
> "The opposite of differentiation," Grover said, drawing an

x-axis, y-axis and curve on his greenboard. "Call this function of x. Consider values of the curve at tiny little increments of x....
"This is integration," said Tim.
"The only kind I ever heard of," said Grover. [186–187]

The full evocative power of this image can only be seen in relation to the whole structure of the story. The boys, full of the innocence of their own trifling sense of being powerful and slightly evil (plots to throw sodium in the school toilets, dropping water bombs on passing cars), initially confuse the two meanings of the word integration. But under Pynchon's control that is an enormously evocative confusion, with its mentions of the bars and a man struggling to be free. Integration in the calculus is:

> ...the inverse process of differentiation. Gives a method of finding the areas enclosed by curves, and of finding solutions to other problems involving the summation of infinitesimals. [Uvarov and Chapman 157]

Integration in racial matters is most certainly the inverse of differentiation, only people rather than numbers are its objects. And there is no doubt that a problem involving infinitesimals is involved, the tiny difference in skin pigment which is the boundary of the area enclosed by the "curve" of the society. There is a suggestion, bounded by two "ifs," that a man could squeeze between the bars and enter the society, but the image clearly conveys a sense of struggle and difficulty.

When this is related to the story from which it is taken, it is further enriched. In "The Secret Integration" the boys, led by Hogan who has joined the AA at the age of nine, go to visit a black musician and alcoholic who has strayed into their white Berkshires community and who is finally dragged off in most menacing fashion by the local police, who have discovered him in an unpaid-for hotel room with the boys. This touches most frighteningly on the image of the man trying to wiggle through the bars no matter how narrow they are and, in touching this physical reality as it bounces off to the larger implications of the metaphor in terms of the way society blocks off integration, makes the details of the rules of exclusion ever tighter, like the declining intervals of the calculus curve. There is also a paradox operating here, for Pynchon offers the contrast between the cool, satisfying abstraction of mathematics, whose elegance naturally attracts the boys, and the messy suffering of human life, which they begin hazily to understand in the story.

For Catherine Hume there is a real pitfall in Pynchon's use of science:

> The problem in science-oriented readings arises when one considers levels of reality and the applicability of principles from one level to another. [190]

I think that the reverse is true. It is anything but the problem when the metaphoric use and control is like that demonstrated above. As with all of Pynchon's manipulations of science, such metaphors reveal an enormous amount about the way the world is (in his mind's eye) by both difference and similarity, the traditional functions of the metaphor. There is no doubt that it is at the very impact point between the scientific and humanistic uses of differentiation that a starburst of meaning occurs and that the burst is managed and controlled by the contexts of plot, the characters of the boys, and the narrator's cool yet essentially sympathetic position.

The metaphorical skills being honed in the early stories are fully demonstrated in *V.* With the foci of the novel on the replacement of humaneness in the twentieth century by the mechanical and upon the incursion of chaos (or our awareness of chaos) upon our time, it follows that the metaphorical language will contribute to those wide premises. Pynchon delineates the era before the mechanization of the animate when he has Slab, the painter, explain his new subject, the Partridge in the Pear Tree:

> The beauty is that it works like a machine yet is animate. The partridge eats pears off the tree, and his droppings in turn nourish the tree which grows higher and higher, every day lifting the partridge up and at the same time assuring him of a continuous supply of good. It is perpetual motion, except for one thing." He pointed out a gargoyle with sharp fangs near the top of the picture. [263]

Not only does the gargoyle, for which the reader will eventually substitute V, and the forces of chaos she/it represents, threaten the cycle, but for the animate to possess the characteristic of the beauty of the mechanical there must be a continuous supply of "good," which could be pears but, in the religious overcontext of the carol, is probably grace. So even the image of this older structure of the world is endangered by the gargoyle and can survive only in the context of belief.

There is no context of belief in the twentieth-century world of *V.* The chaos portrayed on Malta during the 1942 bombing, the aimless "yo-yo" wandering of the American characters, and the devalued overdirectedness of a few characters do not lead to any coherent pattern. One of the novel's central questions is whether Stencil (or his father?) ever want final clarification of the awful anyway. One of Pynchon's prime scientific metaphors for the new chaos is reported by Fausto Majistral:

> The present Fausto can look nowhere but back on the separate stages of his own history. No continuity. No logic. "History," Dnubietna wrote, "is a step-function" [310]

A step function is "any function whose graph is a sequence of two or more horizontal sections with vertical jumps or discontinuities" (eds. Littler and Littler,198) and is represented thus:

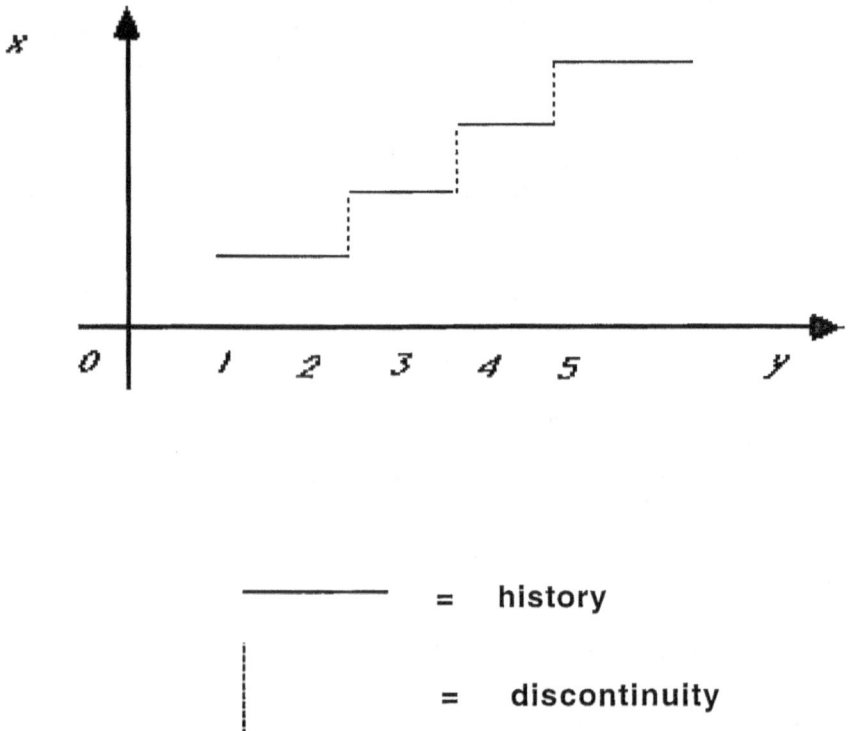

This presents history as discrete worlds broken by sudden shocks and reforming "elsewhere" upon another plane. It is mirrored in Fausto's own division of himself into four, occasioned by the shocks of his twentieth-century experience, and it is also imaged in the returns of V, whose progression mirrors that of the eras in which she occurs, from the virgin deflowered in the shadow of nineteenth-century international intrigue in the Fashoda crisis to the dynamo of the Bad Priest, perpetrator of events on Malta in the Second World War.

3. Thomas Pynchon

The step-function metaphor for history contradicts concepts of historical logic and development and characterizes the chaos of the twentieth century. Perhaps the graphic representation should show a descending pattern or else the x-axis indicate greater chaos as time passes. Faced with sudden discontinuities, man cannot plan and cannot understand, a fact underlined by a mathematical metaphor in which the pattern has no recognizable parallels in reality. A "pattern" of disorder with unknown causes ("discontinuities") for abrupt massive change is a far-reaching image of our times.

The chaos of our times also finds expression as Rachel Owlglass awaits her appointment with Schoenmaker the plastic surgeon and observes his mirrored clock with exposed gears and two mechanical demons. Pynchon's description of this device and his comments on it make it an image of the chaos of the mirror world of our times, with its subjective confusions between reality and images.

> Or was it only the mirror world that counted; only a promise of a kind that the inward bow of a nose-bridge or a promontory of extra cartilage at the chin meant a reversal of ill fortune.... [36]

This vision of nodes where reality meets mirror-reality echoes thinking about matter and anti-matter, but as almost always with Pynchon, the shift to the human generates an interplay for the metaphor. It is the imperfect, the dissatisfied, for whom time needs to be reversed, just as their bodies need to be adjusted by Schoenmaker (beauty-maker) the plastic surgeon, and so the node or connecting point between the chaos of history and other possibilities is located where there is a highpoint of human suffering. And the end of life, coming "quietly as light ceases to vibrate," would be at the end of a process of living falsely through the mirror, wearing the mirror face given by the plastic surgeon. Given that V herself will be many faces and that there will be two Stencils and many other duplications in *V*, this image of the clock with its pendular reversals suggests a suddenness of change similar to the step-function.

The mechanism of the clock links the consideration of historical chaos closely to Pynchon's other pre-occupation in the metaphors in *V*, his representations of the twentieth-century shift from the human and humane to the mechanical. V her/itself is undergoing a transformation from human to mechanical construct and the section "V in Love" deals extensively with the mechanization of love. V's passion for Mélanie places this focus clearly:

> "...moving doll-like in the confines of your costume.... You will drive Paris mad." [379]

This is expanded a page later in Itague's estimation that even a Marxist revolution would be part of a decadence.

The fetishism at the center of the section is the metaphor for this loss of humanity and Mélanie, the girl seeking self-annihilation who dreams with deep sexual pleasure of being wound up with a great key in her back, finds it by becoming V's fetish until her horrible death evolves out of the dance of the automatons in which she is starring. The full horror of the mechanization of humanity (also mirrored in the Baedeker Land of objects and the "breed" called tourists) is described in the inactive "love" which approaches death.

> ...a transvestism not between sexes but between quick and dead; human and fetish. [385]

The machines of death grind not only in the movement to fetish but in the larger world of politics, where it is the Situation, about which Stencil pére is constantly ruminating:

> In his more philosophical moments he would wonder about this abstract entity The Situation, its idea, the details of its mechanism. [173]

He finally deduces that it is extremely subjective as, of course, is all modern physical science, but he phrases it in the language of geometry, suggesting a mechanical logic in the behavior of masses of humanity:

> ...much like a diagram in four dimensions to an eye conditioned to seeing its world in only three. [174]

From the level of the intimate to the whole Situation, reality is becoming progressively more mechanical, and Pynchon's metaphors, from the science of psychology and from mathematics, are the keys to grasping the movement of the central image, V her/itself.

The Crying of Lot 49 is built around the central metaphor of the Tristero (alternately spelt Trystero), the mysterious organization which approximates all of the conspiracy theories of the past thirty years and drives them to a manic, excessive yet terrifying possibility by rooting them in the Renaissance. Oedipa Maas openly wonders whether the Tristero is a fantasy that her psychiatrist should be managing (her sources keep disappearing before they can be verified), but for the reader Pynchon is placing the Tristero in the broader context of the chaos versus order struggle, the presence of entropy. The chaotic Southern California of the novel, the coming apart of twentieth century American civilization in a rush of freeways and a widdershins dance of crazies, is contrasted to the meaningful menace of the Tristero.

When Pynchon looks to entropy for the parallels to this, he picks up on the fact that there are two entropies: one related to thermodynamics and the other to communications theory. The former, which is signified by California, is related to the increase of chaos in the universe, while the latter suggests that the exchange for this chaos is the increase in information which counteracts the loss of order. This strange pairing has been used to argue that human knowledge, or information, acts to contradict the action of physical entropy—resulting in a counterbalancing of the coming of chaos by increased human ingenuity. A physicist would point out the absurdity of this in the long and inexorable run of time, but the subjective human view of the matter (over the short run which humanity will have in astronomical time) may be an accurate representation of a local eddy in the larger pattern.

In *The Crying of Lot 49* the Nafastis Machine, a proposed perpetual motion machine based on James Clerk Maxwell's Demon, purports to be the proof that information (which is supposed to be psychically exchanged between the Demon and a sensitive) gathered by the Demon can offset the natural entropy of a closed system and produce perpetual motion. Maxwell would turn in his grave at this use of his metaphor, for the Demon was strictly a scientific thought experiment designed to prove the Second Law of Thermodynamics rather than overturn it. Students were expected to point out the flaw in Maxwell's closed universe of the Demon in the box which was that, in order to produce energy by sorting the hot from cold molecules, the Demon itself had to introduce the work energy of sorting into the system. Hence, a closed perpetual motion system was impossible. What Oedipa faces when she tries to aid the Demon and fails is a metaphor for her attempt to discover the larger (and perhaps malignant) demon of the Tristero, which would offer a meaning in opposition to the chaos of her world.

The old drunken sailor who gives Oedipa a letter to post through the Tristero system prompts one of Pynchon's more complex metaphors and a contemplation on metaphor itself:

> She knew, because she had held him, that he suffered DT's. Behind the initials was a metaphor, a delirium tremens, a trembling unforrowing of the mind's plowshare....
> The act of metaphor then was a thrust at truth and a lie, depending on where you were: inside, safe, or outside, lost. [Oedipa's memory then leaps backward to a college boyfriend talking] ... about his freshman calculus; "dt," God help this old tattooed

man, meant also a time differential, a vanishingly small instant in which change had to be confronted at last for what it was.... She knew that the sailor had seen worlds no other man had seen if only because there was that high magic to low puns, because DT's must give access to dt's of spectra beyond the known sun, music made purely of Antarctic loneliness and fright. [95–96]

Oedipa recognizes the links between metaphors and reality, how the sailor's DTs are, through the compression of metaphor, like the dts of the calculus which give a painful vision of the immediate frozen instants of reality. Pynchon openly points to the high magic of low puns, the opening of meaning beyond the rational which metaphor can give, characteristically for him, in terms of mathematical science.

After Oedipa has been buffeted about by the mysterious possibilities of the hidden conspiracy of the Tristero, and when all the bits of elusive evidence have passed before her, she sees the summation of the possibilities and the future of America in terms of the language of the computer:

> She had heard all about excluded middles; they were bad shit, to be avoided; and how had it ever happened here, with the chances once so good for diversity? For it was now like walking among matrices of a great digital computer, the zeros and ones twinned above, hanging like balanced mobiles right and left, ahead, thick, maybe endless. Behind the hieroglyphic streets there would either be a transcendent meaning, or only the earth. [136]

This is the perfect image for Oedipa's and America's dilemma. Against the chaos of modern America, typified in this novel by Southern California, there is only the yes/no gate of the binary system. If there is a meaning, it is hidden, and to believe in it forces one outside of the accepted into the realm of the conspiracy theorist. If there is no meaning (Henry Adams' "chaos"), then to believe there is one is full-blown paranoia. The excluded middle, the idea of a liberal and varied America, is not an available choice in a binary system. This image of the absolute, electrical binary choice of the machine perfectly captures the inexorable quality of what Pynchon sees as the American choice—a choice which has no acceptable option.

The great overarching metaphor in *Gravity's Rainbow* is in the title itself, which marries the ballistic arc of the rocket to nature and to the sense of the inevitable force which dominates the text. The novel presents a great struggle between the forces of nature—gravity, dispersal and dissolution, the carbon life cycle, the Zone—and forces of order, which are also forces of evil, and the artificial—the cartels, military organization and the War, the workings of machines, plastics, and Slothrop conditioned by

Jamf. Slothrop is launched in the novel (and eventually becomes Rocketman), either from London or, if one takes the longer view, by Laszlo Jamf and Lyle Bland for the cartel when he was an infant, and his movement toward the secret of Imipolex G is presented as the tiny steps of differential calculus, the ·t of near-infinitesimal events.

This great metaphorical organizing principle of the novel has ramifications in a number of directions. It explains the book's concerns with the Preterite, for lives lived in the arc of the rocket are as inevitable and predestined as the Calvinist damned. It explains the parallel structure of the novel: those firing the rocket—Weissmann/Blicero, Enzian—and those seeking the rocket—Slothrop, Marvy, the forces of governments and shadowy cartels. There are not one but many ballistic arcs in *Gravity's Rainbow*—one for each rocket and one for almost all of the main characters.

And central to this great metaphoric pattern is the path of Slothrop. It is difficult to describe a launched object as a hero, but Slothrop's odyssey, his arc, does override the other patterns in the novel. And insofar as it is possible in a world dominated by the inevitable arc of gravity, through comedy he escapes the inevitable impact awaiting the Preterite. The riotous, farcical closing movements of Slothrop's presence in the novel suggest an escape from the arc of inevitability, as though the human spirit can somehow evade the fall back to destruction.

Pynchon splits the metaphor in his concluding chapters, separating the inevitable action of the rocket, which he associates with Weissman/Blicero, the firing of the A4 and all of the intricate web of government, War, and cartel which lie behind it, from the human principle of Slothrop and the zany Counterforce, who seem to dance away from the last inevitable moments of Gottfried's existence and the Rocket hanging frozen over the theater. But despite this dichotomous conclusion to the novel, it is clearly dominated by the multifaceted colors of the Rocket's rainbow arc, the prescription of ballistic inevitability under which humanity has lived since the first stone was thrown but which blossomed to its full horror with the A4 and the ICBM.

Beneath the overarching metaphor of the Rocket emerges an innumerable range of metaphors which draw science into human lives. Many of these are tied to the Rocket or to the calculus, describer of the arc. At Peenemünde, Franz Pökler, kept in thrall by Weissman by his annual visits from "Ilse," sees how his experience is as controlled as the vacuum cycle with its shutter control in the wind-tunnel:

> ...he has listened, and taken it to imply his own cycle of shuttered love, growing empty over the year for two weeks in August, engineered with the same care. [422]

This is the image of the mechanical manipulation of a man through love, of the desperate inner love drained annually and then so cruelly snapped off. The Rocket, deformed by gravity and air resistance, is a victim of the same forces as Pökler except, of course, without his weakness of love. The dominant feeling in the metaphor is of compulsion, of the inexorable function of the man-made machine ("the shutter") and of the deformation brought about by acceleration and atmosphere which leads to "the same degradation, as death will warp face to skull...." The Rocket (and by implication its ICBM descendant) stand for inevitability, the unavoidable path of machine and natural forces throughout the novel. The behavior of humans is constantly being compared to the world of the rules of scientific effect.

This same resonant parallel to the inanimate is used over and over, as in the description of the mood of the endangered lovers Roger Mexico and Jessica Swanlake:

> ...whippy as sheets of glass improperly annealed, ready to go smash at any indefinite touch in a whining matrix of stresses.... [37]

The richness of this metaphor lies in the seeming perfection of the sheet of glass which, nevertheless, contains invisible faults which will sheer in all directions into the most wholly useless, irreparable, and dangerous pile of fragments. It is rich and effective because it combines a hard scientific truth, which is at the same time a common experience, with the vision of the delicate and beautiful, yet fatally flawed, quality of the love relationship.

The same quality of common experience mixed with physical-mechanical inevitability is used to express Slothrop's relationship to the mysterious masters driving him through the novel:

> There are times when Slothrop actually can find a clutch mechanism between him and Their iron-cased engine far away up a power train whose shape and design he has to guess at.... [207]

When we push in the clutch we do not stop and Slothrop is aware that he is in motion even when he temporarily escapes the driving force of the people engineering his destiny. It is later Slothrop's fate to disintegrate like waves moving away from a center because he reduces his "bandwidth" and lives only for the present. As early as the Anubis era, Slothrop has begun to scatter (see page 53).

> "Personal density," Kurt Mondaugen [said]..., enunciating the Law which will one day bear his name, " is directly proportional to temporal bandwidth." [509]

But while all the sciences are called upon to furnish metaphors in the novel, it is the Rocket and the calculus which describes its behavior to which Pynchon returns again and again. And one of the most important aspects of the Rocket is guidance, the mixture of delicate feedback and adjustments whose mechanical key is the solenoid, the switching mechanism that turns on and off according to current flow from a signal source, such as a gyroscope, and which in turn controls the servo valves that adjust the steering vanes. This delicate balancing can describe human contact, as in the relationship between Enzian and Katje:

> Feedback, smile-to-smile, adjustments, waverings: what it damps out to is *we will never know each other*.... [663]

In this image the proper path, the center, the direction, is for human beings never to get beyond the fencing aspect of the relationship. The path is also known as the Zero, a highly ambiguous idea since the Rocket should have a "Zero" path (that is it should go straight rather than have any degree of yaw) but the "Zero" may also lead to nothing. Pökler experiences this paradox exactly as the Rocket does when one of the control valves is "searching" (in Rocket reality an electrical field is positioning the valve by going repeatedly slightly off center to one side and then the other):

> If he also knew that in something like this extinction he could be free of his loneliness and his failure, still he wasn't quite convinced.... So he hunted, as a servo valve with a noisy input will, across the Zero, between the two desires, personal identity and impersonal salvation. [406]

Tchitcherine, the Russian, is similarly described, as he pauses between his frantic search for Enzian, the black half-brother he seems to wish to destroy, and the appeal of the witch, Geli Tripping, who loves him and has come to find him: "A passive solenoid waiting to be sprung" [734]

These images in which characters are described in terms of machines (most often as parts of the Rocket) are central to the deterministic, Preterite aspect of the novel, the realm in which human lives are controlled, patterned, and victims of the "They" of paranoia. For although Pynchon celebrates both the human comedy and the miracles, clarity, and complexity of the sciences he employs as metaphors and structural frameworks, his pessimistic side is tied to the inevitabilities of Control, whether the control of the Rocket or the control of the chemist in synthesizing polymers like Imipolex-G. Slothrop's own path is structured like the Rocket's flight, and it is not surprising that the metaphors for his situation are often those of guidance and control. The meeting point between the image of control in the Rocket and his Pavlovian conditioning by Laszlo Jamf is the range around the zero. Slothrop quotes Pavlov:

> "...extinction can proceed *beyond* the point of reducing a reflex to zero. We cannot therefore judge the degree of extinction *only* by the magnitude of the reflex or its absence, since there can still be a *silent extinction beyond the zero.*"

Then Slothrop muses,

> Did Dr. Jamf extinguish only to zero—wait till the infant showed zero hardons in the presence of stimulus x, and then stop? Did he forget—or ignore—the "silent extinction beyond the zero"? [84–85]

So Slothrop, just like the Rocket, is searching around the zero for his conditioned direction, following the path towards Imipolex-G just as the Rocket searches for the zero of its guidance-directed path.

Coda: *Vineland* (1990) and *Mason & Dixon* (1997)

Pynchon's recent novels contain only shadows of the involvement with science that predominates in his earlier fiction, but they are deep shadows cast across America in the turmoil from 1960–1990 and America under construction just prior to 1776.

Given *Vineland's* central subject is the ongoing persecution by Right Wing America (the FBI, the Presidencies and their links with the Mafia, the ziabatsus, and corporate America) of dopers, musicians, and radicals; and given that the mode is one which mixes broad satire with personal suffering and flavors the whole with wild conceptual leaps, it is not surprising that science is peripheral rather than a central theme. Pynchon's choice of personal anonymity makes certainty impossible, but this novel feels as though it is written from the inside, that it is personal experience radically altered for presentation by comic and satirical approaches. Its true heart is a dark one indeed and can occasionally be seen emerging directly, as in this exchange about the Darth Vader-like Federal Prosecutor Brock Vond:

> "Then again, it's the whole Reagan program, isn't it—dismantle the New Deal, reverse the effects of World War II, restore fascism at home and around the world, flee into the past, can't you feel it, all the dangerous childish stupidity—'I don't like the way it came out, I want it to be my way.' If the President can act like that, why not Brock?" [265]

This world of persecution is ruled by computers, wiretaps, and all of the other high technology tools of surveillance and intelligence which, turned on domestic America by corrupt Federal forces, make it possible to exert control over peoples' lives. But these are not in the forefront of the novel. They do not dominate it as V or the Rocket dominated earlier novels.

Nor is the language of the novel dominated by scientific terminology or scientific metaphor. There are occasional uses, often in the same pseudo-scientific tone as some of the more zany science in *Gravity's Rainbow*:

> They blasted down to L.A., heading back to the barn only semi-visible and as near as anybody could tell unobserved, Manuel and his auto alchemy team at Zero Profile Paint & Body of Santa Rosa having come up with a proprietary lacquer of a crystalline microstructure able to vary its index of refraction so that even had there been surveillance, the Trans-Am could easily, except for a few iridescent fringes, have been taken for empty roadway. [192]

There are also a number of zany scientific concepts in the novel, such as the television detoxification agency, "…we study and treat Tubal abuse and other video-related disorders" (33), or Brock Vond's fascination with the "criminal" head:

> Brock scanned face after face, registering stigmata, a parade of receding foreheads, theromorphic ears, and alarmingly sloped Frankfurt Horizontals. [272]

But taken as a whole, *Vineland*, because of its subject matter and the requirements of its satiric-fantastic style, marks a departure for Pynchon from his earlier close adherence to a vision of the world as seen through science.

Mason & Dixon is about the science of its times—astronomy, surveying, and peripheral matters such as pharmacy. Pynchon is meticulous in historical accuracy about the state of this science, although his wild and bizarre imagination about people and events is at full throttle. This novel, whose central activity of drawing the line between north and south was quickly rendered nearly useless by political events, is about the world that did not see science as a central trope or mode, where the sciences were not in the ascendant as they were in the nineteenth and twentieth centuries. Read against *Gravity's Rainbow*, it becomes Pynchon's description of the path not taken in modern times, a rollicking saga of colonial America before physics, chemistry, and psychology took it by the throat.

There is at least a hint implicit in this project: the scientific knowledge of any era will look very strange, baroque, and archaic when viewed from a later era. Thomas Pynchon is always aware of the scientific, and in *Mason & Dixon* he seeks to give the reader a rearview look at a culture not wholly in the coils of the serpent science, that image of death as the serpent of the benzine ring.

Conclusion

Writers reach out for stories, modes of language, and associations which confirm and explicate their visions of the world. Thomas Pynchon does this in a world he sees dominated by the inevitabilities of science in the shadow of the technologies of destruction.

It is one thing to assert that he does this because of his training and experience, but it is clear that he has carried this beyond a personal preoccupation to offer a new way of seeing, and that he has begun with his deep sense of the human condition. Pynchon writes about the human dilemmas of fear, insecurity, love, and the paradox of action in the world of the Preterite; but integral to his work is the influence of science on the human perspective in the twentieth century. The actual mechanization of the human is the subject of *V* and the submission of the world to the ballistic arc and the machinations of corporate-cartel science is the subject of *Gravity's Rainbow*.

But he goes far beyond subject matter in drawing constantly on the images of science to describe human experience in his writing. Pynchon writes from inside the world of science, whereas Lessing adapts the particular embodiment of the world in science fiction universes to go beyond the earlier bounds of traditional realistic fiction.

CHAPTER 4

A Bridge Takes Shape: Other Writers

The examinations of the texts of Doris Lessing and Thomas Pynchon in the preceding chapters serve to make clear two important facts about span writing. First, authors like Lessing turn to the tropes formerly exclusive to science fiction to express specific ideas that press the bounds of mainstream writing, to give perspective approaches on the present, and to make the opportunity to project the outcomes of present situations. In Pynchon's case it is science itself, rather than literary tropes, which is integral to the presentation of a worldview. Second, neither author works exclusively in the new genre, but has selected the mode when what they seek to express is best expressed in this way.

Thus *The Children of Violence* quintet (except for the last volume, *The Four-Gated City*), *The Good Terrorist* (1985), and *The Fifth Child* (1988) "surround" Doris Lessing's ventures into span. Likewise some of Pynchon's early stories, a good deal of *V, Vineland,* and *Mason & Dixon* (1997) are only marginally engaged in his articulation of science in our lives.

All this will be seen to be true of the authors to be treated in this chapter. The thesis here is not that authors who write span write only span, but rather that many writers who normally work in the mainsteam of fiction choose, for a fascinating variety of reasons, to venture into the genre in order to take advantage of the freedoms offered and the opportunity to manipulate the tropes of science and science fiction in novel and often intellectually challenging ways. These writers do not feel the entrapment of responsibility characteristic of the traditional writers of science fiction, and they may wish to employ satire, parody or irony, or choose to offer vague or incomplete extrapolations as they direct their work towards other goals. It is not writers, but certain texts by writers, which create a canon of works in the new form.

This chapter will, of necessity, offer only a tasting of the full range of writers who have touched on span and no doubt readers will think of many other texts which fall into the category. The fascination exerted by these texts is partly that of speculating on the motives which lead writers to attempt something different and, of course, partly that of considering the sheer range of imaginative inventiveness which emerges from the imaginations thus freed and stimulated. Where metafictional intent, the desire of the text to comment on its own existence, is usually absent from science fiction, in these texts by writers coming in from the mainstream it may be an important trend. Where only a few science fiction authors (most of whom will be appropriated as span writers in chapter 5) attain high levels of intricacy of language and complexity of characterization, the mainstream writers who venture in are likely to bring with them these aspects of craft and method.

The sorts of opportunities offered cover the categories of subject usually associated with science fiction, such as dystopias, time shifts, future fiction, alternate universes, machine societies (including computer futures), and post-holocaust fiction. As well, and often interacting with these science fictional choices, are approaches ranging from the burlesque of Anthony Burgess' *The End of the World News* (1982) to the serious and philosophical anthropology of William Golding's *The Inheritors* (1955). Within the spectrum are complex metafictions, comedies, prose experiments, satire, and irony, all applied to materials with which the writers are experimenting.

A place to start to consider these sorts of mixed work is a look at texts which begin in a realistic present or historical context and take an unexpected leap, as Lessing's *The Four-Gated City* does. Three strikingly different examples are Nadine Gordimer's *A Sport of Nature* (1987), Julian Barnes' *Staring at the Sun* (1986), and John Fowles' *A Maggot* (1985). In looking at what these three novelists do and in speculating upon their intentions, it is possible to see how variations on the *novum* can assist in elucidating complex ideas and in deliberately complicating fictions for purposes of positioning readers in special relationships to texts.

A Sport of Nature traces the struggles for South African freedom and pan–African liberation through the life of Hillela Capran, a Jewish girl who grows up in the houses of her aunts, flees South Africa with a suspect journalist, marries Whaila Kgomani, a black exile leader, is widowed when he is assassinated before her eyes, and then moves through many countries working for the cause until she marries the General, who regains control of his country and leads it to stability and development. Hillela is a sexual sophisticate whose political awakening is through the body and the senses as much as it is through formal political training. The novel depicts the violence and complexity of the African causes at a human level. As Hillela puts it, after her husband's assassination she will "Do what I'm doing. Looking for ways to free Whaila" (258).

Most of the text involves an interweaving of historical events and personages with the private lives of its fictional central characters. Once Hillela comes into contact with the upper echelons of the African National Congress, she meets historical figures such as Oliver Tambo and later, as the General's wife, she meets Bishop Tutu, Yasir Arafat, Abdu Diouf, and a number of other African leaders. And the real events of Africa, such as the fall of Kwame Nkrumah, the Sharpeville Massacre, and the armed incursions into South Africa from the north, are woven into Hillela's life story. But in the closing sections of the novel two shifts take place. The first is Hillela's relationship with the General and the story of the General's military struggle to recover his country from rebel forces. This portion of the narrative is slightly abstracted, for there is no clear indication of what country is involved, who the General is to be equated with, or when these events are supposed to take place. They simply "follow" Hillela's previous experiences as a lobbyist for African causes in the United States, which take place some time around the beginning of the 1970s without any real sense of a time break, but they do break the novel away from specific historical context.

It is what happens in the last chapter of the novel which is of interest to this study. Suddenly, after several intervening chapters dealing with Sasha, Hillela's cousin who is tried and imprisoned in South Africa for helping black unions organize, and, in no specified time frame, the General (as President of the OAU) and Hillela (who has been given the African name of Chiemeka) are present in Cape Town at the "proclamation of the new African state that used to be South Africa" (350). The chapter begins simply with "This year" but the leap of this *novum* is nothing less than a leap into a future which could not be clearly foreseen by Gordimer in 1987. The short chapter which follows is profoundly moving and triumphant, with great singing masses of people and a ceremony which moves to a crowning moment that brings together Hillela's life and the struggle for freedom:

> Hillela is watching a flag slowly climb, still in its pupa folds, a crumpled wing emerging, and—now!—it writhes one last time and flares wide in the wind, is smoothed taut by the fist of the wind, the flag of Whaila's country. [354]

It is the historical context of the novel which makes this brief leap into the future so telling. Had the novel been "loosely" set in time, with no specific years given and no identifiable historical incidents, it would have fallen within a novelist's normal range to complete the story in narrative terms as she chose. But when a text is set in the past, leading up to the present, a leap to the future is a clear projective *novum*. Gordimer exercises this freedom in order to justify all of Hillela's personal struggle and the larger South African struggle which has gone before, and to put forward her own clear sense of the inevitability of liberation. The reader is hit suddenly by this shift, which is exactly what the author intended. It is the only ending which can make real sense of Whaila's sacrifice and can place Hillela's wandering and variegated life into a framework that illuminates its meaning and purpose.

The motive for this short but telling *novum* is quite simply Gordimer's desire to will a future into existence and to lay out for the reader the justification for all of the suffering and struggle which has come before. Hillela's character is also "at stake" because she has frequently seemed quite ruthless and cold in the latter stages of the work, especially in leaving her American fiancé to marry the General and return to Africa. But when she is present when they raise "the flag of Whaila's country," it brings all of her actions to a comprehensible conclusion. The future is *needed* to complete this novel and the *novum* of a leap in time permits it to appear.

The *novum* in *A Sport of Nature* is the simplest possible exercise of a movement from the present into the future. A considerably more complicated example is Julian Barnes's *Staring at the Sun*, a sophisticated, witty, involved, poetic, and intellectual contemplation of modern death. No summary of this text can capture fully its tonal effects and playfulness with this painful topic. In the course of the novel, a lot of people die and a lot of people contemplate death, but the overall effect comes from the weaving together of these contemplations as they touch the life of Jean Serjeant, a central character presented as consistently unable to carry the burden of articulating the issues at the text's center, yet who finally emerges in possession of a response.

The title image is characteristic of the text's method. The text opens with a description of Sergeant-Pilot Thomas Prosser's unusual experience of seeing the sun rise twice in 1941, by dint of his diving his Hurricane to evade potential German pursuit as he returns from a night mission. At a later point in the text, when Prosser is billeted with Jean's parents, he explains that he was nicknamed Sun-Up Prosser for talking on about the incident. It emerges that he has been grounded because he was frightened of war in the air. He goes on to talk about how one could die by simply flying upwards, always staring at the sun, until one passed out for lack of oxygen. Later in the text Jean discovers from his widow that he apparently did exactly that when he was put back on operations.

Thus staring at the sun becomes a metaphor for facing death, and at the close of the novel, at the age of one hundred, Jean goes flying to see the sun set twice. The narration (it is unclear whether this is Jean's thought or the narrator's generalization) says of this:

> You can't stare at the sun for too long—not even the setting, quiet sun. You would have to put your fingers in front of your face to do that. Like Sun-Up Prosser. [196]

After the sun has set a second time, Jean has fully come to grips with death and the text says:

> For some minutes a glow continued from beneath the horizon, and Jean did, at last, smile towards this postmortal phosphorescence. [197]

There are a whole series of similar epigrammatic musings about death in the text, such as the young Jean's concern with the text under a picture which says, in part: "The Mink is excessively tenacious of life..." (17).

The bulk of the novel outlines Jean's life in a sketchy fashion, settling on the images and incidents that provide the matter for the central theme. Jean was born in 1922 and by the 1970s her parents are dead, she has left her husband, and her son Gregory is a young adult. She travels to the Seven Wonders of the World (she modifies the list to suit herself in her typical self-sufficient fashion), and the narration picks out the things which puzzle her and add to the book's central theme, such as the Fan Zhen's essay on "The Destructibility of the Soul." When the guide at a factory in China says of the grading of jade: "You look at it and by looking you tell its qualities" (93), the statement is an epigraph for the way the text itself, through Jean, peers directly at the "sun" of death throughout.

It is the third section of the text which is of interest to this study. Jean literally ages into the future with her son Gregory as her companion. She is turning one hundred in section three, so it is set in 2022, but it contains a recapitulation of the last decades of the twentieth century and the first decades of the twenty-first century. That recapitulation is very selective, however, for Barnes is not concerned with the type of *novum* which describes the future in great detail. Rather, he is intent on setting the stage for a philosophical discussion between Gregory and a central computer, a discussion that will allow a formal presentation of the themes of the novel so the events and metaphors in Jean's life (and the lives of the other principal characters) can be "positioned" for the reader. Also—and I take this to be very important to what Barnes is trying to do—Jean must be one hundred well into the twenty-first century, or a major part of the formation of her attitudes towards death would be old-fashioned by the standards of 1987. In fact she would be a Victorian, and Barnes clearly wants her to have "modern" attitudes towards death and life. Thus she must be born solidly into the twentieth century and, if she is to have a modest, sage-like nature resulting from great age, she must be projected into the future.

In the last three decades of Jean's life, the elderly have rebelled, using sensational public suicides to gain sympathy for their cause (choosing not to use "soft termination" facilities), and have been given extra rights including the elimination of the word geriatric, free "fun drugs" for the over-eighties, the elimination of old people's homes, and the right to be loved more. Life expectancy has been improved (no one makes any fuss about Jean turning one hundred), and cigarettes have finally been pronounced safe, so Jean took them up at eighty-seven.

There are very few other projected ideas in the section and there is almost no description of technical innovations, other than the computer knowledge service. The quality of what is offered is clearly a mixture of the playful and the suggestive. That old people might rebel is a perfectly reasonable extension of Grey Power and the mounting number of elderly who are demanding center stage in our time, but it does not seem so likely that they will choose martyrdom or that their conditions will include a demand that they be loved more. Barnes is mixing a real projection with a fanciful tone here, and his seriousness lies elsewhere than in this and in smokers' dreams of having their habit finally pronounced safe.

At one hundred, Jean lives with her sixty-year-old son, and it is he who openly wishes to find out about God and death at a point in his life where he has come to feel suicidal. Barnes provides some history of the development and function of the General Purposes Computer (GPC), a free public resource which is information-centered (it searches categories rather than book titles and does not support its information in formal scholarly fashion) and which adjusts its level of presentation to the level of understanding of the individual user. Of special interest is a function called TAT, The Absolute Truth, which is rarely used but is understood to offer those who dare to use it the best available answers to the most difficult and dangerous questions which can be posed.

In his search Gregory begins with GPC, asking it such questions as Jean's "Why is the mink excessively tenacious of life?" and getting in return

"NOT REAL QUESTION." When he relates this to Jean, she illuminates its implications:

> But what were real questions, she wondered. Real questions were limited to those questions to which the people you asked already knew the answers. If her father or GPC could answer, that made the enquiry a real question; if not, it was dismissed as being falsely based. How very unfair. Because it was these questions, the ones that weren't real, to which you wanted to know the answers most pressingly. For ninety years she'd wanted to know about the mink. Her father had failed, so had Michael [her husband]; and now GPC was ducking it. That was the way it was. Knowledge didn't really advance, it only seemed to. The serious questions always remained unanswered. [152–153]

Gregory does not stop at this level of response, but instead thinks carefully through fourteen possibilities for the God situation (God only exists when people believe in him, God did exist and will exist again but is presently elsewhere, etc.) and worries the questions of death and human meaning until he finally chooses to go and ask TAT. The interview is a strange mixture of ironic humor and the most direct and painful exchanges about the nature of death and the fear of death. He is offered NDE, a "near death experience" that has been refined so that individuals may choose to undergo it, and that alleviates the fear of death in over 90 percent of those who use it. He returns to TAT a second time to talk about suicide and religion, and again he gets a mixture of ironic fencing, only this time it seems to be blended in with some public policy on the issue.

Several days after his experience with TAT, Gregory asks Jean his central questions, which are, ultimately, the questions upon which the whole text has been a meditation. Jean, with the wisdom and experience of her long life and her own collection of images and moments which have meant much to her but which she has never summed up before, answers Gregory plainly:

> "Is death absolute?"
> "Yes, dear." The reply was firm and exact, declining the need for supplementary questions.
> "Is religion nonsense?"
> "Yes, dear."
> "Is suicide permissible?"
> "No, dear." [187]

What Barnes achieves at this point is briefly articulated through Gregory's thoughts in the few pages which follow before the closing, in which he and Jean go flying to see the sun set twice. Gregory dismisses all of the knowledge of the machine, the epitome of reason, and realizes that the truth comes out of his mother's experience. For the reader the effect is manifold. First, the complex experience of Jean's life, so vividly illustrated throughout by her odd preoccupations and its strange ironies, is shown to have made her able to answer the real questions. Second, through the use of GPC and TAT, Barnes is able to suggest that there is no revelation of discovery awaiting humankind which will suddenly change its future. He gently mocks the readers' expectations of a future which somehow has different answers to these basic questions.

The leap into the future in *Staring at the Sun* serves considerably more complex ends than that in *A Sport of Nature*. The tactics of telling this story made it necessary to show Jean's unusual and often unarticulated growth of understanding throughout a long life lived in the modernist world, climaxing in a calm wisdom of old age. Barnes also encompasses and controls the modern urge to hope that everything will be better soon by going into a future which is still wrestling with the basic questions and which offers no new answers. The ironic texture of the experiences in the text and the fragmentary quality of its images gradually coalesce in Jean's and Gregory's minds in the closing pages of the text, after Gregory has exhausted logic, reason, and argument in their modern guise as the "neutral" agency of the computer.

Barnes has taken a liberty by projecting into the future, but the liberation is quite distinct from, say, Morris's *News from Nowhere*, because it is in the form of a near-seamless projection from present to future. The ease with which the text follows forward makes it like *A Sport of Nature*, except that it is focused differently in order to accentuate the test of reason against experience in a sort of future vacuum (the effect is rather like a cartoon in that the events of the section are in the foreground and the background is formless), and it is more complexly, and often ironically, woven into the imagery and incidents of the past.

If *Staring at the Sun* takes a complex leap into the future from the present, it is, nonetheless, a leap intended to focus and clarify the thematic patterns and imagery of the text. John Fowles' *A Maggot*[1] is, very much on the other hand, a complex and equivocal integration of different genres that serves to deconstruct the text by focusing upon its unreality through irony, narrative, and authorial attitudes mirrored in the text, and by the way the author chooses to handle the issue of the fictive "believability" of the science fiction intervention. Fowles is interested in mystification and metafiction, and his handling of a lunge into the future is part of his larger exposition of the fixity of human attitudes and comprehension in relation to historical frameworks.

4. A Bridge Takes Shape

A maggot is a brief expansion on a theme (from a use meaning whim or quirk) and was used as a title for a kind of dance, such as My Lord Byron's Maggot. Fowles, who delights in metafictional patterning, tells us this in a Prologue, where he adds that the opening image of four riders in a deserted landscape riding toward an unidentified event was the theme (in the musical sense) of his maggot. He then launches the story with the party (which consists of Mr. Bartholomew, his mute manservant Dick, his elderly uncle Mr. Lacy, Rebecca Hocknell, and Jones, a soldier of fortune) traveling to an inn and some description of the curious relationships among them. It is shortly cut off with a notice from the *Western Gazette* of 1736 that the manservant to Mr. Bartholomew, the gentleman leading the party, has been found hanged by his own hand and the rest of the party has mysteriously disappeared.

The balance of the narrative is the attempt by a powerful and unscrupulous lawyer, Henry Ayscough, acting on behalf of a vastly more powerful but unnamed nobleman, to find out what happened to the party, for it emerges that Mr. Bartholomew was the disguised errant son of the nobleman and the other members of the group were not what they seemed. Fowles exposes brilliantly how the state of human knowledge, social codes, religious beliefs, and human fallibility cloud the search for truth, both by the style of Aysough's questioning (he is a bundle of prejudices and snobbery perfectly suited to his era and age) and by the narrative comments on the states of mind of his bullied victims.

After a long struggle the search comes down to Rebecca's testimony, itself complexly colored by her social position and by the fact she was with child after the events and married John Lee, a member of a Dissenting sect called the French Prophets to which she has been converted. Ayscough deeply distrusts her testimony but Fowles manipulates this distrust and her new-found religious sincerity to present a strange scenario of a meeting with what the reader recognizes as a space-time vehicle. She calls the vehicle a maggot, because it is white and has legs, and she has no frame of reference to see it as a machine.

It cannot be emphasized strongly enough that this explanation of the events is shockingly outside the novel's framework of the eighteenth-century world that Fowles has established, and further aggressively emphasized by authorial-narrator glosses throughout the text about the ways in which the characters are behaving in the context of their times. Over 95 percent of the text has absolutely nothing to do with the science fictional revelation except to heighten the mystery to be solved by Rebecca's testimony. That testimony itself is carefully phrased constantly to remind the reader of the context. And after it Fowles presents Ayscough's conclusion that discounts the testimony. Fowles goes on, in an Epilogue, to explain that Rebecca's baby was Ann Lee, who founded the Shaker sect. The Epilogue includes Fowles' comments on the historical function of religious Dissent, and there are no further comments on the science fictional insert in the text.

What does Fowles wish the reader to make of this unusual interpolation in a text so committed to historical verisimilitude that even the interpolation itself is presented in a legal interview laden with and distorted by the social, religious, and historical context? A first step to an answer to this is to consider that the discontinuity created by the insertion effectively sabotages the whole text. The reader who has become submerged in the eighteenth-century world is shocked out of it by the science fiction interpolation and suddenly both worlds are starkly revealed as fictional. The interpolation plays a primary role in making a metafiction of this text, and it is only one of several things that Fowles does to create that effect. But the interpolation differs from the other methods because the text does not "break stride" to include it. That is to say that the narrator does not interfere with the flow of the text to explain or comment on Rebecca's testimony. Its conjunction with the eighteenth-century context takes place within the language, situations, and characterizations of the larger text, so it comes as a disorienting shock only because it pertains to the different (and post-eighteenth-century) framework of imagination that can encompass such close encounters.

Up to the interpolation, the text has contained many hints and indications of what is to come, but all of them have been presented in equivocal fashion so that they seem to be leading to either witchcraft or a human solution revolving around the relationships between the characters. Mr. Bartholomew was a student of Nicholas Sanderson, the Lucasian Professor of Mathematics at Cambridge, who along with Mr. Whiston and Sir Isaac Newton, his predecessors, had thought most highly of Bartholomew's skills in mathematics. Sanderson had, however, differed with him over the applicability of a sequence of numbers and proportion that Bartholomew had hoped would trace "the history of this world, both past and to come; and thus that were it fully understood, the chronology of the future might be prophesied as well that of the past explained" (188). The papers pertaining to this theory were carried in a trunk that went with the party to the South-West of England and Mr. Bartholomew frequently consulted them. They were burnt the night before the first of May expedition to the cave.

Before that there was a night expedition to Stonehenge, where Mr. Bartholomew, Dick, and Rebecca were visited by strange beings. Rebecca's account speaks of a great rush of wind from directly above, a brilliant light from above, a sweet odor, and the brief appearance of two men. Ayscough dismisses this as lies and, as Rebecca has already given a different account (involving the Devil) of the events to Jones, another member of the party who was not actually present, the reader is thoroughly uncertain of what to make of this story at this point. While later events suggest that this was a preliminary visit of the vehicle, the context at this point is such that a science fiction explanation does not appear likely. Mr. Bartholomew says several things about his intent. He tells Lacy, the old actor whom he hires to fill out the party in the role of his uncle, that:

> ...I have someone I must see, my life depends on it, and there are those who would prevent me.... I am a victim of unjust and unkind fate, which I would try to remedy. [123–124]

He tells Lacy when they visit Stonehenge in daylight:

> For we mortals are locked as at Newgate, he said, within the chains and bars of our senses and our brief allotted span, and as such are blind; that for God all time is as one, eternally now, whereas we must see it as past, present, future, as in a history. [143]

In a conversation with Rebecca on the night before the journey to the cave, Mr. Bartholomew says that those he hopes to meet on the morrow are "but late arrived from their native country," "do not speak our tongue," and he tells her that there are no women of that country like her (that is to say, prostitutes).

On several occasions Mr. Bartholomew also disclaims his parentage, and this is complicated by the presence of Dick, who was born at the same instant as he and who, though mute, serves him with great devotion. Bartholomew says of Dick:

> I am his animating principle, Lacy, without me he's no more than a root, a stone. If I die, he dies the next instant. [165]

And early in the text, before it can have any science fiction overtones, Fowles inserts a strange description of Dick's eyes:

> ...for his strangest features are his eyes, that are of a vacant blue, almost as if he were blind, though it is clear he is not. They add greatly to the impression of inscrutability, for they betray no sign of emotion, seem always to stare, to suggest their owner is somewhere else. So might twin camera lenses see, not normal human eyes. [7]

This presaging of the events at the cave, through hints at Mr. Bartholomew's motives, studies, and his strange relationship to the curious figure of Dick, do not clearly prepare the reader for the events Rebecca describes. The worldviews of the characters and the readers' deep immersion in the eighteenth-century culture, along with Rebecca's initial lying account of a fornication with Satan to Jones, who had spied on the events outside the cave from a hilltop and afterward taken her from the scene: all tend toward a scenario involving the black arts. When Rebecca starts to tell Ayscough the true story of the events, it is shockingly discontinuous. She tells first of meeting a woman in a silver pantsuit outside the cave (Jones has already spoken of this woman in his testimony), who beckons them in and then disappears into thin air.

In the cave they come on the Maggot:

> That floated in the inner cavern, like a great swollen maggot, white as snow upon the air.... [355]
> ...Of white, yet not of flesh, as it were wood japanned, or fresh-tinned metal, large as three coaches end to end, or more, its head with the eye larger still; and I did see other eyes along its sides that shone also, tho' less, through a greenish glass. And at its end there was four great funnels black as pitch, so it might vent its belly forth there. [356]

The vehicle hums and emits the same sweet smell that Rebecca had sensed at Stonehenge. It descends, putting out "feet," and three women emerge, apparently daughter, mother, and grandmother. They then merge into a single woman who embraces Bartholomew and converses with him in a strange tongue, much in the manner of a mother addressing her son. They then enter the vehicle, which is set inside with glowing precious stones with marks upon them, that the reader realizes are illuminated panel buttons. They are shown a complex film of a future world with a white and gold city, orchards, dancers: a pastoral idyll. Then Rebecca alone sees scenes of war and carnage on a world with a triple moon and a child burnt to death, whom she tries to reach through the "glass" of the screen. Finally, the projection ended, Mr. Bartholomew, now dressed in silver, kisses her forehead and tells her to remember him. She wakes on the floor of the cavern, the maggot gone.

Ayscough succumbs to Arthur C. Clarke's dictum: "Any sufficiently advanced technology is indistinguishable from magic."[2] He therefore phrases all his challenges to this account in terms of black magic. Rebecca has named the pastoral scene June Eternal and sees it as the guide to her conversion to her deep new faith in Christ. Neither, of course, recognizes any of the technology, and Rebecca does not even know she has seen a "film." Their frameworks reject the modern readers' perception of the events just as automatically as we, those readers, interpret the events from a framework of science fiction. What I want to consider is how Fowles, who is always fully aware of the fictionality of his texts and the implications of that for the impression he leaves upon his readers, intends us to read *A Maggot*.

First, it seems that he wants to verify the existence of the vehicle. He does this by having Jones see the woman in the strange silver garb outside the cave and hear humming inside the cave, and by having unsuccessful investigations done on an intensely burnt piece of ground outside the cave door. He also does it by framing Rebecca's narrative with the depth of her desire for truth caused by her intense conversion and new life, and emphasized by interrupting her testimony with an interview Ayscough has with her father and new husband, in which their plainness confirms her new honesty and rejects the idea that she is fabricating a fantasy. Ayscough's deep doubt and sharp questioning actually reinforce Rebecca's testimony as well, for she holds up under his vicious private cross-examination.

Having said that, it must be emphasized that the whole framework of the novel is very concerned with levels of belief in narrative. Besides some straightforward omniscient narration, there are the long sections of Ayscough's interrogations, Ayscough's fawning letters to his master (in a style absolutely true to eighteenth-century privilege), the Prologue and the Epilogue, the former with its instruction on what we are going to read and the latter with its discourse on Dissent; and there are pages reproduced photographically from the Historical Chronicle of 1736.

Finally, there is a whole series of twentieth-century interpolations by the omniscient narrator that comment on the cultural patterns of the eighteenth century. Here, for example, is a comment on the perceptions of nature:

> The period had no sympathy with unregulated or primordial nature. It was aggressive wilderness, an ugly and all-invasive reminder of the Fall, of man's eternal exile from the Garden of Eden; and particularly aggressive, to a nation of profit-haunted puritans, on the threshold of an age of commerce, in its flagrant uselessness. [11]

And here is an example of this perspective detachment in the narrative action:

> A modern person would not have had the shadow of doubt that Rebecca was lying, or at least inventing. Gods, except for an

occasional Virgin Mary to illiterate Mediterranean peasants, no longer appear; even in Ayscough's time such visions were strongly associated with Catholic trickery, something good Protestants expected and despised. [411]

This varied range of textual methods reveals a variety of strategies on Fowles' part that "scatter" our responses to heighten the fictiveness of the whole. The pages reproduced photographically from the Historical Chronicle of 1736 tell us nothing about the central narrative and can only be seen as providing texture to historical context. Yet they are more "true" (note my quotation marks) than any other part of the text, so they immediately problematize the rest of it.

Fowles' interpolations on eighteenth-century attitudes and behavior function as narrative "zoom out shots," momentarily pulling back from the main story to prevent the reader from becoming wholly absorbed in the tale and reminding us that we can only read this story from our twentieth-century viewpoint, engaging as we do so in attempts to mentally reconstruct eighteenth-century consciousness. That consciousness is "played out" in vivid detail in Ayscough's aggressive behavior toward his witnesses and in his subservient letters to his employer-patron.

The Prologue further complicates the reading process. By asserting that the whole work arose from the single image of the riders in the wilderness, and by telling us that it is a maggot in the sense of a whim or quirk devised upon a theme, Fowles deliberately trivializes the story to come. In fact, we realize that he is writing against this claim as he invokes the vivid eighteenth-century world and sets up the mystery of the disappearances Ayscough will unravel. Then, at the decisive moment in Rebecca's testimony, she sees, of all things, "the maggot." In this choice Fowles says to the reader that the vehicle and the events surrounding it are as much a whim or quirk of his choosing as the rest of the work, no more and no less fictional than the rest of the text. The reader is immediately drawn to the idea that in his search for an ending, an explanation, Fowles was led to his solution by nothing more than a further verbal play on the form he chose for the whole work.

There are several interesting conclusions to be drawn from Fowles' insertion of the science fictional trope in his text. The eighteenth-century context prepares us for a conclusion rooted in witchcraft, Satanism, or some form of fairy fantasy. Any solution out of context can only heighten the metafictional quality of the text and with it our awareness that any conclusion is artificial. In a sense the trope is deeply insincere. It is Fowles' way of pointing out that readers of science fiction tend to the same suspension of disbelief as readers of the most whole-cloth fantasy teeming with monsters, goblins, and mages. We see this in *A Maggot* because the eighteenth-century context highlights the artificiality of the trope. None of the characters can believe in it because their pre-technological era has no place for the vehicle and its wonders. Is Fowles making an ironic and perceptive leap to the point that our age can believe in such things specifically because we are immersed in the paradigm of a technological world? Viewed from, say, a post-technological twenty-third-century world, would our ready acceptance of a technological solution seem as absurd to some future reader whose frame of reference will have changed yet again from our own?

I can think of only one other text (see discussion of *Toward the End of Time* below) that places a science fiction trope in a similar framework of metafiction, focusing our attention on its "reality" being conditioned by our own context and on the fact that it is, above all, part of a fictional construct. I think it is well worth stopping to consider that the explicit questioning of its own fictional reality is one thing that is hardly, if ever, done in science fiction writing, but that span may opt for this sophisticated stance.

Fowles has had problems with endings. His two novels before *A Maggot*, *The French Lieutenant's Woman* and *Daniel Martin*, have very unsatisfactory endings which weaken texts that begin with great original power. When he came to *A Maggot*, Fowles must have been particularly aware of the problem of endings. Moreover, he seems to have set himself a particularly nasty puzzle in this text, for, however casual its maggoty inception may have been, he has developed a powerful and fascinating view of a complexly dramatic situation, extensively informed by his antiquarian researches and made problematic by its metafictional overtones.

Whether he envisioned the vehicle from the early planning stages or hit on it at the moment Ayscough starts to question Rebecca, it is his choice of ending, and I think it worthwhile to wonder why he chose it. The least complimentary answer is to suggest that he was stuck, saw a Star Trek rerun, and "went for it." Or, again at the low end, perhaps he wished to thumb his nose at those who were dissatisfied with his previous endings, wishing to make the important point that the traditional view of "necessary" outcomes is vastly overrated.

But it seems far more likely that Fowles saw several really important possibilities and exploited them. The science fiction trope dropped into this text is the keystone of its metafictional nature. It throws into question the way in which any culture or period denies or absorbs into an obviously inadequate framework any radical departure from its expectations, thus indirectly posing for us the problematic of close encounters or any other phenomenon that we would offhandedly deny. This complex mixture of historical fiction, metafiction, and a vital science fiction trope clearly places Fowles' text in the grouping I call span.

Twelve years after the publication of *A Maggot,* John Updike produced *Toward the End of Time* (1997), which recasts Fowles' metafiction into a twenty-first-century domestic context. Ben Turnbull, the first person narrator, is by turns a convincing naturalistic narrator (a retired New England investment broker of a type familiar to Updike's readers) and at other times the center of a subtle metafiction quite unlike Fowles' highly wrought and formalistic experiment. Updike's title is a vital guide to the text, a gentle, autumnal apocalypse whose "place" may be in external reality or in the consciousness of the narrator. Ben's experiences are all related to endings, and they dovetail into each other to swing the text beyond naturalism.

On the naturalistic level, Ben is an aging man living comfortably in the country. He struggles with his wife's passion for the garden and her desire that he kill the deer that are eating some of her plants. He also struggles with an aging body, and in the course of the text has a cancerous prostate gland removed, with all the attendant embarrassments of incontinence and impotence. He sees his children and grandchildren and deals with the dangerous youths to whom he pays protection. But even this world is made confusing in the narrative. His wife disappears in the autumn and he does not seem to know why, although he has a vague recollection that he might have shot her. He then takes a prostitute into the house to live with him, and shortly after she leaves him his wife reappears, saying that she has been on a trip. The reader is left puzzled.

On another level there are several first-person narrative sections of the book told in the first-person present yet set in the past. One involves Egyptian tomb robbers at work, another John Mark describing his travels with St. Paul and his start as a gospel writer, in yet another Ben is a Nazi guard in an Eastern concentration camp. These moments are loosely linked to the text. Ben and Deidre (the prostitute) have been exploring Ben's vast old house naked and the frisson from this act causes Ben to imagine himself as the tomb robber. But he does not tell Deidre a "story." Rather, he narrates the event strictly for the reader without explaining why this material, out of time and place with the text, is present.

The world of the text is aging along with Ben. By 2020 there has been a nuclear war between China and the United States, although Massachusetts has been spared the direct effects of war. But there is depopulation, the central government has lost most of its power, there is a local currency, the police are more or less dormant, the space station has been abandoned leaving those on it to die, small metallic life forms have evolved which scatter around the country eating oil off highways, and FedEx is emerging as the national body most likely to bring order to the dispersed society. This middle ground text, set down gently in the future, has a background of these changes but, importantly, they are not central to Ben's life or most of the lives around him. His health, his sex life, his progeny, the deer in the garden—these are as important in the balance of the text as the projections.

Updike even brings in an alien space platform which seems to be watching the Earth[3], although Ben's thoughts about this vehicle leave us in the trap of uncertainty created by first person narration. Quite late in the text the Earth passes through the center of this gigantic torus and Ben reports a transcendent spiritual experience, followed by lassitude and doubt around the world. Yet even this stunning experience has to take its place beside Ben's prostate and the deer in the garden.

The other unusual focus tied to the title is Ben's musing on cosmology. Repeatedly through the text he muses on hadrons, quantum theory, the Big Bang, on the time-symmetric aspects of physics, and the eventual possible ends of the universe. This is unusual and unsettling matter to come from the thoughts of a retired investment banker, but Updike makes them a part of his mosaic of "the end of time," and in so doing places the individual against the larger background of cosmology.

If the new fictional form is partly defined by its domestication of science and its borrowing of science fiction tropes in the service of complex narrative goals, then there is no question that Updike has ventured into this territory. But the narrative, for all its overall autumnal tone (particularly marked by its attention to the slow pageant of the seasons), is technologically edgy, made complex by the deliberately unsubtle blending of different kinds of narrative material. The reader is at one moment in a science fiction future, but that future is subsumed in a novel of old age and contemplation. Being nowhere certainly is characteristic of many span texts and certainly of Updike's melange *Toward the End of Time*.

A Sport of Nature, *Staring at the Sun*, *A Maggot*, and *Toward the End of Time* have in common their leap from the present or past of conventional fiction into a future *novum*. The preceding pages have shown how distinctly different the uses and handling of such *novums* can be, and how their presences can allow authors to make explorations or statements which were not possible without them. The texts use a balance of past, present, and future which is certainly unusual for traditional science fiction and for mainstream fiction, which is framed either in the present or in the past.

Other texts demonstrate a worldview based on science or the effects of scientific language on ways of thinking. Science may remain in the background, driving these texts from beneath, as with William Golding's *The Inheritors* (1955), Kingsley Amis' *The Anti-Death League* (1966), or Peter Ackroyd's *First Light* (1989). Or the texts may relate the contemporary preoccupation with the intrusion of technology into human life as in Don DeLillo's *White Noise* (1985). Or they may be a fantasia of Joycian proportions in which science produces the language and central elements of the plot yet is critically "placed" in its effect on modern man such as in Lawrence Durrell's *The Revolt of Aphrodite* (1974).

Durrell, an Englishman who lived in countries around the Mediterranean throughout his adult life, is best known for his sensuous, erotic, and often evocative fiction describing the interplay between Occidental and Oriental worlds, such as *The Alexandria Quartet* (1968). *The Revolt of Aphrodite* is partly set in Athens and Istanbul and has a distinct Oriental flavor at times, but it is also a venture into the relationship between science and culture in the modern world. Durrell's novel (or novels, for it is actually a two-part novel first published as *Tunc* (1968) and *Numquam* [1970]) is a stylistic precursor of *Gravity's Rainbow*, although I have found no reference to Pynchon having read it. It is, in language, metaphors, and plot elements, very definitely immersed in the world of science, but Durrell is far less interested in technical accuracy than Pynchon and, in fact, lets his imagination carry him into a disorderly and deliberately imprecise middle ground text.

His inventor-hero Felix Charlock tosses off ideas which become marketed products for a multinational called Merlins, usually referred to as the firm, whose commercial tentacles spread out from both London and Istanbul under the direction of the brothers Julian and Jocas. Charlock enters the firm somewhat reluctantly, but is literally seduced in by the sister of the owners, Benedicta, whom he later marries and whose madness is gradually revealed in the story. Charlock is not a dominant, Dr. Frankenstein, scientist but a cultured man with a knack for useful scientific ideas who is caught up in a commercial and international whirlpool.

Other perspectives on the human condition abound in the text. In Athens there is the sensible, affectionate Iolanthe (Io), the young whore who is Charlock's lover and who later becomes a Hollywood star. There is the humane, philosophical Vibart, first introduced as a commercial attaché in Istanbul and later made into a London publisher by the firm. There is Nash, physician and psychiatrist for the firm. There is the sensational, learned, grandiose architect Caradoc, who sees architecture in its role as a measure of the culture and the times. And there is Marchant, the amoral scientist-technician who brings many of Charlock's inventions into existence.

The keys to seeing this text in the context of span are its extravagant use of scientific and pseudo-scientific language and logic, and the central plot devices used in each novel. Science provides the forms of contemplation, the subject matter of conversation, metaphors, and a rich, meaningful play of puns. Here is Charlock considering his nerve for an attempt to escape the firm:

> At what point does a man decide that life must be lived *unhesitatingly*? Presumably after exhausting every other field—in my case the scientific modes: science, its tail comes off in your hand like a scared lizard. [21]

Such a vivid contemplation challenges science, at least as a way of guidance for one's personal destiny, in the language of science itself. One of Charlock's old notebooks yields up his thoughts of love:

> ...the shuddering-sweet melting almost to faintness.... Why, the structure of the genitals is particularly adapted to such phenomena.... The slightest friction of a white hand will alert the dense nerve ganglia with their great vascularity. The affect disperses itself through the receiving centers of the autonomic nervous system, solar plexus, hypogastric plexus, and lumbosacral or pelvic.... Hum. The kiss breaks surface here. The autobiography of a single kiss from Iolanthe. [25]

This kind of thinking is characteristic of the prose of the text, a roller coaster from evocative language like "melting" and "white hand" to the analytic biological description of the event. Whereas Pynchon's use of this always comes down to the basic irony of human aspirations contrasted to scientific fact, Durrell is not willing to confine humankind in the same way. His scientist-narrator has a broad imagination and a perspective awareness of the temptations of science. When Jocas tempts him with the resources of the firm, he is aware of the lure:

> All of a sudden the lust for this vocation—of tampering with the universe and trying to short-circuit its behavior—grew up in me and seized me by the throat. I drank my wine off at a thrust and sat bemused, staring through him. O God! There was also the danger that they might sow these idle speculations broadcast behind my back, that other talents with bigger means might scoop me. I was ashamed of the idea, but there it was! Pure science! Where does the animal come in? [146–147]

Here the crisis is explicit: the temptation to adjust the universe by scientific intervention and the awareness of the base motives of human jealousy and enthusiasm which drive the practitioner. The text abounds with such passages, at once admitting the power of science and questioning human commitment to it.

The construction of the text also centers around things scientific. The opening sections of *Tunc*, the first novel, are discontinuous because Charlock is recovering them from his dactyl, a little transcribing machine he has invented which records and prints out what it overhears. This device (pun intended very much in Durrell's style) permits a mixture of present and past events. From the beginning the text makes mention of Abel, the master computer which Charlock invents towards the close of the chronological narrative to revenge himself on Julian, once he discovers that the latter has been his wife's secret and incestuous lover and a major cause of her insanity, and once he realizes that Julian has entrapped him in the firm. Abel's function is explained by Charlock on the first page of the text:

> "No, but people as destinies are by now almost mathematically predictable. Ask Abel.... I call it pogonometry. It is deduction based on the pogon (όγov) a word which does not exist. It is the smallest conceivable unit of meaning in speech; a million pogons make up the millionth part of a phoneme. Give Abel a sigh or the birthcry of a baby and he can tell you everything." [11]

This wonderful and dangerous device is used on the next page to discover that Nash, the psychiatrist, has had an affair with a patient:

> "Very well, lies; but Abel cannot lie. You must try and imagine it this way—as Abel sees it, with that infallible inner photoelectric eye of his. He X-rays time itself, photographing a personality upon the gelatine surface of flux. Look, I press a button, and your name and voice rise together like toast in a toast-rack. [12]

This extraordinary device is the epitome of Charlock's career, but it is characteristic of him that it is not created for power and gain, but in order that he can kill Julian by booby trapping Julian's "dossier" with a twelve-gauge shotgun. Charlock the scientist is constantly at the whim of Charlock the emotional human being in Durrell's text.

As the novel moves to a close Io is dead, having become a Hollywood star and then dying from abortive breast implants, technology having gone terribly wrong. Julian, shattered by this, forces the secret of the booby trap out of Charlock and Benedicta's son Mark, only to have Mark, out of loyalty to his absent father, commit suicide by triggering the device. All of the scientific marvels have failed and Charlock, who had fled by faking a suicide, is left with the dactyl's bitter residue of experience.

Durrell's *Tunc* positions scientific fantasy in its human dimension. As a man, Charlock is an innocent abroad in an East-West world of sexual, economic, and psychological intrigue and power, afloat in an ocean of contemporary Freudian darkness. His science, which permeates his thinking and is both his living and his only source of power, is pictured as unable to solve his personal and emotional dilemmas. The text ends with his wife insane, his son a suicide, his former lover dead, and his career in thrall to the ultimate industrial cartel. The novel, for all its fanciful science and witty discussions between Nash, Vibart, Charlock, Caradoc, Merchant, and others, is a deep indictment of the modern condition of mankind separated from the emotional self, wandering among the bitter ciphers of science, technology, and power.

"But aut Tunc aut Nunquam—it was then or never!"[4] (66) is Caradoc's translation of the epigraph for the two novels, offered early in *Numquam*. The "then" has been the first volume, the "never" is the action of *Numquam*, central to which is Charlock's creation of a perfect robotic replica of Io to fulfill Julian's desperate desire for the beautiful woman lost in *Tunc*. Charlock is needed because Io is to be a miniaturized incarnate extension of Abel, a talking, thinking, and loving computer. Durrell has a good deal of fun, some of it salacious, with the design of the parts of this apparatus, and it tends to mitigate the dark overtones of the situation. For Io will never live again, and the technologically driven world of Merlins and Charlock cannot overcome this.

The early sections of *Numquam* are set at the Paulhaus, the Swiss sanatorium run by the firm, where Charlock, who has been seriously injured when recaptured by the firm, and Benedicta, who had a major relapse at Mark's death, are recovering and are eventually reunited. Durrell makes this section heavy with Freudian knowledge, at its center the revelation of Julian's castration by his father for his incest with Benedicta and her struggles with Julian's overwhelming of her life. Beside this serious side, Durrell plays with Freud, describing Johnson, a patient incarcerated for a curious affliction:

> "Out in the park there are some lovely trees, and next week when I have my first walk I will try and have a couple. Elms!" It was as simple as that—suddenly in the full flower of his sexual maturity Johnson found he loved trees. Other men have had to make do with goats or women or the Dalmatian Cavalry, but Johnson found them all pale into insignificance beside these long-legged green things

which were everywhere: he saw them as green consenting adults
with diminished responsibility, loitering all round him with intent.
[47]

There is an ambivalence here which is characteristic of much of the text. It is at once scientific and satirical, rich in language play (like the listing of "make do with goats or women or the Dalmatian Cavalry" in that particular order) and humor, yet finally a comment on modern knowledge and the contemporary condition.

The same ambivalence can be seen in the central action of the re-creation of the Io. On the dark side, she is coming into existence just as the much-loved Jocas is wasting away from cancer in Turkey, an exchange of the human for the humanoid. To Charlock, it/she is the subject for a good deal of musing about the modern condition, but to power-driven Julian she is an obsession both erotically and because in life she had managed to remain out of the clutches of the firm. At the satirical level Marchant cautions Charlock that the Io can accidentally make poetry:

> "you will have to make a much stronger temperature control stat, or else she will overheat, and then she's likely to write free verse: I suppose as any normal person might do in a delirium. It all happened yesterday. She lost optimum temperature control and committed a poem." [211–212]

At a more contemplative level, the Io is the subject of a lot of observations which reflect on the human condition. When Charlock is looking at an embalmer's subject in the anatomy laboratory, he makes a telling comparison:

> Surely both were dead in the technical sense? Well, Iolanthe was a little less dead because of a perfect memory which *she could use*: it was her radar. So that dying ... was a case of loss of memory, both mental and physical? [157]

All of the musing becomes action once the Io is brought to life and takes stock of her surroundings. Initially she falls in love with Julian, and there are scenes which are ironically humiliating as this powerful man (but a man who is also castrated) is alternately tormented and rewarded by the charming machine. Before the Io escapes and later kills Julian and is destroyed by Charlock, there is a veritable square dance of ironies. Julian is a man, made rational-mechanical by castration and seeking satisfaction in immense power and control, who is besotted by a mechanical replica of a film star (a profession which makes robots out of its practitioners), which/who is the subject of contemplation by Charlock and others who consistently turn its focus on the mechanized, dehumanized quality of modern life.

Durrell's achievement in *The Revolt of Aphrodite* is elusive and complex. Into a writing life, previously defined by a distinctive rich mixture of modernist experimentation and a Mediterranean-romantic sensibility with strong Freudian overtones, has suddenly come fiction that mixes these with science, the corporate world, and a blend of irony, satire, and judgment of the inroads of science and technology. Bringing fantastic science to a central position, yet constantly integrating it with the human realities of the situation to take the measure of the contemporary world, makes Durrell's text part of the middle genre.

Another writer who emphasizes the bitter humor of our science-permeated world is Don DeLillo. In *White Noise* (1984), and to a lesser extent in *The Names* (1989), and *Mao II* (1991) he demonstrates the omnipresent influence of science and the popular misunderstanding and misrepresentation of the scientific in contemporary American life. His characters are predominantly comic puppets who move in a world overwhelmed by scientific and technological information. Beneath the humor of caricature lies a painful level of angst and the overwhelming fact that all of the information is finally of little or no assistance in the living of contemporary life. Where Durrell envisioned a conflict between humanism and science, with fantastic invention highlighting the division, DeLillo does not see conflict as a possibility. His characters are drowning in a sea of technobabble, breathing it in and out every time they open their mouths.

The title of *White Noise* refers to the susurrous of sound which is used to replace distinct audible sounds in experiments with sensory deprivation or as a calming background to offset disturbing irregular noise in places of work. DeLillo changes the register of the term so it refers to the babble of the modern world: the ground of brand names, background scraps of television news, radio news, scraps of conversation and technobabble, tabloid headlines. Fragments, like this chapter conclusion, are tossed into the text with no narrative reference:

A woman passing on the street said, " A decongestant, an antihistamine, a cough suppressant, a pain reliever" [262]

Or a bit of radio commentary, vaguely menacing, ends another chapter: "The man on the radio said: 'Void where prohibited.'" (303)

Lists of terms suddenly occur in the text:

    Krylon, Rust-Oleum, Red Devil. [159]
    MasterCard, Visa, American Express. [100]
    Leaded, unleaded, super unleaded. [199]

The central character, Jack Gladney, hears his daughter murmur Toyota Celica in her sleep, and muses on the source of such words:

> Toyota Corolla, Toyota Celica, Toyota Cressida. Supranational names, computer-generated, more or less universally pronounceable. Part of every child's brain noise, the substatic regions too deep to probe. Whatever its source, the utterance struck me with the impact of a splendid transcendence. [155]

While the sound may strike Gladney as splendidly transcendent, it strikes the reader as part of the noise junk in which modern life is lived.

This background of white noise makes no particular sense, but its bombardment of our senses makes it the texture of the media-dominated contemporary world. When it is absent there are severe consequences. Babette, Gladney's wife, appears on local cable television teaching posture. Initially seeing her is enough:

> It was the picture that mattered, the face in black and white, animated but also flat, distanced, sealed-off, timeless. It was but wasn't her. Once again I began to think Murray might be on to something. Waves and radiation. Something leaked through the mesh. She was shining a light on us, she was coming into being, endlessly being formed and reformed as the muscles in her face worked at smiling and speaking, as the electronic dots swarmed. [104]

But the sound transmission is not working and, after Gladney's son Heinrich tries and fails to fix it:

> ...as we watched Babette finish the lesson, we were in a mood of odd misgiving. [105]

The white noise is needed, even if no particular meaning can be attached to it. DeLillo implies that the rich world of verbiage is a screen for us, sealing us within a meaningless media world. Several of Gladney's fellow professors concern themselves with the meanings of media, but beyond a certainty that it must all be significant (a certainty useful for their careers), they make very little sense of it.

There is a second brief but telling use of white noise in the text. *White Noise* is a text about death and how it hovers behind all that occurs in life. When Babette and Jack discuss this in bed one night, an underlying white noise comes into focus:

> "What if death is nothing but sound?"
> "Electrical noise."

4. A Bridge Takes Shape

"You hear it forever. Sound all around. How awful."
"Uniform, white."
"Sometimes it sweeps over me," she said. "Sometimes it insinuates itself into my mind, little by little. I try to talk to it. 'Not now, Death.'" [198–199]

This sudden metaphysical sense of the term is characteristic of the angst-laden underpinning of the text. All of the surface white noise of the contemporary world clashes with, or perhaps blends into, the "noise" which lies behind and, in a metaphorical sense at least, beyond the characters' lives.

DeLillo's appropriation of the McLuhanesque description of Babette's face changing "as the electronic dots swarmed" and the whole appropriation of the electronic concept of white noise are illustrative of the ways in which the scientific permeates his text. So too are the two central actions of the text, the evacuation of the town as a result of the "airborne toxic event" and the search for Dylar, the drug which will take away the fear of death. The toxic event is a vast black cloud from a split tank car which causes the evacuation of Gladney's university town. It draws out the way scientific information gets mangled and confused by scientists trying to explain it to the public and by the public trying to pass it on and understand it. The event is first described on radio as "a feathery plume" and then as "a billowing black cloud," which leads Jack to comment:

"That's a little more accurate, which means they're coming to grips with the thing. Good." [113]

Finally it becomes "an airborne toxic event," a piece of Newspeak worthy of Orwell in its efforts to hide its sources ("event" suggests natural causes), and to downgrade it by removing all the negative connotations of "billowing" (suggesting the active nature of the cloud) and "black."

Misinformation surrounds the whole toxic event. Gladney's children have difficulty keeping up with the changing reports of appropriate symptoms:

She [Babette] also said the girls were complaining of sweaty palms.
"There's been a correction," Heinrich told her. "Tell them they ought to be throwing up." [112]

The nausea, vomiting, and shortness of breath are later changed to heart palpitations and a sense of *déjà vu*. This is in spite of the fact that the name of the spilled chemical, Nyodene Derivative, is known from the start.

Then Gladney is drawn into an increasing spiral of confusion and fear because it turns out that he exposed himself to the cloud when he filled the gas tank of his car. To Jack's horror a technician, accessing his record by computer, tells him he is "getting bracketed numbers with pulsing stars" (140). There follows Jack's struggle to get clear information, but the most he can find out is that it is not known what will happen more than thirty years into the future. He has a number of tests and physical examinations after the toxic event and lives in constant fear of death. To the reader this is intensely paradoxical. The "death" being predicted would almost certainly come after Jack's natural demise. The "information" is never clear. First he sees his doctor, who offers one of those physician-patient dialogues which points to the crumbling interface between scientific knowledge and human emotion:

> "Exactly how elevated is my potassium?"
> "It has gone through the roof, evidently."
> "What might this be a sign of?"
> "It could mean nothing, it could mean a very great deal indeed."
> "How great?"
> "Now we are getting into semantics," he said. [260]

The doctor sends him to a laboratory where more tests are performed and sophisticated equipment discovers a "nebulous mass," characterized by the fact that it has "no definite shape, form or limits." (280) This seemingly hilarious vagueness fingers the point of interface between science and human lives, where death, the white noise background to the text and our lives, hovers. DeLillo's black humor around our fears of science is indelible.

While the airborne toxic cloud and its implications are a sharp reminder of the strange cross between false security and terror that scientific information conveys, the second main action of the text is more distinctly fantastic science. Jack discovers that Babette is taking an illegal experimental drug called Dylar, which is supposed to remove the fear of death. She has given her body to a seedy chemist named Mink in order to obtain the drug, and Jack goes to him to kill him for the drug and for sexual revenge. The drug does not work, of course, and Mink, who is eating it "like candy," seems to be a sad mad scientist, spewing senile disconnected thoughts, presumably the result of taking his own drug. But one brief exchange highlights the deeper irony of the situation:

> "You are very white, you know that?"
> "It's because I'm dying."
> "This stuff'll fix you up."

4. A Bridge Takes Shape

"I'll still die."
"But it won't matter, which comes to the same thing." [310]

It would be hard to better this bit of dialogue for a mixture of spurious logic and irony focused on the modern perceptions of pharmacology and medicine. Gladney finds out from the medical profession that he is menaced by death, but the terms are so vague that all modern medical technology can really tell him is that death is the essential human condition and he will die sometime in the future. The whole aura of scientific knowledge and "expert" counsel frightens him a great deal. Then he ends up talking to a crazy scientist in an Hawaiian shirt and Budweiser shorts in a seedy motel room, where the miracle drug is available, but it is both illegal and memory-destroying. The price of not fearing death is not knowing what is going on in life.

Tabloid journalism plays a prominent role in the popular distortion of science in the text. DeLillo's thrust here is sharply different from, say, Pynchon's respect for the final equations of the ballistic path, for he is focusing on the interface between science-technology and the culture. He demonstrates that in bits of abstracted half-truth:

> "Mouse cries have been measured at forty thousand cycles per second. Surgeons use high-frequency tapes of mouse cries to destroy tumors in the human body." [236]

He describes technologically tagged idiocies like "The Stanford Linear Accelerator 3-Day Particle-Smashing Diet" (145), and weird psychic predictions:

> "Earth's only satellite, the moon, will explode on a humid night in July, playing havoc with tides and raining dirt and debris over much of our planet. But UFO cleanup crews will help avert a worldwide disaster, signaling an era of peace and harmony." [146]

Such are the general public's distorted contact with a complex world that otherwise overwhelms modern consciousness.

Yet this misinformation only underlines the way that a confused respect for science and technology dominates people's thinking. Murray Jay Siskind, ex-sportswriter turned lecturer in popular culture, sums up the attitude when he and Gladney are discussing death:

> "Technology is lust removed from nature."
> "It is?"
> "It's what we invented to conceal the terrible secret of our decaying bodies. But it's also life, isn't it? It prolongs life, it pro-

vides new organs for those that wear out. New devices, new techniques every day. Lasers, masers, ultrasound. Give yourself up to it, Jack. Believe in it. They'll insert you in a gleaming tube, irradiate your body with the basic stuff of the universe. Light, energy, dreams, God's own goodness." [285]

In the black comedy of *White Noise*, DeLillo comes to grips with the complexity of our response to a Niagara of information and misinformation about the scientific. For all its humor and irrationality, this is a text which is concerned with "the terrible secret of our decaying bodies" and the way contemporary culture, permeated with scientific thinking, latches on to a language it rarely understands as a blanket of protection against the essence of the human condition.

Whereas *The Revolt of Aphrodite* has a balance between science, traditional fiction and satire, elements that are disparate and rammed together for Durrell's effect, and *White Noise* gets purposefully lost in a confusion of science and jargon, Kingsley Amis *The Anti-Death League* (1966) aims at the metaphorical qualities of science and technology in order to produce a novel whose moving undercurrent belies Amis' usual comic surface. In this text a British armored group is preparing to test nuclear rifle shells at a site in England and a series of deaths occurs in the area. These begin with an unknown person, a motorcycle dispatch rider, and move "inward" to Fawkes, a young enlisted man. The text, while often comic and ironic in Amis' manner, keeps death always in its sights. The weapons are being tested as part of a concrete plan to use them immediately in an Asian war, and all the officers have been told there is a high level of risk in the Asian operation. The title refers to a mysterious notice and a poem which appear in the camp, the notice purporting to start an association opposed to death. The issue comes to its head when the weapon is tested, one rifle and shell goes missing, and someone uses it to destroy an unused priory in the night. Congruent to this and in the foreground of the story is the intense love affair between James Churchill and Catherine Casement. Just as the nuclear shell tests are about to happen, it is discovered that Catherine has breast cancer, and this furnishes the center of the death pattern in the text.

For the central idea, as much a metaphorical "theory" as Pynchon's ballistic arc, is that there is a pattern to all this dying and threat of dying. James Churchill, moved by Catherine's danger, sums it up:

"Something out of the tactical mumbo-jumbo they keep throwing at us fitted the situation better, I thought. You've probably heard of these things they call lethal nodes. You don't have battles or fronts any more, you have small key areas it's death to enter. Well, we're in a lethal node now, only it's one that works in time instead of space." [224]

Later Churchill has a drowsing dream of the pattern of the lethal node:

> It was in the form of a broad horizontal disc, vague and granular at the periphery, thickening towards the middle. Through the exact center a taut vertical thread ran both ways to mathematical infinity. You entered the node, or it moved across you, until you arrived at the thread. [225-26]

Those in greatest danger of death are stranded on the vertical thread (Churchill sees Catherine and himself in this position) while others are moving across the disc, presumably to emerge from the node.

The rest of the text seems to confirm this patterned vision. Just as the center had been approached through the deaths of the anonymous dispatch rider and the slightly known Fawkes, so the route out leads through the death of the slightly known Private Deering (a spy flushed out in the camp) and the almost anonymous Dr. L.S. Caton, a civilian visitor caught in the crossfire surrounding Deering. At the conclusion of the text Catherine may be out of danger and the community is enjoying a concert, when, in the background, Major Ayscue's dog, Nancy, is run over by a truck with faulty steering. This sudden final twist leaves open the nasty possibility that the lethal node is beginning once again and may plunge the characters back into a cycle of death.

In fact, by using the idea of the lethal node, Amis has effectively shaped the idea that the cycle of death is continual. This in turn conveys the essential pessimism of his text which runs like a dark river beside the mannered and comic surface. The technology of the atomic tests (and a speculation about biological warfare for which the tests may only be a cover) seems to flow over into the language of the lethal node. Amis does not seek the pervasive and intrusive scientific presence that DeLillo does but he gets a powerful effect by planting a "scientized" explanation for the menace of death. It is as though there was something serious that this usually comic-ironic writer wished to say, and he has found a means in the semi-scientific realm of the lethal node.

William Boyd's *Brazzaville Beach* (1990) is an example of a text which draws on the sciences for its frame, and like *The Anti-Death League*, sees metaphorical function in the science it uses. But its use of mathematics and ethnology investigations and their implications for the lives of the characters are more complex than Amis' and lack his comic-ironic overtones.

Brazzaville Beach is a complex, retrospective narrative centering around Hope Clearwater's two recent crises. In the first person past she relates her experiences on a chimpanzee research project in the Congo, where she has caused a sensation, overturning the received knowledge that the chimpanzees are peaceful social creatures by uncovering their brutal cannibalistic side, thus undermining the work of the Director, Eugene Mallabar. A congruent omniscient narrative deals with her marriage (before her trip to Africa) to an obsessive mathematician, John Clearwater, which ends with his insanity and suicide. Interpolated into these narratives in italic type are a number of technical explanations of things including ethnology and mathematics but extending to such matters as the neural clock, ECT therapy, and the history of volleyball. The inexorable need for the reader to establish the interconnectedness of the interpolations to the rest of the text infuses their science with human meaning and allows the human to be seen as a realization of the theoretical.

Two major examples of this in action are archtectonic in that they provide the very shape of the text. An italicized definition of chimpanzees establishes that their classification truly makes them "mockmen" (the Angolan word's meaning), the closest genetic relative to human beings. The significance of this emerges as Hope gradually discovers their violence to one another and, at the same time, she becomes progressively more alienated from the "tribal group" of the research project scientists. Just as the northern group of chimpanzees silently invades the southern territory to kill and eat their fellow creatures, so Hope finds her evidence destroyed and her journals and records burnt in an "accidental" fire. Finally, when Hope takes Mallabar (whose "Alpa male" status as director of the project has been established by his intellectual dominance and by his sexual attraction for several of the women) to actually see the violence, he cannot believe it, turns, and in wild anger physically attacks Hope, irrationally blaming her for what they have seen. Thus the narrative confirms the animal behavior and the animal behavior predicts the narrative.

The other archtectonic pattern centers around John Clearwater's mathematical pursuits. At the start of his relationship with Hope he has moved from Game Theory, where studies are made within strict formal limits and there are "winners" and "losers," to studies of Turbulence, the attempt to predict and understand the infinite confusion of ocean waves or the surface of a ball of string whose *"erratic behavior terrifies mathematicians"* (55). Turbulence comes to signify Hope's relationship with John, John's twisted inner life, and the crazily unfolding events in Africa.

4. A Bridge Takes Shape

John makes brilliant initial advances and is then totally stymied, turns wildly from obsession to obsession, and then goes mad. Hope falls deeply in love with John, then realizes she will never be able to follow him into the arcane realms of mathematics, and finally sees the relationship disintegrate in a random series of disagreements and misunderstandings.

Boyd's method with these analogies is open comparison. Hope, who presents the scientific interpolations (except for a few in which she is a figure), precisely draws out the correspondences:

> But people were learning, now, that the key response to a divergence syndrome was not to be startled, or confounded, but to attempt to explain it through a new method of thought. Then, often, what seemed at first shocking, or bizarre, can become quite acceptable.
> As I stroll the length of this beach I consider all the divergence syndromes in my life and wonder where and when I should have initiated new methods of thought. [55]

In Boyd's employment of these comparisons there is an acceptance of both the metaphorical and the practical relationships here. Mathematics is trying to describe all reality, human behavior not excepted. So as science it is directly applicable. Yet talk of game theory, chaos theory, turbulence, and divergence syndromes tempts the reader's sense of metaphors, a temptation stimulated by the architectonic use of the science to parallel the major plot elements. This is a rich integration of the language and shapes of science with the language and shapes of life, that both acknowledges the scientific descriptions of life phenomena and holds open the gap which shows that life is more complex than science can manage. John Clearwater smashes against the wall of that complexity and Hope is badly mauled by the discovery that mockmen and men share attributes of violence.

A number of other texts stand further away from the use of accurate science or the accurate employment of scientific language yet have framing devices drawn from science fiction, scientific knowledge at their crux, or may be users of a scientific background. Texts such as William Golding's *The Inheritors* (1955), Graham Swift's *First Light* (1989), and Marge Piercy's *Woman on the Edge of Time* (1976) are examples of these more distanced uses of science or science fiction tropes in fiction.

William Golding's *The Inheritors* is a speculation based on the evolutionary moment when Neanderthal man encountered Cro-Magnon man some 30,000 to 40,000 years ago. It takes into account what is known about both groups: the general differences in stature and skills, the fact that both groups occupied areas of Europe, and the vital fact that Neanderthal man was a dead end in the tree of human development. From this basis Golding's soaring imagination takes flight to envision an encapsulation of this transitional moment as the meeting of two small groups in the forest, embodying in this conflict both the human emotions involved and the implications for all radical human change and transition.

The first four-fifths of the text presents the Neanderthal view of reality, dominated by the immediate needs of survival and the close family structure of seven individuals. They gather food, have fire, think in pictures (imagine and plan), worship Oa, a fertility goddess, and endure the death of the eldest male, Mal, whom they bury in a fetal position. Then their world is shattered by the coming of the Cro-Magnon others, hunters who steal their baby and small child, and are distinctly different in that they have rituals, alcohol, dugout canoes, and bows and arrows, and walk upright. In a mixture of accidents and aggression all of the Neanderthals except Lok (and the stolen baby) die.

Then the perspective switches so Lok is "the red creature," "it," walking on four legs and picking up objects with his/its toes, and is followed briefly as he/it grieves the loss of his fellows and finally lies down in the fetal position to die. The perspective switches a final time to that of the Cro-Magnon people traveling across a lake after their frightening engagement with the horrible creatures whose baby they have taken to replace a baby of their own which died at birth.

Golding's focus in *The Inheritors* is first and foremost upon the real human experience of both the Neanderthals and Cro-Magnons. The psychological portraits are entirely fictional, in that he can only speculate as to how they felt and behaved based upon the remains of their cultures. He endows the Neanderthals with great warmth of feeling and immense fear of their surroundings, and a very limited ability to comprehend that makes their days chaotic, trying, and very human. He relates their efforts to remember from last year, their primitive attempts to improve their existence (by shifting a log over a stream to replace another bridge-log that has disappeared during winter), and their struggle to think things through with limited thought processes. The reader becomes sympathetically attached to their life struggles and then undergoes the two sudden shifts of perspective: the "creaturizing" of Lok and the Cro-Magnon view. These shift the text from a simple anthropological recreation to a challenge about the meaning and value of human life. The Neanderthals are destroyed by the cruel and absolute dictates of the survival of the fittest: they seem to change from the human species to the animal and then they die off in the course of the text. But the Cro-Magnons are not purposefully destroying their predecessors through some sort of intellectual choice. The meeting is an accident, the Cro-Magnons act out of blind desperation, and only their technological superiority and superior organization allow them to survive.

While it is full of human suffering and struggle, Golding's text yields to the biological inevitability which is at the root of its situation. In thus humanizing scientific knowledge, he indirectly raises the issues of the shifts taking place since the late eighteenth century with the rise of industrial technology and the post-industrial technology of the computer world. A deeply moral writer, Golding carefully reaches backwards to another greater change, when a whole branch of the human tree was lopped off, to suggest the implications for the individual beings caught in the inexorable movements of change and progress. The moment he chooses is known only through anthropological science, its implications are replicated whenever humans face incomprehensible change.

Peter Ackroyd's *First Light* offers the past as it emerges in the present in a brilliant blending of archaeology and astronomy with a contemporary tragicomic situation. This complex and fascinating text begins with Damian Fall, an unhappy minor astronomer, speculating on the formation of the cosmos and man from swirling energy and on the way the ancients must have looked at the sky and at Aldebaran, one of the brightest stars. The main plot concerns the excavation of a 4000-year-old tumulus grave site and the mysterious events which surround it. It gradually emerges that the ancients buried an astronomer-priest in the star-oriented site and that the isolated Dorset community contains the descendants of the Old Barrren One (tied to Aldebaran), who seek to prevent desecration of his tomb and person.

This summary cannot convey the levels of the text, which vary from moving relationships between death, the stars, and the awe invoked by the dig to the low comedy of chases and deceptions and the presence of a retired wise-cracking music hall comedian who discovers that he is part of the ancient family. All of this is jumbled together in the present time, but the real power of the text lies in the connections which it establishes between pre-history and our own lives. Whereas *The Inheritors* has meaning for the present only by analogy, Ackroyd telescopes the past into the present. Mark Clare, the local archaeologist who manages the dig, is married to a crippled wife who goes into depression and commits suicide, and he undergoes experiences in the tomb beneath the valley and in Damien's observatory which lead him to resolve his grief. Alec, Damien's assistant, tells Mark:

> "But didn't you know that we were made from the ashes of dead stars? All the materials of life come from the cosmic trace elements." Alec put his hand upon Mark's shoulder. "You have a universe inside you, my friend. The real thing."
>
> "So perhaps the story is right, after all. Perhaps our souls do become stars."
>
> "And there's something else, too." Alec sounded as if he had discovered all of these things for the first time, and was eager to share his knowledge. " If you ever put blood plasma under a microscope, do you know what it looks like?"
>
> "No."
>
> Alec was triumphant. "It looks exactly like a star field." [263–64]

This newfound revelation profoundly affects Mark:

> "But if we are all part of the same pattern," he said, "then nothing is destroyed. Things just change their form, and take up another place in the pattern. No one really dies." He put his hand up to his face, feeling a happiness that was also unhappiness, and both were mingled, and both were the same. [264]

Like the other writers treated in this section, Ackroyd has met Wordsworth's criteria of "carrying sensation into the midst of the objects of the science itself." The archaeological and astronomical knowledge flows into Mark Clare's life, where its human meaning asserts its human value. For the Dorset community the archaeological information is lived in their lives in the veneration of the Old Barren One, and where astronomy comes together with the archaeology in the siting of the tomb, the text communicates an awe for the lineal connection of human achievement. Alec and Damien Fall, huddling in the cold dark and looking at the night sky from their observatory, feel its mystery and majesty much as the ancients must have perceived it when they carved a star map on the blind entry stone of the tomb. The events of 5,000 years ago are, in a feeling way, linked to the present in a story which is both science and art. Damien actually articulates the link in terms of the narrative act:

> "Science is like fiction, you see. We make up stories, we sketch out narratives, we try to find some pattern beneath events. We are interested observers. And we like to go on with the story, we like to advance, we like to make progress. Even though they are stories told in the dark." [159]

First Light sees science in the human realm, where it is a vital part of the human story.

4. A Bridge Takes Shape

The most radical possibility offered to writers of conventional fiction to attract them to span is the utopian-dystopian opportunity that all science fiction, set in the future or the far elsewhere, opens up. All writers create their worlds, but there are exceptional possibilities for imaginative creation when every custom, practice, social and psychological reality, and the physical world itself are wholly open. Then writers are put in the position of considering what the world could be like, should be like, or will be like: speculating around human circumstances in a projected reality which may or may not center on scientific advances. The pure utopian convention (beginning with Sir Thomas More's *Utopia* [1516]), with its stress on change of place rather than time, preceded modern science fiction, but the projection of scientific-technological change, and most recently of such changes combined with radical changes in personal and social conditions, have made future speculation the center of the contemporary utopian impulse. In fact, it is perhaps more accurate to describe it as a dystopian impulse, for almost all twentieth-century texts deal with negative possibilities, beginning with H.G. Wells' *The Time Machine* (1895) and coming forward through such classics as Aldous Huxley's *Brave New World* (1932), Ayn Rand's *Anthem* (1946) and George Orwell's *1984* (1948).

Span writers come from the mainstream of fiction writing to the utopian-dystopian model because the range of their possible expression of the human situation is vastly expanded by the move. They are able to manipulate ideological possibilities by realizing them rather than by having characters discuss them in the abstract. They are able to isolate characters in strange environments in order to better examine the human experience itself. They are able to offer indirect but powerful social commentary through the extrapolation of particular trends or possibilities in the current world. They are able to model by contrast: that is, to have both future and present worlds in the same text through the devices of time travel, or having beings from a future culture examine the artifacts or texts of our present time. The comparisons, be they implicit or explicit, offer immensely powerful and flexible possibilities for ironies.

The treatment of the human, the effect of scientific progress, scientific speculation or scientific viewpoint on ordinary lives, has been the central thread of the new form considered in this chapter. The utopian-dystopian models complicate this because they may have powerfully coherent and logical projections of humanity's material conditions, as well as their focus on individual lives. Here, on the new middle ground, speculative fiction in the utopian-dystopian mode meets the science fiction which focuses on the human condition (as opposed to the formulaic science fiction overwhelmed by ideas in which characters are functional ciphers), which will be the subject of chapter 5. The only real difference will be the writers' previous experience—whether in science fiction or in conventional fiction.

Darko Suvin's ideas about the *novum* function with a vengeance in most dystopian fiction. One change may be at the root of a dystopia, but it almost always reaches tendrils out into all facets of human life, creating a whole jungle of the new and strange. The features which distinguish span dystopias by traditional writers from science fiction dystopias arise from their writers' interest in the complexity of human responses and from the opportunities for highly tuned ironic perspectives. Some of these dystopias even push their irony to comedy, and here it is clear that the writers are not struggling to wholly capture their readers by belief but rather seek to play with the dystopian concept. Few science fiction dystopias risk such an equivocal position (Stanislaw Lem's texts and the Frederick Pohl—Cyril Kornbluth *The Space Merchants* (1953) are among the few exceptions) because the demand for belief in the generated world is part of their readers' pattern of expectation in reading the genre.

A starting point for the examination of dystopias by traditional writers is Margaret Atwood's unsettling modern masterpiece *The Handmaid's Tale* (1985). This text differs from traditional fiction because it is set in the wholly imagined *novum* of a claustrophobic, extreme right-wing dictatorship called Gilead in a near future Cambridge, Massachusetts. It deals extensively with the immediate effects on individuals of such a world, but it does so with such integral attention to language, psychology, style, intertextuality, and complexity of construction and design, including metafiction and irony, that it is, in sum, unlike any work of strict science fiction. Its middle ground status depends upon its place as a small branch on the generic tree of modern fiction rather than as a part of that strong but separate seeded sapling beside it which is science fiction.

The most prominent feature of *The Handmaid's Tale* is the intensity of the emotional experience it offers through the brilliantly managed first person narration of Offred, the handmaid of the title, who is trapped in this society where viable women are property to be used for reproduction by prominent males. The full horror of entrapment is the driving force of the narrative and it depends upon a carefully selected and sustained writing style, particular qualities of play on language, metafictional intimacy, variation between an agonizing present and a criticized past, the handling of intertexts, irony, and the striking and equivocal Historical Notes at the close of the text.

Offred's writing style is clipped, plain, and full of absolute and irrevocable statements:

4. A Bridge Takes Shape

> A bed. Single, mattress medium-hard, covered with a flocked white spread. Nothing takes place in the bed but sleep; or no sleep. I try not to think too much. Like other things now, thought must be rationed. [17]
>
> Doctors lived here once, lawyers, university professors. There are no lawyers any more, and the university is closed. [33]

The description of the bed, early in the text, contains ominous, constricting overtones. "Nothing ... but sleep" indicates, but does not explain, a loss of the sexual and of companionship. The "no sleep" leads on to the danger of thinking, once again enforcing the sense of oppression and control, ending in the idea of rationing. The phrases are loaded with constricting and limiting words: nothing, no, not, rationing. In this fragment, as throughout the text, the style evokes limits, controls, restrictions. The second quotation is characteristic of the absolute fashion in which whole segments of the world as we know it are erased. Erasure, reduction, and elimination are mirrored in the stripped writing style that expresses unchallengeable absolutes.

The texture of the text is reinforced by word play which consistently demonstrates the ideology of repression and its costs. Offred is the absolute proof of the effect of Gilead on the individual:

> I avoid looking down at my body [she is in the bath], not so much because it's shameful or immodest but because I don't want to see it. I don't want to look at something that determines me so completely [72–73].

The rich complexity of these sentences focuses precisely on how, in an authoritarian state, all individuality is sacrificed to function—determined. It also calls up the rhetoric of sociobiology. Atwood forces the implication to its maximum with the "something," Offred's separation of herself from her own fertile body which, in a very real sense, is her prison. Her deprivation is so great that even her name has been taken. She is Offred, of-Fred, a name she and the other handmaids (like of-Warren, of-Glen) take only while attached to a particular Commander.

One of the most painful plays of language in the text is the tense corrections which Offred makes when thinking of those she cares for.

> What I feel is partly relief, because none of these men is Luke [her husband]. Luke wasn't a doctor. Isn't. [43]
>
> And he [Luke] was, the loved. One.
> *Is*, I say. *Is, is,* only two letters, you stupid shit, can't you manage to remember it, even a short word like that? [239]

Each of the above passages marks the end of a section of narrative and points to Offred's desperation and loneliness as she tries, by correcting her own tenses, not to let go of those she loves.

The sentence-by-sentence awareness of words is framed by an extraordinary metafictional intimacy. Atwood makes Offred's situation intense for the reader by having her describe the most intricate details of her situation and feelings, but at the same time has her narrate self-consciously, telling the reader that she is telling a story and commenting on the pain of that activity and on the choices she makes in the telling. So, for example, Offred prefaces her account of what happened to Luke with, "Here is what I believe" (114), and then relates possible scenarios, ending with the contradictory idea that she believes all three of them. Later, when she has sex with Nick [the Commander's chauffeur], she offers different versions of that event as she seeks to assuage her guilt in "betraying" Luke.

Offred is constantly aware of her story as story and, through that, Atwood adds to the sense of desperation, and, with the paradoxical effect common to metafiction, to the sense that the story is real. Having a narrator, under great pressure, tell the reader that this is a story but that she is trying to make it as real as possible (i.e. close to true events and scenes) actually adds to the reader's belief in both narrator and events. This metafictional device not only adds to the reality, it powerfully accentuates Offred's isolation and uncertain destiny.

> I would like to believe this is a story I'm telling. I need to believe it. I must believe it. Those who can believe that such stories are only stories have a better chance.
> If it's a story I'm telling, then I have control over the ending. Then there will be an ending, to the story, and real life will come after it. I can pick up where I left off.
> It isn't a story I'm telling. [49]

Entrapment, desperation, the denial that this fiction is a fiction, and, on a more expansive level, a reflection on the common human situation of being in a story (life) from which there is no exit, are all compressed into this metafictional ploy. Later in this same passage Offred wonders who will hear her story, imagines a reader, and then, in despair, decides that no one can hear her. This essential deprivation, a storyteller apparently without the necessary listener, stresses, through the very rules of the fictional act, Offred's desperate isolation.

Another vital tactical decision, without which a great deal of the power of the story would be lost, is the use of time contrasts in the tale. Offred has only been in Gilead three years, and so she is constantly comparing her situation to the "before" in which she was with Luke and her daughter and in the broader world which prompted Gilead. Atwood deals extensively with this richly paradoxical material, making clear that radical feminism and social decadence (such as the Pornomarts and militant Christian fundamentalism) were the causes of the revolution, while the horrors of the outcome are simultaneously held in focus. The final time twist is the Historical Notes, the bitingly ironic picture of scholars living one hundred and fifty years after Offred's time who have unearthed and reconstructed the tale but from whom it elicits not a shred of human sympathy: "Our job is not to censure but to understand. (Applause.)" (315). This awful tribute to those who suffered and died in historical persecutions (the book is dedicated to Atwood's ancestor Mary Webster, who survived hanging as a witch in Salem when the rope broke, and to Perry Miller, the Harvard professor with whom Atwood studied the Puritan era) leaves the reader indigestibly angry at the fate of human individuals caught in the social-material-political web of history and produces the most lasting effect of the text: an awareness that we overlook the play of power at our gravest peril.

This text, a projective fiction with more complex fictional techniques than any science fiction, is further enriched by a bewildering display of carefully chosen ironies and by a rich and far-reaching intertextuality. The Gilead society was designed by the Sons of Jacob Think Tanks, comforting product advertising names are used for awful "Aunts" who indoctrinate the Handmaids, the Eyes of God are patterned after the F.B.I., the justification for polygamy is dredged up from the Bible, and such advertising terms as Prayvaganzas and Particulation (for a mob execution—a mixture of Participation, the Canadian national physical fitness campaign, and "making into particles") are attached to ceremonies designed to manage the society.

The greatest ironies are more global ones: a religiously based society practicing slavery and murder, the former Harvard University a center for secret police torture and murder, and all of this done by ideologically driven men who cannot see the havoc they have wrought.

The intertextual complexities begin with the title, which is described, in the Historical notes, as a tribute to Geoffrey Chaucer. But Chaucer's world was one where humans followed the faith with joy and warmth and the movement of the pilgrimage is in bitter ironic contrast to the static, involuntary imprisonment of Gilead. In the second of the "Night" sections, Offred evokes Marlowe's Mephistopheles in the intensity of her painful isolation:

> ...and step sideways out of my own time. Out of time. Though this is time, nor am I out of it. [47]

> Faust. How comes it then that thou art out of hell?
> Meph. Why this is hell, nor am I out of it:
> Think'st thou that I, that saw the face of God,
> And tasted the eternal joys of Heaven,
> Am not tormented with ten thousand hells,
> In being depriv'd of everlasting bliss? [1, iii]

The overwhelming physical and psychological permanence of Offred's condition is evoked through this link, for she can no more be out of the time she is in than Mephistopheles can *ever* change his state of damnation. These two figures also offer an eerie visual echo, the demon disguised as a Franciscan friar and the fertile woman disguised by Gilead as a "red nun."

Other intertexts are much more open, such as the quotation of the first stanza of *Amazing Grace* which Offred points out can no longer be sung because it ends with the word free. She then quotes from another banned song, "Heartbreak Hotel," ending with "I feel so lonely I could die." Personal emotions and personal faith are formally excluded from Gilead.

By far the largest body of intertextual reference is biblical and it features the bitterly ironical reversals that arise when the manipulators of the Word use it for their own ends. The handmaids are told that "Gilead is within you"(33), a horrifying distortion of "The Kingdom of heaven is within you" which secularizes the holy, contains the idea of brainwashing dear to this state, and, at a deeper level, refers to the physical reality that only these women's wombs can contain the future of the state. The women are also told "From each, says the slogan, according to her ability; to each according to his needs" (127), a distortion of the original biblical idea of sharing (Acts 4:35), which speaks of every man (in the sense of human) but does not say that women must yield to this sexist view of need. Offred also contemplates Genesis 30:1–4, the text upon which the regime bases its ritualized polygamy:

> *Give me children, or else I die.* There's more than one meaning to it. [71]

In Genesis it is envy which moves Rachael to her plea, but for Offred it is a life and death imperative, for she will be executed or exiled to die by the regime if she does not conceive. In the Genesis passage, which is one of the text's epigraphs and is read during the ceremony leading to the Commander's monthly attempt to impregnate Offred, Jacob is angered by the accusation of his infertility, and the regime has codified this into a denial of male sterility which makes the handmaids wholly responsible with their lives for a failure to conceive.

A final example of intertextual distortion is the hymn "A Balm in Gilead" which is sung at the Prayvaganza. Offred's lost friend Moira parodied it, "There is a Bomb in Gilead" (230), an act of verbal rebellion against the state. More importantly the hymn, which the regime takes as a confirmation of the blessings rained on the state, is based on an incorrect reading of the biblical original. The original, taken from the bitter admonitions of Jeremiah to the erring Israelites, reads: "Is there no balm in Gilead; is there no physician there? why then is not the health of the daughter of my people recovered?" (8:22). There is no balm (soothing ointment) for the anguish of those trapped in this evil and erring state, particularly for the "daughter" Offred.

The intertextual complexity is abetted by the intensely ironic metonymy of the text. Metonymy usually involves substitution of one object to evoke another (a frequent example is "the crown" for "king") but from a wider perspective it is the insertion of all the cultural markers in a text, the things which relate the text to its cultural-historical moment so readers can "place" it in their world picture. Mention of golden arches, for example, conjures late twentieth-century American mass commercial culture with strong class undertones.

Atwood's text is an example of the modified way in which metonymy operates in dystopian texts with future settings. The rich and varied cultural echoes do not so much reflect the Gilead culture she is portraying as serve to contrast it with the culture of our present. This is a site of powerful irony, for the present is caricatured by the metonymies selected and Offred's comments on them and, simultaneously, the traces of the ordinary markers of our lives serve to underline the world which Gilead has destroyed. Offred, trapped in the enforced idleness of her role in Gilead, remembers Pig Balls, which were used to keep pigs active, and wishes she had one. Pig Balls capture the strangeness of the popular culture of our historical moment, for while they may be useful in the raising of pigs, their popular echoes are to the way they simulate human behavior in the directionless ease of late twentieth century middle class western culture. When Offred wishes for a Pig Ball in Gilead it brings into sharp focus the way in which she is being used like a breeding animal and accorded no credit as an individual thinking person.

As she puts her veil on after bathing, Offred remembers seeing a film of women having their heads shaved in public. She wonders, "What had they done? It must have been a long time ago, because I can't remember" (75). This fragmentary memory of the French punishment for World

War II collaborateurs is very evocative. The reader immediately compares the fate of these women to Offred's fate, for while they were shamed, they were not imprisoned in an endless and degrading servitude. Mention of them raises all of the questions around Offred's cooperation with the regime; both had little choice if they were to survive. And the reference beckons Nazi Germany, with all of its repressive brutality and mental coercion, into the reader's consciousness. The Nazis have come to occupy a mythic monster status in late twentieth-century Western culture, they are the "other." But when they are brought into this text, the policies and style of this ideologically rigid American dictatorship bring the "other" home. This accentuates Offred's entrapment and sets the reader to work comparing the regimes.

Mentions of Weight Watchers, *Vogue* magazine, a Tennyson garden, Playboy bunnies, anti-pornography and pro-abortion demonstrations, and television evangelism are all metonymies of our times, which stand out starkly against the time being pictured in the text. Their presence at once criticizes them for excess, vagueness, narrow self-absorption, and chastises the Gillead regime for its denial of freedoms and narrowing of the human perspective. Atwood peppers Offered's speech with scraps of clichéd speech that take on powerful and ironic overtones, reminding the reader that words change their meanings against different historical backgrounds:

> The house is what he [the Commander] holds. To have and to hold, till death do us part. [91]
> One false move and I'm dead. [99]

The Handmaid's Tale has all the attributes of a contemporary literary text in terms of language, metafiction, intertextuality, metonymy, complex time scheme, and its subtly controlled intense emotional focus. But its dystopian thrust, with its particular mixture of imagined elements projected as developments upon our historical moment, moves it to the new middle ground. Atwood is a mainstream writer (although she has written several other middle ground fragments[5]) who has brought an essential projective trope to bear not to sell books to science fiction readers but because it suits her need to speak about what she perceives as dangerous present trends.

Paul Theroux, best known for his travel writing and for mainstream novels such as *The Mosquito Coast* (1981), has also ventured into dystopic fiction in *O-Zone* (1986). He envisions a future America with a wealthy, isolated fortress New York City populated by "owners," a reduced rural America, and an Outer Zone, or O-Zone, in the Ozark Plateau which was

Missouri. O-Zone has been contaminated by the release of nuclear wastes stored in its caves, although it emerges in the text that it is once again possible to live there.

The complex story begins with a party visiting O-Zone to celebrate New Year's Eve and discovering "aliens," a roving party of people living in the forbidden territory. Later Hooper Allbright returns, fascinated by a young girl (Bligh) he has seen in the alien group, and kidnaps her, accidentally leaving behind his fifteen-year-old nephew Fisher (also known as Fizzy and Fish). As the story unfolds Fisher, superbly intelligent but stranded away from technology and his luxurious confined life, gradually attains his manhood among the aliens and gets their cooperation in a trek back to New York.

Set against this are the lives of the other members of the party, whose closely delineated natures are the keystone in Theroux's complex observations of the dystopia. For while this text presents a physical dystopia it is the expansion of the way that the characters in it feel and function that establishes the middle ground position of this text. Theroux, whose travel writing and other fiction make him a very gifted creator of place and cultures, sees that it is not technology or storied places that have meaning for readers of dystopias, but what it will feel like to be there and what it will do to human nature.

In the opening sections of the text the characters verge on caricatures, like so many science fiction exploration parties used by authors to discover the wonders of strange planets or different eras, except that they are motivated by boredom and purposeless wealth. But Theroux places emphasis on their isolation, first by having them encased in flyers, portable shelters, and suits and later by descriptions of their tightly controlled world of New York City with its heavy security, frivolous pursuits, and meaningless relationships. Gradually it becomes clear that this world of plenty and power is also a world without intimacy or even close contact between individuals.

Fisher's shattering experiences with the "aliens" (who in fact turn out to be intelligent humans exiled into O-Zone) bring him into real touch with people who care for each other and even for him. As he gradually becomes their leader, he becomes less and less isolated. He has found what was never offered to him in New York—human caring and contact. So important is it to him that he abandons New York for O-Zone and his new-found companions.

Fisher's mother, Moura, whose aimlessness is partly driven by her arid marriage to Hardy Allbright, becomes increasingly dependent upon her memory of the release of passion fifteen years earlier, when she went monthly for two years to a licensed contact clinic to conceive Fisher through intercourse with a selected "donor," both of them wearing only decorative masks. After Fisher's disappearance she is drawn back to the clinic, not for sexual pleasure (the fashion for contact donors has palled and the clinics are now exclusive brothels) but to seek information about Fisher's biological father. She becomes progressively less sympathetic to her New York friends and as the novel closes she has fled to the post-earthquake West Coast to the confusion of Landslip and believes she has found the man who has been haunting her. Significantly, he is not a wonder of youth, but a confident man worn by struggles in a real world.

> But if it was this man, time had wrecked him and caused him pain. Yet oddly it had also given him more life. He looked a little dangerous and if it were truly him he looked a lot freer and stronger. [532]

Moura, the man, and his son Fisher are all pictured as better and stronger because they have broken out of the confines of New York. Hooper Allbright's fascination with Bligh changes from lust-for-property to sexual obsession to a flowering of love. Bligh is O-Zone come to New York, but she is hardly the wide-eyed innocent Savage of *Brave New World*. She seizes the chance for luxury and it is Hooper, who goes through a voyeuristic phase of watching her with remote cameras ("Photography was foreplay" [388]), who is initially the reluctant player in their sexual duet.

Theroux's repeated theme is distance and barriers, people who avoid contact with the physical world through technology and whose society has closed itself from contact with much of the world, including most of America. It is in this context that O-Zone takes on immense metaphoric importance, standing at once for reality ravaged by technology, for the raw and dangerous America of the frontier, and for the human space so lacking in this claustrophobic world. When they first fly over O-Zone, Moura says of it:

> "Something that's been lost—that you can't see or touch or ever have again—can grow in your mind and acquire wonderful associations. It can become almost magical." [8]

Once the first traumatic trip is over, there are continual references to "before O-Zone" or "since O-Zone." The enclosed lives of the characters are forever changed and opened out by this engagement with the unknown.

> Had the world changed, or had he? The O-Zone trip gave him a way of dating his life. He now had a sense of time, a feeling of before and after. It was scratched on his memory in a long raw stroke that would heal but always remain as a narrow scar. In that sealed wound were the discoveries he had made—the forbidden place, the friends he had seen in a new way, the shock of having seen those aliens in an area believed to be empty. And he had to accept the strange simplicity that O-Zone was America, and aliens were human. [89]

It is depicted as a fascination not only for these travelers but for all of America:

> People dreamed about it and used it as a backdrop for their fantasies…. O-Zone had been like that. One day it was just the Ozarks, and the next day it was an island revolving in outer space. It was lost beauty—spoiled, people said, ruined and poisoned. But now Hooper knew better, and somewhere down there so probably did Fizzy. [330]
> They [Americans] thought about it all the time. It was an area of darkness in most people's consciousness, and Fizzy was lost in it. [384]
> O-Zone is nowhere. Moura smiled: No. O-Zone was not a wilderness or a riddle—it was a condition and it was probably eternal, and it was everywhere. O-Zone was the world. [518]

With its clear attempt to offer an American echo to Conrad's *Heart of Darkness,* Theroux's complex and metaphorical idea of O-Zone is pervasive and enigmatic. It may begin in the realm of the dystopic future disaster science fiction novel, but as it moves into the psyches of its characters and of America, it becomes a complex literary variation on the frontier novel, that form of the romantic expression of America as the unfulfilled dream. Lacking the precision of the standard science fiction extrapolation (despite its particle beams, its visions of a fortified New York), it is a way of getting at the curious mixture of the utopian American Dream and its desecration and the way in which it is finally centered in the soul and not the physical body of America. Despite all of its dystopian tendencies, this is a text which finally finds human hope in the desire for real intimacy, in a breaking through the embellishments of technological America to the individual dreaming of the heart.

That same troubled dreaming of the human heart is central to Walter Tevis's *The Steps of the Sun* (1983), a text whose real center is the midlife crisis of Ben Belson. For very interesting reasons the text is set in a dystopic era around 2063, for Tevis wants to use science fiction motifs to highlight aspects of the crisis in metonymic fashion. The science fiction and buccaneering aspects of the story provide excitement and direction but, as the text progresses, it becomes more and more the story of an individual's turmoil rendered in metaphors of space, science, and dystopia.

The future Tevis envisions is one in which North America has run out of nuclear fuel and is reduced to burning wood for domestic heat and coal for transport. New York city has empty skyscrapers whose elevators and lights no longer function but is still a style capital and a tourist center for the rich and powerful Chinese (who continue to exploit their dangerous uranium resources).

Ben Belson is an aggressive multimillionaire who has become impotent at fifty and has staked a major part of his future on an illegal space venture to discover a "safe uranium" which scientists had predicted would exist under certain circumstances. Belson, the first planet he visits (and names for himself), has no uranium but has a strange polymeric grass which can sing and shows other signs of intelligence and a plant which yields an immensely potent analgesic drug with no side effects. A second planet yields the uranium.

Belson chooses to stay alone on Belson to contemplate for four months and goes through remarkable personal changes, climaxing in a symbiosis in which the grass feeds him. His ship's crew brings the news that he has been made an outlaw in the United Sates, and the action line of the remainder of the novel involves his finding ways to recover his wealth and to find Isabel, the actress he had loved but lost through his impotence.

The real center of the text is Ben's personal transformation from an action figure to a person in a midlife crisis to a reconstituted whole man. The text, which he is dictating to a computer, reviews his whole life and so brings the memories of his unhappy childhood and his struggles throughout life into a present context, where they are played against his ongoing experiences.

Early in the text Ben seems less a person than the personification of an "action figure" of American success. His decisiveness and his polite but authoritarian manner are reminiscent of the entrepreneur kings of American soap opera. This apparent caricature is in keeping with the vitality of the adventure plot. Tevis employs the dystopian hero to place an action line on what would otherwise emerge as a static study of middle age angst. As it is, all of the stages of the angst are played out within the span context, as Ben develops into a progressively more nuanced character whose struggles with himself have correlatives in the technology and situations.

4. A Bridge Takes Shape

This is a first person memoir without the implied conventional context of someone "speaking" to a reader because Ben is recording it on the computer. His time alone, during which he reassesses his life and regains his potency, is spent on Belson, the planet with the sympathetic polymeric grass. The experience is a metaphor for spending the time with oneself, finding energy within (he and the planet do, after all, have the same name), and becoming able to nourish and support the self. On the narrative level he is alone, having sent his ship and crew back to Earth with the uranium. But his isolation is a willed and psychological thing as well, for he has abandoned the Eden-like planet where the uranium was actually discovered for the harsher isolation of Belson. The planet seems to act on Ben, first depriving him of his connections with material comfort and then, when he is *in extremis*, coming to his aid with nourishment and reassurance. This is clearly metaphoric, representing the stripping away of externals so that he can find inner strength whose source is Belson, the self. The polymeric tendrils (whose roots go "miles below the surface") nuzzle up into Ben and nourish him, wordlessly sing to him, and share his agitated response when the ship (representing the world outside the self) returns:

> What glory, to relearn it [orgasm]. I relaxed and my whole body softened. I fell back to sleep.
> When I awoke to a distant roar Fomalhaut was high in the sky and I saw descending, riding a bright silver flame, the *Isabel*. A moment later I felt the ground of my planet receiving her, with a profound subcutaneous shudder. [116]

Another metonymic sequence is Ben's coming to terms with the memory of his alcoholic mother, who had made no real effort to offer him the love that his failed and distracted college professor father had withheld. On his return to Earth, Ben tries to contact his psychiatrist by viewphone but is offered only a computer surrogate briefed with his file and using the psychiatrist's synthesized voice. Ben asks to talk to his mother and the surrogate obliges by animating an old photograph in an eerily lifelike way. In the ensuing argument his "mother" explains her own pain, tells Ben that he was an unwanted accident, and tries to blame her failure to love her son on both Ben and his father. To his surprise, Ben finds himself with an erection (which his "mother" can see through the vidphone) replaying the Oedipal moment and, in his anger at her failure to love him, tells his "mother" that she is not worth either his lust or his anger. He breaks the connection and when he phones back tells the surrogate therapist that his anger has faded. The technology has relieved the Oedipal tension, allowing Ben to play out the scenario which he needs to clarify his experience. This metaphor for inner resolution is characteristic of the opening offered to represent internal experience through speculative elements.

This text is not Tevis' first experiment with span to investigate the human heart. His Martian visitor, Thomas Jerome Newton, in *The Man Who Fell To Earth* (1963), was in many ways a study of human sensitivity and despair framed by the rubric of an alien visiting earth and finding it horribly wanting. But in Ben Belson, Tevis has created a man with the more specific aspects of middle age angst and found the frame which allows the experience to be viewed in a new light. When Ben finally liberates his uranium and gives half of it to the United States, the relighting of the Empire State Building and New York City recapitulates the remaking of his life, with Isabel found and a surrogate mother, a Chinese scientist and sage, in his life to replace the mother who would not take the responsibility of loving him. Tevis has successfully blended an external adventure in the dystopic mode with Ben's internal adventure, using the openings provided by the speculative imagination to generate metaphors which enliven and enlighten our experience of Ben's transformation.

Walter Tevis' complex and sensitive use of metonymy to frame a human crisis is in stark contrast to Anthony Burgess' alternatively savage and hilarious dystopias, *A Clockwork Orange* (1962) and *The End of the World News* (1982). Burgess, whose interests in the often comic or cosmic twists that language can produce often rival James Joyce's, engages in much of his fiction in a relaxed, zany, and inventive search for the forms and genres suitable to what he wants to say.

A Clockwork Orange is a bitter dystopia of stunning moral complexity that features a manufactured street language. Alex, its narrator and central character, leads his droogs (the pseudolanguage is a Russian-influenced slang English) or toughs on adventures centering around "the old ultra-violence," a career of beating, raping, and cutting based on the 1950s British Teddy Boys. Finally jailed for a murder, he becomes a test case for a cruel and aggressive form of operant conditioning (called Ludovico's Technique) in which he is forced to watch films of violence and listen to his beloved classical music while drugged to make him feel vile.

His aggressive tendencies suppressed, he is released, helpless, into the violent world where he promptly beaten senseless by his old droogs, who have become policemen. He stumbles to the home of a writer whom his gang had once assaulted and he is "saved," only to be made a political example as the victim of the government's vicious conditioning scheme. To further this the writer drives Alex to attempt suicide by locking him in a room with music. The state then "cures" him by deconditioning him while he is in hospital recovering from his injuries and releases him to the world, once again moved by music and ready to enjoy violence.

The span elements in this text are rooted in the character of Alex. He is, on the one hand, a fierce horror capable of really enjoying violence and without a shred of morality. On the reverse side, he is quick, observant, enormously amusing, and deeply devoted to his classical music, normally a marker of high culture and sensitivity. Alex is a conscious first person narrator who directly addresses his readers:

> ...my brothers and only friends....
> ...against your Friend and Humble Narrator.... [75]

and, because he performs his acts of violence with panache and without guilt, he emerges as a strangely attractive narrator. This sets the stage for what is done to him, where Burgess brings on the conflicting forces that focus the moral issues at the root of his text.

The reader's mixed sympathies for Alex are essential for the propositions that the text examines. The operant conditioning makes Alex docile (a clockwork orange, as F. Alexander, the antiestablishment writer who takes up Alex and later makes him attempt suicide, calls the conditioned) but, as the prison chaplain points out, this is not done through free will and thus makes Alex less than a person. Alex is manipulated by both sides in the debate, and Burgess leaves us with the pointed paradox of choice between the "clockwork" Alex who eschews violence and classical music and the "cured" Alex with his love of music and violence restored. For the moral dilemmas of the text to function, Alex must be a complex character, not rooted in the science fiction traditions of reason and action but in the richly contradictory realm of mainstream fiction. Placing that character in the dystopic, linguistically experimental future produces the special hybrid which is *A Clockwork Orange*.

A Clockwork Orange is a tightly unified, almost claustrophobic future, but in his 1982 entertainment *The End of the World News*, Burgess treats the serious issues of our times as a burlesque. The text combines three stories written in different registers. There is a sketch for a very bad and inappropriate opera (complete with excruciating lyrics and stage directions) about Trotsky in New York, his failure to move the prosperous American workers, and his eventual embarkation to join the Russian Revolution. There is an enriched "treatment" meant to create a television drama about Sigmund Freud, that weaves his life around his escape from

Austria to England and his death but is full of ironic humor about Freud's personal failings and emotional blindness which humanize the great man. Finally, there is a dystopian sketch of a bad science fiction disaster scenario, in which a wandering planet, Lynx, destroys the human race except for a tiny community which escapes in a space ship. Central to this story is Val Brodie, a science fiction teacher and a moderately bad science fiction writer, who ends up aboard the escape ship, a non-scientist whose generalism makes him its leader.

It is probable that Burgess wrote the disaster plot, with its caricatures of government, culture, religion, and classic natural disaster novels, partly to put to use the other fragments which he may have been tempted to abandon. But the outcome is fascinating, for it is a twentieth-century mélange of the driving forces of Marxism, Freudianism, and the fear of Armageddon, all treated comically yet with an underlying sense of panic and interconnection. Produced almost before the term, it is a postmodern pastiche that insists throughout that readers make their own connections, although Burgess brilliantly collapses the tales together at the conclusion of the text by revealing that the catastrophe "novel" has actually been taught to a much later generation of children of the survivors, who do not believe it is any more than myth (there never was an Earth, man has always lived in a ship), and by placing the other two scenarios as tapes which have survived onto the voyage and which are viewed as fantasies and given wildly distorted meaning by the space children.

The End of the World News is a prime example of the management of science fiction conventions for span purposes. Burgess offers three stories, of which only the Freud story borders on literary realism. Even it is affected by the comic tone and overwhelming ironies. The Trotsky story is frankly parody, but parody about one of the most important political movements of our time. Set beside the science fiction plot they obviate the possibility of the reader suspending disbelief in the disaster scenario, and so make that scenario both a revelation of the weaknesses of such plots and direct the reader to see it as fiction. Yet even this "destroyed reality" is telling, for Burgess wants the reader to consider what is worth saving in the human experience, and a plan to save fifty people, set against the background of the whole culture responding to catastrophe, focuses that issue wonderfully.

The text also evaluates the other two great stories of our century in perspective, both by the way they are treated in the writing and by their final position as mythological fragments of future human experience. Finally, in Val Brodie, Burgess has placed a critic of science fiction within a science fiction story, and this opens the way for a metafictional consideration of the genre. Brodie and his graduate students discuss the genre and he offers a definition which proves to be ironically relevant:

> This, I think, is what our genre is about—the ways in which ordinary human beings respond to exceptional circumstances imposed unexpectedly upon them. The bubonic plague, a Martian invasion, global dehydration, the end of the world.... [29]

Later, at a dinner party, Val describes what might happen with Lynx as just such a scenario, so the reader has a fiction fulfilling the requirements of science fiction, were it not for the other fictions it is interspersed with and the Preface, a Swiftian letter in which the assembler of the fragments (he thinks they belong together only because they were in one container) quotes a letter from the author as saying that the three great events of our times were Freud, Marxism, and the space rocket.

The End of the World News offers a token formal integration of its science fiction portion with its other sections. Unlike all of the other variations on science fiction that this book has been considering, it does not integrate the mode into more complex fictions, but places it beside, thus making it one of the tools for Burgess' ideas. While Burgess may entitle the text "an entertainment," he has the very serious intent at its roots of considering the modern condition, and behind its consciously invoked humor, irony, and implicit critique of science fiction as a subgenre, he is able to use the form in a context which helps to focus on our times and our condition.

The authors of two other British dystopias offer contrasting levels of success in the employment of the middle ground. *The Children of Men* (1992) by detective fiction writer P.D. James is a model of what can go wrong when some science fiction conventions are not properly understood. James began with an interesting idea, that births might simply cease to happen in 1995 and that the population of Britain and the world would slowly age to the end of the human race. But the resulting text is flawed on two levels.

On the level of conventional fictional construction the first person narrator, an Oxford history don named Theodore (Theo) Faron, is clumsily handled, fails to engage the reader, and emerges as an unbelievable action hero in the later stages of the book. His narration is further weakened by sudden intrusions of omniscient narration, which give a feeling that James, familiar with powerful third person narrations driven by the excitement of the intellectual chase in her detective fiction, stranded herself in unfamiliar first person narration.

But it is the failure to adequately manage the new conventions which most seriously flaws the text. Despite some nice span touches such the Omegas, the last generation born who have set themselves off as cold and potentially violent, or the distraught women who push about dolls in prams, James fails to offer any coherent pseudo-scientific rationale for the events of the text. Were she creating a myth or parable this might not be necessary, but there are frequent mentions of compulsory fertility testing for men and women and the fact that science has been unable to find the cause of the world's barrenness.

Confusion occurs in the central action when Julian, a devout Christian woman, becomes pregnant in an adulterous relationship with a priest, Luke, who is later murdered by the Omegas. Julian's husband, Rolf, believing himself to be the father, delights in the idea that he will be able to take over the dictatorship of England because his fertility will allow him to impregnate many women and create a new race. Why then, the reader wonders, were women being tested regularly for fertility, if the problem lay only the motility of sperm? And why, given the current state of molecular biology, was not a solution quite quickly found through either cloning or parthenogenesis? James does not even dismiss these options. Nor is there any explanation, beyond the indirect implications that the religious zeal of the couple who become pregnant has some connection with what is happening, as to why a pregnancy has finally occurred and as to why, by general agreement, it is assumed that the boy born at the story's climax will be the source of racial regeneration once he reaches sexual maturity.

The Children of Men provides an unfortunate example of a writer turning to the new conventions without a grasp of the minimal requirements. It would have been possible to pitch the text in a register of myth or parable and avoid this challenge, but James is prosaic in her rendering, a legacy of her detective fiction background, and this unfortunately focuses the reader's attention on what is not explained in any adequate way.

A far richer and more rewarding dystopia is Anglea Carter's *Heroes and Villains* (1969), whose vision is enriched by a stunning and subtle mixture of myth and postmodern irony. From science fiction Carter takes a root story of a post-holocaust Britain "surviving the blast" in which the survivors have divided into several groups. In the towns there are Soldiers, Professors, and a populace engaged in basic agriculture. In the wilderness, which has proliferated and exploded in mutated variety, there are lions escaped from zoos, feral cats with poisonous saliva who drop on prey from trees, and groups of wandering Barbarians who survive by hunting and raiding the towns. There are also Outpeople, disorganized groups of mutant humans, and Fisherman who live by the sea. In the central plot Marianne, a Professor's daughter, rescues Jewel, a Barbarian man, during a raid and then chooses to join the Barbarians, who are led by Dr. Donally, a rogue Professor.

The story and setting first appear to be a conventional science fiction text written by a writer otherwise known for both fantastic and realistic texts. But Carter has additional aims which texture the text and make it self-conscious. On the one hand she engages in deliberate mythmaking, stressing elements of the human tendency to see things as absolutes. Thus the Townsfolk tell their children that the Barabarians wrap little children in clay, bake them and "gobble them up with salt," and the Barbarians believe that the Townspeople similarly bake and eat their prisoners with salt.

Marianne's relationship with Jewel is established as a myth, for he rapes her in a wood, marries her and they live in a tower where she discovers passion, they journey together to the sea, and he is killed in battle leaving her to bear their child. Behind this and other constructions, such as the meting out of ritual punishment, lie principles enunciated in two of the epigraphs to the text:

> There are times when reality becomes too complex for Oral Communication. But Legend gives it a form by which it pervades the whole world.
>
> Alphaville
—Jean-Luc Godard

> The Gothic mode is essentially a form of parody, a way of assailing clichés by exaggerating them to the limit of grotesqueness.
>
> *Love and Death in the American Novel*
—Leslie Fiedler

Alphaville, itself an urban futuristic nightmare, attempts a legendary style, as does *Heroes and Villains.* The Gothicism of her text offers rich potential, for Carter evokes strong colors, rituals of power, violence, passion, coincidences like Marianne's lover murdering her brother, and the high romance of a lion licking a man's face. As Fiedler suggests, such obviously emotional overwriting is finally parody, and Carter makes absolutely certain this ambiguity will be uppermost in the reader's mind by offsetting the Gothic and mythic riches with the characters' heavily intellectualized self-consciousness. Marianne, Jewel, and Dr. Donally are educated and aware of sociology and psychology, and their observations shock the reader because they are deliberately presented inside a "Barbarian" reality in full-fledged academic form. Hence:

> "You're a gift from the unknown, young lady," said Dr. Donally, smiling sufficiently to reveal his curiously uncompromising teeth [they are sharpened to points]. "You provide these unfortunate people with a focus for the fear and resentment they feel against their arbitrary destiny." [51]
>
> "Why?" [Marianne asking why Jewel wishes to make her conceive]
> He was silent so long she began to wonder if she had actually spoken aloud.
> "Dynastically," he said at last. "It's a patriarchal system. I need a son, don't I, to dig my grave when I'm gone. A son to ensure my status."
> "Give me another reason."
> "Politically. To maintain my status." [90]

This apparently Gothic-Romantic myth-like dystopia actually mentions Teilhard de Chardin, Lévi Strauss, Max Weber, and Emile Durkheim by name, and rarely wavers from a distonal course of social self-awareness. Donally is manufacturing a religion for the Barbarians, and generates artificial fits in order to maintain his status as a shaman.

The effect of this double layering of myth and intellectual analysis is to deconstruct the text. This is furthered by Jewel's introductory line to his rape of Marianne in the forest:

> "Isn't it a nice day," said Jewel at last. "After all the rain we've been having." [53]

and by other strange formal echoes and exhibitions of wit in the wilderness. The potpourri of styles and attitudes destabilizes the reading of the text, creating a postmodern pastiche that it is at once Gothic, Romantic, science fiction dystopic, and full of intellectual ironies of self-consideration.

Finally, the text has to be seen in light of feminist considerations, for Marianne is intellectual, vital, strong, and angrily aware in her responses to being dragged into a primitivist narrative full of rapes and male power. Carter is exploding male romantic-sexual fantasies by offering up one that is pointedly undercut by Marianne's attitudes, by the seediness and filth of the wild paradise, and by the intellectual ironies and self awareness the characters display. When Jewel has raped Marianne and says that he now

4. A Bridge Takes Shape 153

must marry her, he is not so much following a social custom as a narrative one, and it stands exposed as such to the reader.

Carter has brought her towering fictional-tactical intelligence to the span post-holocaust dystopia and the result hits a pitch unlike any text which precedes it. It is Carter's "management" of the new elements as some among many that makes *Heroes and Villains* an exemplary text for this book. She is putting the science fiction element on display for examination, placing it in its true center between myth on the one hand and intellectual rationalism on the other, in order to perform the double act of using the form and implicitly commenting on its nature.

Marge Piercy has also taken span elements from the dystopian-utopian tradition in three of her thirteen novels. (She is also a significant poet.) Her first such text is *Dance the Eagle to Sleep* (1970), which envisions a counterculture revolution taking place in the United States circa the end of the twentieth century. This text, with its depiction of a youth uprising in the United States, initially appears to be a very conventional near future projection. It follows a number of young people from their home lives to their mixing in the revolution and traces the ways the hands of authority slap them down. The characters are sketches and much of the action is based on the history of the commune movement and the urban guerillas of the 1960s. It reads today more like an historical text than a projection.

But there are several aspects of it which suggest that Piercy was interested in the potential for the dystopian form to be altered to vary its conventional approaches. The text is highly self-aware in its social analysis, and several of the characters delineate Marxist inspired examinations of the way the American society oppresses youth through schooling, advertising, and through a variation on the military draft called the Nineteenth Year of Service. The sections describing the characters' home and school lives, while generalized and typified, have a texture of critical condemnation of the society. The text makes a real case for social change and has a particular edge because the state and its institutions are not caricatured by projection into a distant future like *1984* but are relatively realistic and immediate.

The other feature which differentiates *Dance the Eagle to Sleep* from most science fiction that projects a revolution is that the attempt fails. Instead of the usual pattern of a few dissatisfied rebels gradually coming together to overthrow a regime, the text ends with the defeat of the uprising and the participants' near destruction. Parallel to the analysis of the society is analysis of the failings of the rebels, as their personal desires for power and their inability to gauge the will of the authorities contribute to their downfall. Piercy goes against the romanticism of much science fiction in *Dance the Eagle to Sleep*, varying the form and the outcome for her own purposes.

Her second and most famous experiment in the utopian-dystopian tradition is *Woman on the Edge of Time* (1976). On first examination this text appears to be a conventional utopian fiction in which Connie Ramos, a woman from the late twentieth century, is taken into the future by Luciente, a person from that future, who "moves" her through mental projection to the community of Mouth-of-Mattapoisett in 2137. There Connie sees Piercy's complex projection of a society that has abandoned cities ("We don't have big cities—they didn't work."[68]), returned to the land abetted by non-intrusive technologies, adjusted the roles of the sexes, rediscovered the ritual rhythm of life, eliminated racism by interbreeding, and begun to recover the world from its descent into the horrors of pollution, heavy industry, and big government.

Were this society simply visited and described by Connie, *Woman on the Edge of Time* would be very much a conventional science fiction text, even if it was written by a mainstream writer, but this text is powerfully different. Most utopian-dystopian projections are either launched by a brief takeoff sequence in the present or the reader is simply in the future throughout the text. *Woman on the Edge of Time* is only half set in the future and it focuses on the relationship between Connie's situation in the early 1970s and the future she escapes to. Piercy deliberately plays with the possibility that Connie is hallucinating this future, for she is a mental patient who spends most of the text in asylums.

The portion of the text set in the real historical world is a coruscating attack on the mechanisms of poverty in the barrio culture of New York City. Connie is an intelligent woman but she has been a victim in many ways, culminating in her gross mistreatment by the public mental health system. The narrative of her struggle begins with her reincarceration, forced on her by her niece's pimp, and follows her struggle in institutions, culminating when she is forced to participate in a surgical procedure to implant electrodes which will "control her violence." The descriptions of medical attitudes, institutional horrors, and Connie's struggle would themselves have made a moving novel but Piercy seeks to focus them, heighten them, and give them depth through Connie's contact with the future.

Mouth-of-Mattapoisett is an intensely vivid locale and many of its features answer Connie's needs. There is no social violence, the sharing of food, other necessities, luxuries and human affection are uppermost in social values, and, in particular, children are treasured. It is close to utopia but without the sterility which often accompanies mechanical utopian models. The possibility that it is her hallucination occurs to the readers and Connie herself frequently articulates the possibility.

Mouth-of-Mattapoisett is at war with shadowy combatants who represent the old ways of technology, and, near the end of the text, Connie finds herself in combat with Luciente and her friends against enemy ships apparently manned by the very doctors who are persecuting her. And, despite the references to enemies and the reconstruction of the ruined world, there is a pointed narrowness to the future vision, which seems to end at the borders of the township in which it is set.

But if Mouth-of-Mattapoisett is Connie's hallucination it is a surprising one, for there are features of it that are hardly part of a consistent dream. She is very upset by the childrearing practices which see breeder-produced (rather than woman-produced) babies being breast-fed by both men and women. She finds the relaxed sexual mores confusing and mildly unpleasant and, as a city woman, is uneasy about the pastoral Massachusetts seashore community.

Moreover, there is a sequence in another and awful future New York City where she meets a distorted sex-toy woman living trapped in a sex contract in a high rise above the gross ground pollution of New York City. Luciente makes it fairly clear to Connie that she has been brought into the future because she is needed to help actualize it in her own time, and Connie responds by poisoning the doctors who were experimenting with electronic mind control on her and her fellow patients.

By deliberately not being bound to convince readers of the "realism" of the future world, Piercy foregrounds the way utopian projections are the products of present injustices, problems, and desires. Mouth-of-Mattapoisett answers many of Connie's deepest needs for social fairness and a world without the torments of poverty and male authority. And Piercy places her focus on a fact of enormous importance to those who think and write about the future: what is done in the present will make that future. Utopian visions are essentially important because they spur social and political action, just as Connie is driven to fight by the realization that she will be fighting for something, the world of Mouth-of-Mattapoisett.

Piercy has made a text which is deeply moving in its portrait of Connie's suffering and struggle in the present, and wonderfully suggestive about the future, without attempting to prove its existence to the reader. By riding the boundary line between utopia and hallucination, she creates a text that focuses on the socio-political issues and the story of human struggle rather than the usual issue of verisimilitude.

He, She and It (1991) is strongly influenced by Piercy's reading of

William Gibson and his fellow cyberpunk writers[6]. It depicts Tikva, a twenty-first-century Jewish commune community near Boston which lives by creating softwares used to protect the net–Base sites of the twenty-three vast multis which control much of the world, excepting the Glop, a version of Gibson's Sprawl, and similar unprotected peasant masses. Palestine and Israel have been destroyed by a terrorist with a nuclear device in 2017. The world has suffered horrifying effects of global warming. Against this background the central plot is the illegal making of a cyborg, Yod, by Avram, and the cyborg's emergence as a "person" who falls in love with his trainer Shira.

While the text is thoroughly and richly imagined, with a dystopian-utopian mix characteristic of cyberpunk, it is Piercy's variations on the form which mark it as a middle ground text. The Pgymalion theme is handled in remarkably subtle and aware terms. Shira is initially asked to help socialize Yod and she gradually moves from describing the cyborg as "it" to using "he" as she recognizes his emotional sensitivity, self-awareness, and ability to grow and change. When she falls in love with him, their sexual relationship is depicted as remarkable and satisfying for Shira, and Yod becomes progressively more capable of participating in the complexity of what is usually thought of as a human experience. Yod introduces the idea that humans are as programmed as he is:

> "What does it mean for you to feel pleasure?"
> "How can I answer that? What does it mean to you? I know that it's entirely mental with me, but mammals, too, have a pleasure center in their brains. You're programmed to like sweet tastes and avoid bitter ones. I'm programmed to find some things pleasurable and others painful." [106]

This theme is repeated frequently enough that it is the philosophical center of the text and it is augmented by the second major variation in the text: Malkah's narrative of the Golem of Prague. Malkah, Shira's grandmother, has been responsible for programming the social and emotional side of the cyborg, and, having been barred from continuing her tutelage, she places this narrative into the Base computer for him to read.

Piercy has taken great care in recreating the events of 1600, and not only is the Golem, created to save the ghetto from Christian persecutors, a clear parallel to Yod's function as a defender and ultimately as a weapon, but in the sections Malkah narrates she is in a position to speak complexly about the whole act of making persons to protect the community. Chara, the daughter of Rabbi Loew of Prague, is loved by Joseph, the Golem, but he is forever denied her love when he is returned to the clay from which he was summoned. This denial of humanhood is also Yod's fate, for he is finally used to self-destruct (as the weapon he is) to destroy the enemies who would invade Tikva.

As in *Woman on the Edge of Time* Piercy enriches her text by calling on a different time to reflect the action, but the effect here is rather different. In *He, She and It,* the effect is to make both the Yod and Golem stories mythic, to draw out in detail the implications of the human relationship to manufactured beings and, in so doing, to raise questions about just what it is to be human. Both Yod, a technological marvel of grace, beauty and independent intelligence, and Joseph, a great hulking warrior-servant made of clay, are being used by their masters, and the reader cannot help but feel a great deal of sympathy for their situations.

The strong feminism that informed *Woman on the Edge of Time* comes into focus in Shira's relationship with Yod, a "man" so much more loving, considerate, self-sacrificing, and fascinating than the other men in her life. The end of the text puts an unexpected twist on her relationship with Yod. He has destroyed his creator, Avram, and the lab where the information about his manufacture is kept, by explosives that detonate at the exact moment that he self-detonates to save those he loves and the town. Shira, mourning his loss, suddenly realizes that she can recreate him from information crystals that escaped the blast, and she could be expected to begin to create a perfect lover without the mechanism that made him a weapon.

> Let men make weapons. She would make herself happiness. She would manufacture a being to love her as she wanted to be loved. [427]

But she does not do so. She destroys the crystals, deciding in an act of love that Yod's wish that there be no more cyborgs must be respected. Human emotion overcomes technological progress, in keeping with a text that has focused on issues of what is human and what can be seen to be lacking in the human male in relationships.

The predominant intention in Piercy's text is the focus on the human in a mythic frame. Span provides a modern myth of value to Piercy, set beside a quasi-historical myth of "man-making" in the Golem to offer reflections and refractions. Span is *among* her tools in her study of human nature and the history of created beings.

There are too many examples of the span utopia/dystopia motif in texts by mainstream writers for this study to treat them all exhaustively. Among the others worth noting are *Love in the Ruins* (1971) and *The Thanatos Syndrome* (1987) by American Southern physician and Catholic thinker Walker Percy. *Love in the Ruins,* best described as a metaphysical satire on the American way of life, depicts a black uprising in a slightly futuristic America where the Catholic Church has trifurcated, the United States is at war with North Ecuador, and Gore Vidal is the grand old man of American letters. The central character, Thomas More, has invented More's Qualitative Quantitative Ontological Lapsometer, a device that measures the state of the human soul, and in the multifaceted action of the novel it is very much the soul that is central.

In both *Love in the Ruins* and *The Thanatos Syndrome,* Percy uses span devices (in the latter it is the discovery of a plot to reduce crime and human misbehavior by putting radioactive heavy sodium in drinking water) and scenarios, but a good deal of his focus is elsewhere. His religious concerns, his depictions of alcoholics and depressives, his astute searing yet affectionate characterization of the American South, and his irrepressible sense of satire and irony place his dystopian text on the middle ground.

Russell Hoban's *Riddley Walker* (1980) is a challenging post-holocaust dystopia depicting Britain some 2300 years after nuclear near-destruction. Riddley, the narrator, is a boy-man of twelve in a Southern England world reduced to spears, arrows, and primitive tribalism. Hoban, a writer of children's fiction, has created a language ("not even in proper English but in a broken-up and worn-down vernacular of it" [Introductory page]) which reflects the breakdown of knowledge and history. There is a myth of "Berstin Fyr" (28), the bursting fire of nuclear holocaust, and of Eusa, presumably the European nuclear agency, which has been personified as the human agent of the holocaust. Knowledge is a mixture of distortions and myth, with vague ideas that a group of people traversing a circle around Canterbury can reproduce the function of a nuclear accelerator and regain the powers lost in the mists of time.

The text is excruciating in its presentation of hardship and in the realization that its twelve-year-old narrator knows as much as anyone in this shattered kingdom. It is weirdly satirical in such survivals as the "Pry Mincer" (Prime Minister) and "the Littl Shynin Man the Addom," which conflates Adam and atomic power. And it has a finality extremely rare in the new fiction since it offers no suggestion of any movement forward in either the understanding of history or in the possible growth of a more complex or technological civilization. The text is a struggle to read, like primitive glyphs discovered on a wall, and every revelation is of pain and anger that man could have done this to himself. From a modified dystopia it takes the post-holocaust scenario, but Hoban's address, in the twisted and wholly original dialect, is to the hopelessness of such a future rather than to some moment of a new dawn of technology or rediscovery of history.

Far from the bleak, Beckett-like world of *Riddley Walker,* whose only mitigations are touches of bitter irony, are the works of comic and satiric writers who have chosen to experiment with span themes and tropes. Pre-eminent among these and the most controversial is Kurt Vonnegut Jr., whose fifteen novels, collections of short stories, and autobiographical fragments reflect wholly original perspectives on the modern condition.

The central issue in the relationship between the new fiction and the work of writers like Vonnegut is the effect of humor, comedy, satire, and irony on the necessary "fabricated realism" of a science fiction text. While there may be room for gentle humor of personal situations in science fiction (Genly Ai's distresses in *The Left Hand of Darkness* by Ursula K. LeGuin come to mind) and occasionally for farce (Brian Aldiss and Philip José Farmer), the need to make the reader accept an alternate or future universe generally requires an steady seriousness on the part of the writer. Comic writing produces a constant undercutting, a form of distancing that challenges the requirement for the science fiction text to be accepted, despite its strangenesses, as a "real" mental place where "real" events, however strange, can happen to "real" characters, no matter how many arms they may have.

Vonnegut's directions have never been towards a realistic new form. His first novel, *Player Piano* (1952), is a satire on American corporate manufacturing based on his own career with General Electric. While it is set slightly in the future, after America has won the "big war," become almost entirely automated, and thus created a vast unemployed class who rebel against their uselessness, the text is really about contemporary American corporateness and the patent blindness of its attitudes towards the rest of society. It features an absurdist satire on a management wilderness weekend outing and a "peasant revolt" of the unemployed, which fails partly because of state power and partly because the American fascination with machines causes the proto–Luddites to start repairing the things they have destroyed.

Among Vonnegut's other texts *Mother Night* (1962), *Jailbird* (1979), *Deadeye Dick* (1982), *Bluebeard* (1987), and *Hocus Pocus* (1990) contain only traces of span. The touches are a neutron bomb killing the population of a single American town without damaging any property in *Deadeye Dick*[7] and a minimalist extrapolation in which American prisons are racially segregated and privately managed by Japanese companies in *Hocus Pocus.* In neither of these cases are the extrapolative elements central to the plot.

In the texts that caused him to be misidentifed as a science fiction author, Vonnegut consistently devalues realism and actually parodies it. *The Sirens of Titan* (1959) explodes the galactic history motif by having Salo, a seven-million-year-old creature from the distant planet Tralfamadore, organize the entire history of Earth and the lives of all the human characters throughout the text, for the sole purpose of having them provide a small jagged piece of metal to him on Titan to repair his spaceship, so he can cross the void for more millions of years to deliver a message that says "Greetings."

The Earth history includes a deliberately futile invasion from Mars by zombies formerly kidnapped from Earth, a "chrono-synclastic infundibulum" that allows a man and his dog to be in many different places without transport (and without control), and a religion entitled the "Church of God the Utterly Indifferent." The dazzling and hilarious perspective leaps of such thinking parody predestination, wave mechanics, conventional religion, and much of the inventiveness of traditional science fiction. They stand completely outside any attempt to make readers believe in these events and such devices as Combat Respiratory Rations, oxygen "goofballs" used on Mars because there is no oxygen in the atmosphere, flying saucers, and the infundibulum are guarantors that the science fiction elements will not be taken seriously.

On the other hand, there is something very serious about Vonnegut's observations of the human condition that is woven into the text. His Martian army, every man with a wire in his skull to force obedience (and provide marching music) is a sharp comment on the nature of military practice, a sort of general staff dream. His trivialized Trafalmadorian explanation of the meaning of the universe confronts the myriad of philosophical-religious explanations available. And in Earth's response to the Martian attack, there is an encapsulation of essential human violence:

> Earth laughed and got ready. All around the globe there was the cheerful popping away of amateurs familiarizing themselves with small arms. [171]

The "cheerful popping away" is characteristic of the surface style of much of Vonnegut's writing, revealing as it does the almost secret pleasure people take in violence and making arms training sound like a popular game.

It is treating what might otherwise be science fiction themes to his unique style that most clearly demonstrates how Vonnegut is only putting such themes to use in his complex fictions. *Cat's Cradle* (1963) turns on the existence of ice-nine, a substance produced for the Marines to freeze water and mud on contact but which, like other tools produced for the military, would have an unconsidered side effect. In this case that side effect is the end of the world, for everything touches everything else and the world freezes solid. This violent innocence, which can also be seen as the great flaw of modern science, is brought into focus in an anecdote about the discoverer of ice-nine that parodies Robert Oppenheimer's famous remark about the Alamogordo nuclear test:

> ...a scientist turned to Father said, "Science has now known sin." And do you know what Father said? He said, "What is sin?" [21]

Cat's Cradle is the first of Vonnegut's texts written in short sections with leaps of logic between them. This fragmentary construction, along with the aphoristic and frequently comic quality of the prose, gives Vonnegut's texts the aspect of a series of small objects to be viewed at a distance rather than the "realism" usually required of science fiction.

Slaughterhouse Five (1969) has three "stories" which come at the reader interspersed and, while they are connected by the figure of Billy Pilgrim, their clash of content assures the distancing effect. Yet Vonnegut goes further than that, for the "stories" interlock to comment on one another in order to make up the most painful of modern odysseys. In this text Vonnegut first makes his narrative self a central figure and takes full control of his style. In order to tell of the horror of the firebombing of Dresden in 1945, he has Billy Pilgrim be there (as he, Vonnegut, in fact was and pointedly states, thus establishing himself as the model for the bumbling Billy Pilgrim), but also be in America in the years after the war in his family life as an optometrist who marries the boss's daughter, and be an exhibit in a zoo on Trafalmadore with a film starlet in a wholly absurd science fiction plot. Billy is "unstuck in time" and veers from one of these stories to another. Vonnegut thus illustrates the monstrous irony of trying to live a "normal" life after Dresden and, through the Trafalmadorians' vision of time, a spatialization in which everything always exists, he accentuates the horror of the losses of the lives at Dresden and the futility of the lives lived in the outwardly prosperous United States.

Throughout this text about death and violence, Vonnegut further distances readers by repeatedly employing the phrase "So it goes" after all of the frequent mentions of death. The aphorism reflects the supposed Trafalmadorian attitude that a dead person is only dead at that moment but is alive at other moments. The effect on the reader is overwhelming in its ironic bitterness, for the Trafalmadorian attitude to time and death is simply unacceptable to human sensibilities and the repetitions become hammer blows. This is characteristic of Vonnegut's method—stylized, absurd, painful, at once funny and metaphysical. Vonnegut will similarly use "Hi. ho." in *Slapstick* (1976), the idea of the "innocent wisps of undifferentiated nothingness" whose "peepholes" open when they catch life and shut when they die in *Deadeye Dick* (1982), and asterisks besides the names of the all the characters about to die in *Galapagos* (1985).

One of Vonnegut's most consistent foregroundings of his attitude to traditional science fiction is the frequent presence of science fiction writer Kilgore Trout or summations of Trout's plots. Trout first enters a Vonnegut novel in *God Bless you, Mr. Rosewater* (1965) and he appears or is mentioned in *Breakfast of Champions* (1973), *Jailbird* (1979), *Galapagos* (1985), and *Hocus Pocus* (1990). When he is an active character in *Breakfast of Champions*, he is described as a hopeless little man who sells aluminum windows because his hundreds of wild science fiction novels have brought him no recognition. *Breakfast of Champions*, and other novels are filled with the synopses of the wildly silly plots that he has written, but in *Breakfast of Champions*, Vonnegut makes himself a character who tells Trout that he has created him and that he will make him famous. Trout stumbles through the novel on a trip to Midland City, where his only fan has arranged for him to be invited to the opening of an Arts Center. Vonnegut is in fact manipulating a situation (as he constantly tells us) in which a car dealer named Dwayne Hoover meets Trout and reads a portion of his novel *Now It Can Be Told*, whose plot tells Hoover that there is only one human being and everyone else is a robot. Hoover, tottering on the edge of madness anyway, goes on a spree of violence, stimulated by this idea.

Vonnegut creates a set of intricate paradoxes in this text. Kilgore Trout, whose name probably echoes that of science fiction writer Theodore Sturgeon, is part of Vonnegut's attack on science fiction both in the absurdities of his plots and his life story. But the character-narrator Vonnegut makes it clear that he is the only real person in the book, whose jagged style, crude cartoons by the author, and absurd structure balanced against pungent satirical comments on American society all put stress on the fictionality of the situations. Vonnegut, in fact, is living the idea of Trout's novel as all *novelists do*, for all the characters are his robots and this is stressed by the way he openly announces the engineering of the meetings and events of the plot. The exposed narrator is one of Vonnegut's devices in other works, where the voice of preface sections in texts like *Slaughterhouse Five*, *Slapstick*, and *Deadeye Dick* cannot be separated from the voices of the first person narrators (even though those narrators have "identities").

Where science fiction may use characterization verging on caricature in its haste to deal with projective imagining, Vonnegut uses caricature for humor, irony, and distance, pillorying American stereotypes such as enthusiasts for guns and violence. Further distancing comes from the inserts of poetry, songs, and dramatized sections (in *Deadeye Dick* the narrator can only handle high emotional moments in this way), but above all the jerky, brief, television-shot-like sequence of narration forever bars the reader from the suspension of disbelief necessary to weld together a science fiction text.

Vonnegut's approach to science is eminently disrespectful and brilliant in the ways it mocks traditional scientific thinking. In *Galapagos*, for example, Vonnegut sets his narrator (the ghost of Kilgore Trout's son Leon) one million years in the future where, as a result of human stupidity (the atom bomb at Hiroshima) and natural disasters, the only "humans" left have fur, flippers, and small brains but are superb underwater hunters of fish. In Galapagos, where in 1835 Charles Darwin found some of the most substantial evidence for his theory of evolution, Vonnegut plays a trump card: the possibility that evolution will have to "dumb down" the human race in order for it to survive. The fittest humans may well be the best fishers, focused on survival and lacking those damnable opposed digits which led from the cave to atomic missiles.

This dark comedic view of human stupidity and violence, and the stylish mocking of science, are qualities that Vonnegut has in common with Jonathan Swift. In an introduction to Swift, Vonnegut has written lines that could well be applied autobiographically:

> Human reason was in the process of assuming powers to change life such as only armies and disasters had possessed before. So Dublin's first citizen found it urgent that we take an unsentimental look, for the good of the universe, at the great apes that were suddenly doing such puissant thinking. Lambs indeed! [*Palm Sunday*, 256–257]

If anything, Vonnegut has a less pathological response than Swift, at once funnier and less deeply pessimistic. While Vonnegut's characters may come to very awful ends as a result of twisted science scenarios, readers are kept clear of sympathy by the cartoon-like quality of the narratives. The narratives of Vonnegut's plots are exoskeletal, on open display while he works around and through them with comic and satiric effect. We know these stories cannot happen, but the people in them are unaware of the implications or outcomes of their actions, and the reader watches in horror as things unwind in predicted ways. This powerful use of narrative irony is Vonnegut's most distinctive feature, as writer and reader share the knowledge of what is always around the corner for the characters.

Vonnegut is, finally, just what he has frequently asserted he is: a fiction writer and not a science fiction writer. But the texts he has written that carry burdens of science fact/fantasy could not exist without his awareness of science and of the conventions of old "hard" science fiction with its precise rational scientific projections. Taking that seriousness, and undermining it through parody and satire, has been the key to most of Vonnegut's work in the middle ground.

Kingsley Amis, whose poignant *The Anti-Death League* had only touches of his normal acerbic comic style, is much more in his normal mode in *The Alteration* (1976). This text proposes an alternate time line of history, as a result of which the Roman Catholic church controls all of Europe (Martin Luther was a Pope, albeit one opposed to excesses), while America is a breakaway Presbyterian theocracy. The central story is the fate of ten-year-old chorister Hubert Anvil, whom the Pope's delegates decide must be castrated so that he can go to Rome to sing for fame, fortune, and the greater glory of God. Amis, known primarily as a comic writer of social comedy, is also author of an early study of science fiction, *New Maps of Hell* (1960). He was fully aware of the amazing potential for satire and comic mischief possible in alternate-time-line universes, and *The Alteration* can take its place beside the masterpiece of this form, Philip K. Dick's *The Man in the High Castle* (1962).

The mechanics of alternate universe texts center around the ability of the author to create backgrounds and situations that comment upon actual history. He can pick up historical figures and give them alternate lives that comment upon their actual lives, and at the same time offer a sharp critique on the outcome of a world dominated by whatever pattern drawn from history has come into power and authority in the alternative world. The unnatural practice of castrating young boys so they could sing castrato parts in church and secular music existed from the sixteenth to the nineteenth centuries in actual history, and Amis selects this practice to center his critique of the powers of the Church and to write a comic novel rich in sexual overtones, as young Hubert tries to find out what he is going to be missing if he submits to the alteration.

In *The Alteration*, the choristers secretly read TR (Time Romance) and CW (Counterfeit World) stories, and as they are about to begin *The Man in the High Castle* the omniscient narrator offers a definition of CW that explicates Amis's own purposes in the text.

4. A Bridge Takes Shape

> ...a class of tale set more or less at the present date, but portraying the results of some momentous change in historical fact.... [27]

In the succeeding description of "Dick's" text, Amis makes clear how thoroughly he understands the original. *The Man in the High Castle* depicts America around 1960, fifteen years after the Axis powers have won World War II and Japan has occupied the American West coast. In it Hawthorne Abendsen has written a banned novel, *The Grasshopper Lies Heavy*, that describes the defeat of the Axis in World War II, but it does not accurately describe the "real" history of our world. In it President Roosevelt and his successor, Tugwell, make America strong enough to block the creation of the Axis, advance warning prevents Pearl Harbor, and British armies fight at Stalingrad, so there is a *third* reality involved that is neither the reality of the text nor our known history. The version of *The Man in the High Castle* that the boys read in *The Alteration* has Henry IX as the English King who broke from Rome, an America that declared independence in 1848, and a Northern Pope, Germanian, who refused to go to Rome and stayed in Almaigne as plain Martin Luther but did not begin a schism (and who, in the world of *The Alteration* went to Rome as Pope and was responsible for the austere interior of St. Peter's). It is a world in which Mozart lived and wrote eight years longer and Beethoven wrote twenty symphonies.

Amis also transposes the work of a number of other "real" writers into his alternate universe. Children read *St. Lemuel's Travels, Wind in the Cloisters, Lord of the Chalices,* and the Father Bond stories (a neat conjointment of G.K. Chesterton and Ian Fleming) (80). There is mention of *The Orc Awakes* by J.B. Harris (one of John Wyndham's pen names) (102) and, importantly, of a text called *Galliard* by Keith Roberts in which Elizabeth Tudor was kidnapped and converted by the Schismatics (135–36). This is a tribute to Keith Robert's 1968 text *Pavane* in which Elizabeth Tudor was assassinated, the Spanish Armada conquered England and the Reformation never took place, a close parallel to Amis's own text. Note that the plot of *Galliard* is, like that of *The Grasshopper Lies Heavy*, a description of a third reality, neither ours nor that of Amis' imagined England.

When Hubert is kidnapped briefly by the Jewish underground, his captor gives Shylock's famous defence speech "Have we not eyes?" and it emerges that Shakespeare's theater was burnt down, he was excommunicated and exiled to the New World, the only place where his plays are still performed. This last remark is characteristic of Amis' ironic treatment, for it implies both that Shakespeare gets relatively little attention in America in our real time and that he gets either too much or too little in Britain. There is also mention of Burgess (203), probably in reference to Anthony Burgess, one of whose texts, *Earthly Powers* (1980) is about the powers of the Catholic Church. Percy Shelley, "excommunicate English runaway and minor versifier" (202), had set fire to Castello Gandolfo and then committed suicide, and one Monsignor Jean-Paul Sartre, a Jesuit, has written *De Existentiae Natura* (171).

Amis is at his witty best in his adjustments to the historical lives and achievements of the famous in the world of *The Alteration*. Historical figures are cleverly transposed into the text. Edgar Allan Poe was a general who died young in battle against the forces of Louisiana and Mexico (181) and Nelson had died at Lipari, presumably fighting against the Turks. Wren, Blake, Gainsborough, and David Hockney have done the art at the Cathedral Basilica of St. George and Coverley (Cowley), and Rudyard Kipling has been First Citizen of New England (1914–1918). The irony is heavy in these last two references, for Hockney is the epitome of a modernist secular artist and Kipling, of course, was viewed as a foremost advocate of the British Empire.

The world that Amis constructs has advanced in very different directions from our own. A church official sums up the key position:

> And, in the last fifty years, Christendom has finally drubbed a power much more awful than the Turk could ever be, one that now lives on as it can in New England among boors and savages: science. [99]

Inventors are permitted but their range is strictly limited. There are diesel cars but no electricity, and Hubert is rushed to Rome on an express steam train, The Eternal City Rapid, across the English Channel on a bridge (built by a Sopwith who did not design aircraft) and at speeds of up to 195 mph. The society is distinctly early industrial, with its focus of attention upon matters which the Church considers to be important. The Brunel who constructed the spires of St. George's is probably Isambard Kingdom Brunel, who is the epitome of the great nineteenth-century British industrial engineers who built bridges, railways and factories, but not churches. Transport is frequently by horse, and cities are lit by gas. The progressive New Englanders have giant dirigibles, there is a digital clock in their embassy, and Hubert is told that the Wright Brothers have just achieved powered flight (in 1975). But Europe is in the firm grip of the Church, and science is a threat to it.

Amis' text is aimed at the Church but is not wholly opposed to it. He has a great deal of fun with things ecclesiastical, such as naming the bell of the Basilica "Great Dick" in place of Great Tom, the real bell of Saint Paul's. The prelates wear gaudy silks, dine in luxury, and their word is law. Islam is still the enemy after six hundred years and there are such institutions as the Chapel of St. Cecelia's, the choir school where Hubert is in training, with its Abbot, prefect of Music, and Chapelmaster. The Church is more liberal than Renaissance Catholicism and rules of all of Western Europe and much of the rest of the world (from Japan to Brazil). Rome is the center of it all, even more wealthy, florid, and powerful than Renaissance Rome.

If one considers what Amis is doing, its twofold nature is revealed. The Pope, a Yorkshireman who does not eat Italian food and who covers the art on the walls and ceiling of his private apartments ("he saw enough of it at other times to make its absence refreshing" [200–201]), is pragmatic and political, exercising his power to obtain Hubert for Rome because it expresses that very power. There is a lot of political infighting in the text, as the English Church spars with the Pope for Hubert and for a measure of independence. Near the end of the text, it is revealed that the Church is facing a horrible crisis—the birth rate in Europe. John XXIV curses his predecessor, who published a Bull against "artificial regulation," and he is scheming to spread a controlled plague (that does not work) or secret birth control in the water supply by adding Crick's Conductor. This last is presumably in ironic honor of Sir Francis Crick, who with Dr. James Watson unlocked the DNA molecule, the key to reproduction. When these methods fail he unleashes a war on the Turk in Bulgaria that takes thirty million Christian lives. This cynicism, as well as the uncaring treatment of Hubert, is sharp irony indeed.

But Amis is also having fun with the reverse side of the coin, the modern world overwhelmed by science and technology. The New Englanders, "boors and savages," are the proponents of technology and science, users of the feared electricity. There is a nostalgic warmth in the text towards a pre-industrial past, with glowing brass on public taxis, beautiful music, domestic stability, and some of that comfort and confidence that a community united in faith offers. And, as a final twist, Hubert's escape to New England is thwarted when one of his testicles gets twisted and he must return to an English hospital where only "alteration" can save his life. God's will is done, in a way, and at the close, fifteen years later, he is singing at a high pitch in Rome.

The Alteration alternates between humor and the underpinnings of serious irony about abuses in the name of power and art. It has delightfully comic moments when ten-year-old Hubert is trying to discover why people find sex so compelling, and its "modern" Catholicism is treated with wit and imagination. For readers, Amis' venture into the realm of the high castle keeps the tone and treatment of his naturalistic texts but offers the escape that it was intended to be.

Peter Carey's *The Unusual Life of Tristan Smith* (1994) defies categorization within the range of span texts. In the manner of Swift and More, it features a new geography centered around an island country, Efica (a vague mixture of many former colonial territories) set in an indefinite time, and Voorstand, a post-colonial imperialist power modeled on a mixture of South Africa and the U.S.A. It is at once a political tract on the partly hidden wellsprings of American cultural, military, and political domination; a wicked satire partly focused on the theatrical arts, particularly cartoon and circus (spelt Sirkus) and their distortion for profit and cultural hegemony; and a deeply moving story of the deformed son of an actress-manager who longs to be an actor. Its interest as a middle ground text lies in casually imagined technical innovations such as holographic satellite Sirkuses for neocolonial peoples, spectacular innovative technologies in the Voorstand Sirkuses themselves, and such things as simulacrums of Bruder Mouse, the Mickey Mouse replacement in the strange puritanical-mythic-ethical-vegetarian cultural scheme of Voorstand. (Corrupt as they have made it, the Sirkus was originally an outgrowth of a Dutch Reform Church influenced by a Franciscan belief that the Bruders, i.e. animals, should not be caged. So their Sirkus used costumed humans, holograph or simulacrum of the figures from their animal myths.)

Carey's creation of a slightly technologically advanced world serves to keep the readers aware that they are elsewhere but fairly near our time and political realities. Tristan's mother, a fierce anti-colonial (as is so often the case, she herself comes from the imperialist state), has made her politicized theater a combination of dramatic speaking and the physical expression of Sirkus (although without Sirkus' exaggerated high-tech accessories). The style is slightly baroque and grotesque, owing something to both Swift and Gunter Gass' *The Tin Drum*. The Voorstand capital, Saarlim, is Hollywood and New York City rolled together: tawdry, energetic, squalid, overrun by immigrants called POWs from conquered countries. The technology, as with so many span texts, is woven into the background of a text it does not dominate but to which it adds an exciting sparkle to place and situation. Carey keeps a constant sideways focus on the sensations of being neocolonial: vassal to the debased art form of Sirkus, subject to political interference and dirty tricks if one's politics don't suit the imperial power, longing for the glitter of the power yet embarrassed and shamed by that very desire.

At the climax of this intense, intricate tapestry of a text, Tristan is in Saarlim, has been reunited with his father, and is the target of a Secret Service assassin. Carey at this point gives Tristan a voice (his speech has been severely impaired from birth, as he has no lips) in a dramatic technical way. Jacqui gives him a two-pin throat voice patch, the kind they have heard at the Water Circus, and Tristan is suddenly able to articulate what the reader has known him to be capable of. This dramatic moment must have been in Carey's mind from the beginning (he has had Tristan's other major congenital defects fixed in childhood but his mouth was not touched) and it is in light of it that the level of technology for the whole text was set.

Span opens a vista here. It is not a far-flung future, but a restrained yet powerful innovation with a profound dramatic effect, that is central to the text. Had it been written several centuries ago, the plot would have demanded a miracle, but with the middle ground's integration of technology into fiction, the change is important for its effects on Tristan rather than for itself. The whole of the text has apparently been Tristan's spoken defence of his actions, words that he could not have given without the patch.

The Unusual Life of Tristan Smith is a characteristic middle ground text, its language opened by technology and science, its content a mixture of a moderate high-tech world (with zines and vid) and a complex Bildungsroman lived in "another place." Carey stands on this new ground with ease.

In 1977 Joseph McElroy published *Plus*, one of the most unusual of all the span texts. McElroy, known for sprawling multifaceted realist-postrealist American texts such as *A Smuggler's Bible* (1966) and *Women and Men* (1988) and a tiny sensitive Bildungsroman *The Letter Left to Me* (1988), turns in *Plus* to a cross between a "hard" genre SF text and a study in what could be appropriately termed epistemological agony. The story certainly sounds like genre SF. In it Imp Plus, a human brain installed in an orbiting space vehicle, comes to consciousness and undergoes a mysterious transformation into a being beyond itself, before being burnt up in reentry (there is some doubt about this final moment). Much of the language is technical, and McElroy has done a good deal of study about brain function. Nor is this idea unique, as a number of science fiction stories (such as Anne McCaffrey's *The Ship Who Sang* [1969]) and films (such as Kubrick's 2001) have explored the theme.

What makes *Plus* different is the attention to the *cogito*, to the meaning of and function of human consciousness. René Descartes' assertion that the self exists because it thinks is given a physical reality with a vengeance in *Plus*, for Imp Plus has lost all of his sensory equipment. The only things preventing a perfect solipsis are some inserted probes, one of which, the Dim Voice, permits verbal communication to Cap Com (capsule communication) on Earth. It is as though Samuel Beckett, the twentieth-century master of the text of reductive consciousness and solipsism in texts such as *The Unnamable* (1959), had chosen to attempt a text in genre SF.

The resulting product is a *tour de force* exploration of what it is to be conscious, of what it might be like to have no sensorium (although the strange miracle of the text is that the awakening Imp Plus creates a sensorium of a sort), and of what it is like to be absolutely alone forever, with only fragments of memory and the mysterious transformation process as activity.

Before Imp Plus, who apparently was suffering from a terminal bodily illness, had the surgery to completely remove the brain from the body and nervous system, one of the project scientists had said to him:

> *You don't want to go on forever, do you?* [29]

In realistic terms this referred to the fact that the proposed Imp Plus experiment, project Travel Light, was to test the ability of equipment to "feed" Imp Plus with sunlight acting on chlorella and would end when the orbit decayed. But in human terms, this was the inexorable promise made to us all, that in any condition of life there will be limits and death. The situation of Imp Plus (Interplanetary Monitoring Platform [20] or possibly Impedance Plus [168]) is the desperate and helpless one of the essential human condition augmented by a total lack of physical ability. Imp Plus has fragments of memory—a woman friend, a child, a blind newsvendor, several of the project scientists, and these emerge as he struggles with sentience and function in the capsule. For the reader these connect him to the ordinarily human, but the central emotional pull of this text is Imp Plus' struggle to perception.

That struggle is in an intricate, hypnotic, and difficult prose that mixes hard scientific terminology with new metaphors and language that imaginatively attempt to depict movement within an unmoving mind. Imp Plus has forgotten much common language and one aspect of the text is his remembering such words as ellipse, capsule, and camouflage. The real density of the language is not vocabulary but involuted structures that reflect the involution of the experience. The brain begins to "see" without eyestalks, almost with its surface, and the language traces this virtually inexpressible experience.

> It [something that appears to be growing from the brain] did not come to him. It went from him. He could not stop knowing that it was to be taken away from him.

> If everything was to go away from him maybe it would go away after dark came. Through the lessening light he made out no change in the membrane spokes. Except what began to be a bend in one.
> He saw that his sight was not shifting as frequently now from widespread haze to clear and back. And saw that while he was able to think his sight into his outlying limbs he did not.
> Because he wanted not to. And the desire had outstripped the memory of why he'd wanted not to.
> This thought turned into the caving and burned him inside out. Not on an outlying membrane but close to home, though with that same feel of being independent of him. [80]

Pain and desperation are at the center of this text, in a way they are not in most genre SF, and there is no release or solution possible. A person is suffering this, being alternately treated as a person and as a lump of experimental matter. The situation is terminal, a technological tragedy virtually in the Classic Greek sense of the term tragic. For Imp Plus rises in the text, exerting his human energy and ingenuity and being mysteriously transformed by hard radiation into a lattice that is partly him and partly more, following a tragic curve until Earth command seals his fate by forcing reentry and burnup.

This text is far from the overwhelming genre SF model of science in triumph, yet it is scientific in language and situation and projective in nature. It is a span text whose prose poetry, as convoluted and puzzling as the surface of the brain, and focus on the *cogito* makes it distinct from genre SF and the mainstream: a text in the new genre.

The pursuit of other texts in the span genre quickly becomes a race against the writers, for so many new texts continue to emerge that can be placed in this range of writing, where science and fiction intersect, but not to produce classical science fiction. Texts that could have expanded this chapter include Robert Persig's *Zen and the Art of Motorcycle Management* (1974), Ronald Sukenick's *98.6* (1975), Don DeLillo's *Ratner's Star* (1976), Raymond Federman's *The Twofold Vibration* (1982), Christine Brooke-Rose's *Amalgamemnon* (1984) and its trilogy partners *Xorander* (1986), *Verbivore* (1990), Kathy Acker's *Empire of the Senseless* (1988), Umberto Eco's *Foucault's Pendulum* (1988), Faye Weldon's *The Cloning of Joanna May* (1989), Ken Kesey's *Sailor Song* (1992), Alan Lightman's *Einstein's Dreams* (1993) and *Good Benito* (1994), T.C. Boyle's *A Friend of Earth* (2000), Michael Ondaatje's *Anil's Ghost* (2000) and Margaret Atwood's *The Blind Assassin* (2000).

The body of texts is growing exponentially and this is itself the most convincing of proofs that a new genre form has emerged.

CHAPTER 5

Border Skirmishes: Span and Science Fiction

"SF's no good," they bellow till we're deaf.
"But this looks good."— "Well, then, it's not SF."

This wry couplet, which Brian Aldiss attributes to "Kingsley Amis and/or Robert Conquest"[1] will *not* work in establishing the relationship between span and science fiction/speculative fiction. Genres are not divided by quality but by characteristics. There are excellent detective stories, excellent mainstream texts, and excellent fantasies, but they are not excellent science fiction. The confusion over the boundary between mainstream fiction and science fiction was one of the reasons for creating span in the first place, and as there is room for a new genre between them, there are clearly going to be territorial struggles around the newly created boundary of science fiction and span: struggles as intricate as those I have been demonstrating at the juncture between mainstream fiction and span.

One reason the line between science fiction and span is not going to be a clear one is that the middle ground is in part defined by its partaking of science fiction tropes and its respect for the scientific imagination. Likewise the characteristics that would redefine a science fiction text as a span text are combinations of the aspects that such texts have and science fiction texts usually do not. So many span texts will be heavily endowed with science fiction characteristics but will be made distinct by the addition of these other aspects. Nor will a single span characteristic necessarily make a science fiction text into a span text. It will be a matter of weighing and measuring the span aspects of a text, an admittedly subjective evaluation in close cases.

A pivotal aspect of this evaluation was discussed in my introductory consideration of the *novum*. It is unusual for it to be science fiction writers' intent that their *readers partly believe in the world presented*. Generally science fiction has departed from the known world aggressively, as writers struggled to maintain a tight and integrated world built on cognitive logic, enticing readers to believe by coherence and imaginative brilliance. But it is clearly a characteristic of much span fiction to challenge and undercut its own embellished *novum*. It is, for example, characteristic of metafiction in all its varieties, and much span fiction uses elements of metafiction to expose its own fictionality and to play with the reader's tendency to "fall into" an effective work of fiction.

Thus a mixture of narrative voices, often including the supposed "author's" voice, may throw the imagined universe into relief for the reader, emphasizing its fictionality. Or a foregrounded, self-conscious use of language experiment may emphasize the fictionality of a text. Or literary pastiche, a conscious and exaggerated mixture of styles or objects of representation, may force the reader away from the suspension of disbelief. Or parody, the deliberate exposure of the weaknesses of the science fiction form and conventions, may distance the reader from commitment to the novum. Insofar as science fiction is a popular literature form characterized by the highly structured and conventionally rewarding plot with resolution, it stands exposed to the potential for parody or satire. Humor may also affect belief, although there is clearly a place for humor in science fiction proper, if its sticks to the ridiculousness of its premises with a rigorous, pseudo-scientific intent.

Another group of texts that should be seen as span are those that push their *novum* as far aside as possible in the pursuit of other intentions. These texts would be judged deficient in pure science fiction terms, for their *novums* would be incomplete and vague. Frequently they would function better viewed as experiments in psychology, but their authors choose to clothe these experiments in at least a dash of a *novum*, so they hover near science fiction. Christopher Priest's *A Dream of Wessex* (1977), *The Affirmation* (1981), and *The Glamour* (1984) are good examples of such texts. *A Dream of Wessex* deals with a social research project in which a group of people collectively dream a future for the South of England while their bodies lie suspended in "coffins." Priest makes little of the device and everything of psychological struggles that ensue when the sadistic former boyfriend of one of the participants forces himself into the projection, creating a chaos of contending and violent visions of the future. Priest, like Samuel Beckett and other modern prose fictionists, has a special gift for quickly jumping from one reality to another, making each real and absorbing after only a few pages.

The Affirmation moves even deeper into the middle ground, for in it a man in turmoil tries to write his life to understand it and ends up fluctuating between a "real" world in which he may be marginally insane and a world he consciously manufactures as an allegory. In it he has won a lottery that gives him a biologically managed eternal life at the cost of total amnesia. The story used in that imagined world to reteach him his life is a "fiction" set in what the reader thinks of as the real life world of London. The intermingling of story and reality would be fantasy were it not for the powerful overtones of mental illness which move the text closer to scientific thinking.

The Glamour deals with the phenomenon of persons who can will themselves invisible and who live in our world. This would be purest fantasy were it not for the fact that the central character has been severely injured and is attempting to reconstruct an amnesiac period with professional assistance. When his former lover, one of the characters with this strange gift called the glamor, comes to help him, various voices tell various stories, some involving quite scientific explanations of the phenomenon. The twists in the closing section of the text do not dispel or tie up the fiction. Without closure no view of the events is privileged, and so the text falls short of science fiction. But it does dwell on possible marginal "scientific" answers to the phenomenon, making it span.

Besides the narrative that is partly to be believed, there is a category of stories that stay close to science itself. They not so much have a *novum* as a focus on some aspect of science that becomes a dominant way of seeing the world. The partly science fiction world of Michael Crichton's *The Andromeda Strain* (1969) or *The Terminal Man* (1972) are examples of this. Crichton's only *novum* in *The Andromeda Strain* is the actual substance that comes to Earth from an orbital probe. The exciting complexities of the scientific method used by scientists to solve the problem posed by the substance were drawn from American plans for the management of biological attack. *The Terminal Man* arose from Crichton's medical studies at Harvard, and while the device inserted in the patient's brain to control psychomotor epilepsy does not presently exist, it is tantalizingly close to our present technological capabilities. Crichton's books stick very closely to contemporary science and are best described as span texts within a thriller sub-genre.

No one would deny that Stanislaw Lem's *Solaris* (1961), *The Invincible* (1967), and *The Cyberiad* (1967) are science fiction texts. But *The Investigation* (1959) and *The Chain of Chance* (1975) are in the span universe. In *The Investigation,* Lem pretends to set out to demonstrate the effectiveness of statistical analysis in the solution of multiple murders in and around London. But the premise comes apart, finally arriving at no reasonable or acceptable conclusion. This undercutting of the scientific method comes to its hilarious conclusion in *The Chain of Chance* when the astronaut-hero, after struggling for a whole novel to link a series of deaths around Naples, comes to the triumphant conclusion that "random causality" caused them. The reader pauses over that phrase, then grasps that Lem is denying the ability of the mounds of evidence and theories put forward throughout the text to give any useful meaning to the events. Lem's method in these span texts is to weave a clutch of very scientific-sounding discussions that seem to be leading to an amazing scientifically verifiable conclusion, and then to undermine the whole.

One of the key issues of differentiation between science fiction and span is characterization. Numerous classic science fiction writers, such as Robert Heinlein and Theodore Sturgeon, have emphasized their understanding that science fiction must center around human behavior in human situations affected by science[2]. But the pressures of popular literature for vigorous narrative, demanding action and closure, plus the additional burden of richly detailing the *novum*, have often forced science fiction writers into using stereotypes or characters constructed on firm and inflexible scaffolds like hard Freudianism. Edmund Crispin, who wrote detective fiction and edited science fiction anthologies, saw the characterization problem thus:

> The characters in a science fiction story are usually treated rather as representatives of their species than as individuals in their own right. They are matchstick men and matchstick women, for the reason that if they were not, the anthropocentric habit of our culture would cause us, in reading, to give altogether too much attention to them and altogether too little to the non-human forces which constitute the important remainder of the *dramatis personae*. Where an ordinary novel or short story resembles portraiture or at widest the domestic interior, science fiction offers the less cozy satisfaction of a landscape with figures; to ask that these distant manikins be shown in as much detail as the subject of a portrait is evidently to ask the impossible.[3]

The modernist exploration of the complexity of human character and behavior, the territory from Conrad and James to Beckett and Murdoch so fraught with the indefiniteness of human nature, our inability to know the other, has not usually been the terrain of the science fiction writer. The natural balance of the mass market popular fiction called science fiction has been towards the *novum* and its demands, but as "soft" science fiction (or speculative fiction) has dwelt more and more upon the social sciences, including psychology, texts have been written that are harder to place. Span is a natural home for these texts, for they have scientific pretensions but neither dwell upon nor completely explain their *novum*. Characters in these texts tend to be inward and puzzled about their selves and the *novum*, doubting it even as they are caught up in its function. Christopher Priest's texts cited above are characteristic of such texts.

Most of the span writers at the juncture with science fiction are also writers of science fiction. Some of them have seen themselves as science fiction writers at all times, but I shall argue that some of their work is more properly span. Among the writers in the border zone are Ursula K. Le Guin, Philip K. Dick, J. G. Ballard, Samuel R. Delany, George Alec Effinger, Joanna Russ, and Christopher Priest. Harlan Ellison is omitted from this list solely because I have kept my focus primarily on the novel.

In what follows in this chapter, I shall briefly examine some of the span works by these authors, aiming not for an exhaustive analysis but rather to demonstrate tests of criteria. Ursula K. Le Guin's early work is clearly and without doubt science fiction, albeit science fiction with a particular tendency to feature complex and self-questioning central characters quite different from the heroically certain scientists and action figures of Golden Age science fiction. But by the time she comes to the sophisticated mature texts, *The Left Hand of Darkness* (1969) and *The Dispossessed* (1974), science fiction and span fiction are vying to claim her for their own.

Her imagined worlds are richly complex and in them characters struggle with dilemmas of self knowledge and knowledge of the other. The situations in the two books rely heavily on anthropology and psychology, and *The Dispossessed* centers around a metaphorical physics problem. Yet Le Guin focuses her texts on the struggles of the great central figures—Ai and Shevek—and the *novums* are pushed into the backgrounds. Genley on the Gobrin Ice alone with Estravan, in their joint struggle for knowledge of the other and survival, and Shevek as a lone figure in an anti-government demonstration are the still centers of these texts, the place Le Guin wants to take the reader. There space vehicles, ansibles, and the other paraphernalia of technology are superseded by the humanist project of relations among persons. Le Guin is not sloppy about the science in these texts, but her depiction is not centered on a *novum* and its outcomes.

These two texts clearly cut deeper into the human dilemma than most science fiction texts. Le Guin's controlled style, capable as it is of lyric outbursts, is the vehicle for fictions that take clear steps towards span. Her readers are presented with the Hainish genotype (of which Earth humans are a sub-group) and so make the mental transition to viewing the characters as human and seeing their dilemmas as the readers' dilemmas in knowing the other and coping with power. The domestic quality of her writing, her ability to depict social minutiae, "ordinary" events, and the humor of daily life in unordinary places, and to give them importance in stories, is very much a skill normally associated with mainstream naturalistic writing.

The novels are complexly structured. *The Left Hand of Darkness* is Genley's report interspersed with other reports and with folktales that both help to realize Gethenian culture but also offer commentary on the events of the report. Images of duality and unity predominate, encompassing light and shadow, sexual division, and the yang/yin principle. *The Dispossessed* is constructed to mirror the complex interrelationship between circular and linear concepts that Shevek is seeking to relate to one another in the temporal physics problem that is the ostensible center of the text. I stress ostensible because the physics problem is in turn a metaphor for the relationship between the planet Urras and its moon Annares, for Shevek and Takvar, and for the ways different cultures view reality. The intricacy of language and metaphor (walls, the temporal physics) also shift the text towards span.

Le Guin has ventured in many directions in her writing. *Malefrena* (1979) and *Orsinian Tales* (1976) are set in an imagined nineteenth-century Europe. *The Beginning Place* (1980) is an adult fantasy novel ostensibly for young adults. Her children's books won a National Book Award, and *Searoad: Chronicles of Klatsand* (1991) is a set of linked naturalistic stories.

But beyond *The Left Hand of Darkness* and *The Dispossessed*, which truly sit on the knife edge border between science fiction and span, is her later text, *Always Coming Home* (1985), which quite clearly is a middle ground text and was not well received by the science fiction community. This sprawling text has several narrators including the tellers of the fiction and history of its imaginary community. It also has the writer, who starts by describing the project without identifying herself but who transforms into Pandora in later inset portions of the text. Le Guin/Pandora foregrounds the fictionality of her choices openly:

> Many as we [the world's population] are, there's still too much to carry. It is a dead weight. Even if we keep breeding ten babies every second to bear the load of Civilisation forward into the future, they can't take it. They're weak, they keep dying of hunger and tropical diseases and despair, puny little bastards. So I killed them all off. You may have noticed that the real difference between us and

the Valley, the big difference, is quite a small thing really. There are not too many of them. [154]

Pandora actually enters the valley to hold a discussion with the Archivist:

>   Pan: How old is the scroll?
>   Arc: Oh, four hundred years maybe, five hundred.
>   Pan: Like a Gutenberg Bible to us. [333]

This metafictional talent for being in a text set in the future is Le Guin's way of reminding the reader of the fictionality of the whole. So is the jumble of geography, customs, poetry, drama, fiction, drawings, and music that compose the whole text (a tape of the music comes with the text). This cultural pastiche is a rich stew, a three-dimensional portrait of future peoples of the American West Coast who have placed technology much more carefully in their lives than the twentieth century has. It has not gone. It is simply not used much because a balanced style of life close to nature has developed.

Le Guin also decenters the principal plot events of the text, Stone Telling's narration of her life story. The central story takes up only three of the many sections of the book, giving way to others' stories, poems, plays, etc. Her narration ends completely just over two-thirds of the way into the text and the remainder, called The Back of the Book, is devoted to detailing the culture. The reader comes to realize that all of the text is really part of The Back of the Book, and that this text notably lacks the solution-oriented action plots of most science fiction. It lovingly depicts a complex society, self-aware in all aspects of its behavior, employing metafictional narrative techniques that allow the author to both show and tell. Because the Kesh have come (chosen would be too strong a word for the slow progress of the generations) to a pastoral way of life, the City (the hub of the ethereal technology with its Exchanges or terminals in every community of over fifty people) remains deep in the background. It is used briefly by the aggressive Condor people, but their attempt to develop a high technology stumbles on the lack of materials. It is a source of learning only for those who feel they need to know of the past in a culture that lives close to the phases of the natural year.

This text, metaphorical, metafictional, decentered and without closure, yet set in a future that is a sophisticated version of tribal pastoralism, is a span text. Its focus is on the domestic and on the human, on how we might choose or be forced to live after some catastrophe; but its answers are not drawn from the power of technological complexity. It is a bumpy, awkwardly shaped artifact, demanding that the readers turn it over in their minds to see its bulges and serrations. Le Guin guides and manages her readers openly, controlling our disbelief so that we can see the present mirrored in her future. As the reviews suggest,[4] this text was not very welcome in mainstream science fiction. But seen as a span text, its rich and varied originality need not be measured by the quality of its story line or the absence of the science fiction utopia's need for explaining how the future came to pass. Its metafictional narrative experimentation takes it to the middle ground, as does its blend of genres and media.

Only one of Philip K. Dick's attempts at mainstream fiction writing was published in his lifetime[5] and the majority of his writing is inarguably science fiction. His science fiction is itself unusual, frequently involving events so deliberately wooden and cartoonlike that readers' attention is focused upon the philosophical concepts that he both animates and has characters discuss. His work touches frequently on issues of sanity, reality, and the relation of science to theology, in such a fashion that readers are aware of the agonized personal intensity of these issues for the author. There is nothing cool and scientific about Dick's science fiction. Rather, it is driven by twisting logics and shimmering illusions of the real.

His last texts, the Valis trilogy[6], are rooted in his metaphysical-psychological agon and demonstrate different formal approaches. *The Transmigration of Timothy Archer* (1982), written last and published the year he died, is a naturalistic novel about death, afterlives, primitive Pre-Christian scriptures, and the kind of wild and agonized philosophical entanglement typical of Dick's thinking. Its most unusual feature is its female narrator, who appears to be Dick's projected slightly distanced version of his own concerns and uncertainties.

The middle text, *The Divine Invasion* (1981), is Dick's science fiction realization of the Gnostic vision of a fallen world in the hands of Belial awaiting the attempt of Yah (God) to invade reality and right the universe. The edge of madness haunts this text, as six-year-old Zina (who is the Torah personified) and six-year-old Manny (Emmanuel—Christ) discuss their functions as masters of reality, and as Elias (who is Elijah) and the confused protagonist, Herb Asher, co-own an audio store while being caught up in the metaphysical combat.

Valis (1981), the first volume, is a span text. It features a split narrator:

> I am Horselover Fat, and I am writing this in the third person to gain much-needed objectivity. [3]

This narrator is P. K. Dick (Horselover Fat means Philip Dick[7]):

> I am, by profession, a science fiction writer. I deal in fantasies. My life is a fantasy. Nonetheless, Gloria Knudson lies in a box in Modesto, California. [4]

The text frequently plays with this separation ("The night before, Bob and I—I mean, Bob and Horselover Fat—...." [4]) and at one point the two figures blend, a moment which his friends claim indicates his recovery. But after a catastrophe, the death of the child Sophia who Fat/Dick thought was the agent of external salvation (the same idea that had been treated strictly as science fiction in *The Divine Invasion*) the figures diverge again, so that at the close Fat is searching the world and sending letters to Philip Dick, whose books are selling very well.

For the author to be so present in the text is metafictional, and Dick employs the device to communicate and toy with his desperate psychological hunger for sense in the world and his ongoing pain at the suffering of himself and others. The root of this text is Dick's anguished struggle (no reader can fail to feel the personal quality of the desperation) to get meaning out of the world, which leads him into maelstroms of reasoning about conspiracies both good and evil. Just when these seem wholly absurd, events in the text will seem to confirm the wildest speculations, creating much the same fragmenting of reality that Dick was personally enduring.

In this personal, half-crazed struggle for sense, Dick interjects some science fiction devices. The half-crazed makers of the science fiction rock film Valis (Vast Active Living Intelligence System) tell Fat and his friends that an alien power is seeking to inject itself into the world to overcome evil and confusion, and that Sophia, their two-year-old daughter who spouts adult prophecies, is its agent. But Dick/Fat has said his life is "fantasies" and these people and their ideas are depicted as unstable. Thus Dick, the author, challenges the *novum* of the text, leaving the reader with the feeling that the nearly insane, split person who asserts he is writing this text (the fictional P.K. Dick) would envision intricate conspiracies and explanations in science fictional terms.

There are no final clarifications in *Valis*. The Horselover Fat/ Phil Dick who experienced God as an information blast of pink light in 1974 is two divergent yet holistic things for the reader. His conspiracy reasoning and wild adventures make him an absurd figure who nonetheless drags the reader into desperate gambits to understand reality. At the same time he is the man raw to the world, emphatically dragged through the suffering of others and himself until he is turning on a spit of pain. The science fiction fragments in Valis do not make it a science fiction text. They are undermined by their sources and overwhelmed by the text's fictional complexity and the immediacy of its psychological pain. The result is a span text. In science fiction Dick had found an audience for his vivid allegories of his disordered struggle to understand the world and its pain, but in *Valis* he shows a direction towards a confessional writing that he might well have practiced had death not cut him short.

Like Dick, J. G. Ballard firmly asserts that he is a science fiction writer,[8] but both writers pushed the envelope of the definition in the direction of their needs and visions. They pushed it, in fact, all the way to span. Familiar with the rigors of science through his assistant editorship of *Chemistry and Industry* and backed in his extensive private investigations of psychology and psychiatry and his two years of medicine at Cambridge, Ballard, aided by the perspectives borrowed from surrealism, set up worlds to meet one essential aim:

> The serious answer to your question is that my fiction is *all* about one person, all about one man coming to terms with various forms of isolation....[9]

After his first disaster novel, *The Wind from Nowhere* (1961), Ballard tightened his focus on that one man in *The Drowned World* (1962). In it and in most of his other texts such as *The Drought* (1964), *The Crystal World* (1966), *Crash* (1973), *Concrete Island* (1974), *High-Rise* (1975), *The Day of Creation* (1987), the central character is measured against progressively more bizarre circumstances.

But whether surviving world-changing flood or drought, the crystallization of matter, or the ravages of modern urban reality run wild, Ballard's central characters are undergoing inner transformations, psychic modifications to adapt them to external reality. For Kerans in *The Drowned World* this means that he recognizes that his body and psyche are finding stored genetic memories—"the archaeopsychic past"—which lead him to seek union with water and heat. To the reader, Kerans' choice to move towards dissolution in the southern jungles seems suicidal, but Ballard intends it to be a curious sort of triumphant reconciliation between the inner man and the changed world about him. The same can be said of the doctors, teenagers, film producers, architects, and others who are central to his texts. They adapt, changing both physical and mental states to meet a violent, often media-image-soaked present or near future. The settings of many of the later novels are timeless, filled with events that could happen now or in the near future. The abnormal psychology of the characters and of the distanced, low-affect interplay between them and their environments are Ballard's focus. The focus is like that of science, but the writer's attention to the abnormal and driven characters is lifted to a poetry of obsessions by a hypnotic style.

Ballard has spoken of himself as concerned with inner space[10] and, after early short story experiments with perceptual variations and the shapes of insanity (climaxing in the amazing *The Atrocity Exhibition* (1970), the bulk of his fiction has focused on inner states in relation to varying external worlds. Some of these worlds are science fictional but they are not the focus of the text. Like other middle ground writers, Ballard pictures exceptional things, such as the abandoned wreckage of the space age, only as backgrounds for central probes of human nature, in his texts often seen stylized through the distorting lens of pathology and the low affect of clinical language.

His is a new fiction. Like Pynchon he is always aware that we live and think in a scientific world. While he may toy with strange worlds, Ballard's real focus is on the complex anguish of modern, violent, often perverse life. His texts usually deal with massive natural changes or the contemporary crazed urban world that none of his characters even envision changing in the manner that aggressive, optimistic scientists fix their worlds in traditional science fiction. Both in his loaded, painterly, massed prose and in his psychologically centered subjects, he projects outside the frame of science fiction into span.

Samuel R. Delany does not merely protest that he is a science fiction writer. He has devoted a good deal of effort as a critic based in the tenets of structuralism to defining what the genre involves. In *The Jewel-Hinged Jaw* (1977), *The American Shore* (1978), *Starboard Wine* (1984), and elsewhere he has enunciated a theoretical description of science fiction as a genre based on structuralism and other aspects of literary theory, particularly those associated with discourse. He has produced a major body of science fiction writing but has also written memoirs and complex fantasy fables such as the Nevèrÿon books. In a few of his texts, such as *Dhalgren* (1975) that I shall discuss below, he appears to be writing span, but in his case it is not a matter of attempting to prove this. Rather, with a writer so aware of the implications and characteristics of genre and so clear in his assertion that most of his texts are science fiction, I take it to be a case of asserting that there are two options for approaching his texts on the margin. Delany may be expanding the territory covered by science fiction in his more adventurous texts. His desire to do this is rooted both in his early successes in the genre and in his wide-ranging respect for the tradition of the masters of the field. But, despite his own assertions, he is creating texts that should be viewed as span.

In *Dhalgren*, for example, the city, Bellona, is presented as an American city as it would appear if the urban disintegration evident in the 1970s had continued. It is entered by walking across a bridge, but it is isolated in that it has no telephones or television and it seems to live inside a persistent pall of smoke. Strange events take place in the city, such as the sighting of a second moon during a break in the cloud cover or the appearance of a gigantic sun that covers half the horizon. No scientific explanation is ever offered for these events.

The central character, the Kid, has lost much of his memory and seems to lose periods of time during his stay in the city. The text has a metafictional overlay that involves breakdowns in the third person narrative for brief first person sections and some circularities that suggest that the Kid himself is writing the narrative. For example, the truncated last sentence is completed in the truncated first sentence of the text. Within the general picture of this strange and inexplicable place, the narrative is chiefly about a radical domestic life involving gangs, parties, a commune, the Kid's creation of a book of poems, and a good deal of graphic sexual activity. While the setting is unreal, within it is a bohemian life lived in the late 1970s.

The Encyclopedia of Science Fiction states that *Dhalgren* was "controversial" and that is entirely understandable when it is placed beside hard science fiction texts of its time. While Delany saw himself as expanding the genre in which he had already won Nebula and Hugo awards, it is arguable that within span, as I am proposing it, his broad concerns with sexuality, race, metafictional construction, and linguistic experiment find their true home. When the choice was simply between mainstream fiction (mundane fiction, as Delany labels it) and science fiction, his choice was clear. But seen from a critical perspective where a new middle genre exists, *Dhalgren* is at the very least on a cusp between science fiction and span.

A similar case can be made for the fiction of Joanna Russ. While she sees herself as a science fiction writer and has written about the genre,[11] her range of experiment and the focus of her texts suggest that she can also be viewed as a span writer and might well accept the designation. To see where her texts venture outside the normal boundaries of science fiction, I want to look briefly at aspects of *The Female Man* (1975) and *We Who Are About to...* (1975). *The Female Man* is a book with science fiction premises (alternate reality lines and time travel), but its employment of these devices is as a setup for the strong feminist center of the book that is itself largely satire of the present or other times, achieved by describing the responses of "present" characters to strange realities.

Once Janet Evason from Whileway, an alternate Earth eight centuries in the future populated only by women, has come to twentieth-century America to an historically but not socially altered Earth, the bulk of the novel is about what she sees and experiences. She is sometimes in the company of Jeannine, a twenty-nine-year-old library assistant from the 1940s who is under immense pressure to marry and much concerned with appropriate feminine behavior. At other times she is with Joanna, who is at times the narrator but at other times a character viewed by a narrator-author; and Laura Rose, a small town teenager whom Janet seduces. But much of the text is satiric vignettes, such as this overheard at a party:

> A Simultaneous Round of
> "Ain't it Awful"
>
> Lamentissa: When I do the floor, he doesn't come home and say it's wonderful.
> Wailissa: Well, Darling, we can't live without him, can we? You'll just have to do better.
> Lamentissa (wistfully): I bet *you* do better.
> Wailissa: I do the floor better than anybody I know.
> Lamentissa (excited): Does he ever say it's wonderful?
> Wailissa (dissolving): He never says *anything*! [35]

The extensive portion of the text set in the 1970s "present" offers a full round of situations concerning women's roles and also features extensive metafictional interventions by the narrator, including one in which she sums up the fragments of criticism that she expects to see leveled at the text:

> ...destiny is anatomy ... sharp and funny but without any real weight or anything beyond a topical ... just plain bad ... we "dear ladies," whom Russ would do away with, unfortunately just don't *feel* ... ephemeral trash, missiles of the sex war ... a female lack of experience which.... [141]

Clearly Russ's text explores a wide range of ways of getting at the power imbalance between women and men, not the least of which are two other sections, one set on Whileway where the women capably manage rich lives without men and the other set in a violent world where women are fighting men in brutal warfare. What this wildly varied text most clearly does not demand is the kinds of consistent belief that a classic science fiction *novum* asserts. In fact, the metafictional inserts, the range of situations, the satire, the pointed comedy of Janet handling Earth males aggressively, and the authorial interpolations overrun the science fiction devices. Russ has used science fiction only as a starting point for a far more complex venture in fiction, one driven by the intelligent passion of her cause and infused with her pointed playful wit.

We Who Are About To... appears at first glance to be a far more conventional science fiction text about a party of eight who are stranded with no apparent hope of rescue when a space ship crashes on a wholly unknown planet. But the narrator, a complex and unclear figure who dictates the story to a recording device, does not tell us a story of heroism and human ingenuity ending in some sort of rescue. Instead she murders the others, partly out of anger and party out of a wish to spare them, and then she settles in a cave to await her death. Nearly half of the text depicts her slow decline into starvation as she muses on fragments of her life and has hallucinations of the presence of those she has killed. Russ has undercut all of the conventional optimism of science fiction versions of *Robinson Crusoe* and focused instead on the inner life of one character, a powerful but puzzling woman who finally takes her own life with a poison ampoule she has been saving. The shock of this outcome and the attention paid to this dying individual make something entirely new and shift the text from its setting and science fiction trappings to an existential agon.

Summing up her career, *The Encyclopedia of Science Fiction* states: "For 30 years, JR has been the least comfortable author writing SF, very nearly the most inventive experimenter in fictional forms, and the most electric of all to read" (1035). That discomfort, which I would suggest is as much about form as it is about content, suggests that span would be a natural place for her work. Many other feminist writers (such as Ursula Le Guin, Joan Slonczewski and Marge Piercy) have found in science fiction itself a place to explore their positions, but Russ' eclectic imagination and irrepressible edged wit drive her work to the edge of the classic genre and beyond.

The thrust of this chapter has been to show that some of the work which has been classified by both its writers and its critics as science fiction, in fact is not comfortable in that definition but would fit into span fiction. The discomforts of the science fiction categorization for these texts lie principally in their metafictional playfulness and in the fact that they focus not on a seamless *novum* but on other matters. The *novum* is demoted for the sake of play or from a desire to examine individual human behaviors with an intensity that was characteristic of traditional naturalistic fiction but in new and revealing circumstances.

The science in these texts may be thin. Joanna Russ makes no effort to explain the leaps her characters take through the continuum in *The Female Man*, although she is perfectly capable of the planetary construction practiced in *We Who Are About To....* There are obviously two ways to look at this situation. As they exceed the boundaries of traditional science fiction (boundaries consisting of pressure to tell exciting tales in the straightforward forms of popular adventure fiction, buttressed by the often highly innovative and carefully wrought "science" of the *novum*) these writers are either expanding the genre of science fiction or they are working in span.

The unease of the science fiction community is indicated by the fact that neither Priest nor Ballard nor Lem has won a Hugo or Nebula Award, and Le Guin, Russ, Dick, and Delany have most certainly not won for the texts under consideration in this chapter. So it appears that, for all of the imagination about subjects that has marked science fiction, there are genre demands for borders around fictional innovation and for conventional adventure stories crowned with concrete resolution. While subject matter revolutions have happened in science fiction, most notably the breaking of sexual taboos by Philip José Farmer and Harlan Ellison's *Dangerous Visions* series, there seems to be a decrease in appreciation and response from the field for structurally radical work and for some radical themes. Thus the science fiction writers who seek to broaden the field have often been met with silence from their fellow writers or with urgings that they return to the kind of work they have done that has met with genre approval in the past.

The alternative way to look at the situation is to place these works in the new and flexible middle ground. Here the expectation is for fictional originality and daring in subject matter in the directions that conventional science fiction has tended to reject. Here writers wishing to work in these ways will find readers whose genre expectations and contextual preparation for reading fits them to appreciate such work within the framework that the writer is seeking to present. Texts in this field will be expected to make use of science fiction tropes but they will be free to undercut them, satirize them, or deconstruct them. Here they will meet with other texts by the writers entering span from the mainstream side. It is likely, and writers like Delany and Le Guin have already demonstrated, that writers of span can also be writers of science fiction, just as writers entering from the mainstream side can drop the science fiction tropes that they have been experimenting with and return to mainstream writing.

I have only sampled the range of science fiction writers who have produced some work that can be seen as span. Ian Watson, George Alex Effinger, Michael Bishop, Neal Stephenson (particularly for *The Cryptonomicon* [1999]), and Harlan Ellison are among others who could be considered here. But it is important to recognize that much excellent contemporary science fiction does not aspire to be span. While given to verbal descriptive experiment, the cyberpunk writers such as Pat Cadigan, Rudy Rucker, Bruce Sterling, and William Gibson are not span writers. They stick to the action plots and limited characterization of the science fiction. Nor are many of the newer generation of science fiction writers—such as Nancy Kress, Linda Nagata, David Brin or Kim Stanley Robinson—span fiction writers.

Science fiction is alive and very well but beside it span offers a different sort of mental liberation for the writers whom it suits and the possibility afforded by genre recognition for a readership whose expectations are in accord with the writers' intentions. Span plays on and exceeds the expectations of the popular fiction form that is science fiction, and it requires new readers to read differently from those of the traditional genre.

There will undoubtedly be a definitional battleground around texts at the experimental edge of science fiction, which may or may not be defined as span. As I suggested in my introductory chapter, the importance of such a struggle lies not so much in placing a text in science fiction or span, but in the approaches to reading that are opened when the possibilities are being weighed.

It is repeatedly the case that texts of the sort that I have been considering above benefit from being read as span, for a number of their "deficiencies" (such as a lack of a wholly consistent *novum*) become positive features when the filter-glass of genre expectation is changed. Within a genre there are, finally, only a certain range of things that can be said because of the cultural expectations for that genre. One can see this in the essential failure of mainstream fiction to embrace modern scientific and technological reality that has led some mainstream writers into the middle ground. It can equally be seen in the limitations of science fiction to cope with the reflexive and deconstructive playfulness of postmodern writing and in the failings of many science fiction texts to pay sufficient attention to the human personality (Edmund Crispin's "representatives of their species") as it is presently understood.

Span offers a location, an definable node of textual aspects, where such work can be done and understood on its own terms.

CHAPTER 6

The New Alignment

> ...he will be ready to follow the steps of the Man of science, not only in those general indirect effects, but he will be at his side, carrying sensation into the midst of the objects of the science itself.
>
> —William Wordsworth,
> Preface to the Lyrical Ballads, 1800

This book has been a proposal for the creation of a new genre, span fiction, and has been based on a consideration of texts written over the past thirty-five years. This is a retroactive argument and, as chapter 5 has demonstrated, a number of the writers whose work can be seen as span see themselves and have been seen as science fiction writers. Those in chapters 2, 3, 4 would generally see themselves and have been seen as mainstream writers who were merely borrowing from science fiction or took into proper account the way in which science penetrates modern life and thinking.

My assertion is that the work of both groups of these writers can be better understood within a new genre, where the expectations of the uses of science in and as fiction may be more clearly defined and where various experimental uses of form can be domiciled with the scientific elements.

This concluding chapter will recapitulate the salient points of the argument: the necessity of the concept of genre and the distinctions that identify span. Finally, it will seek to answer, however tentatively, the question of why this phenomena is appearing when and as it does.

Genre goes far beyond the arbitrary descriptive act of the literary critic and beyond the typing identifications used in the publishing industry. Genre is a vital element in the active process of writing, reading, and understanding texts. Readers understand a text in terms of their previous experience of texts of the same type and within the cultural-historical context of what is expected in such texts in their own moment.

In the context of this book, that means that many readers of traditional science fiction find span texts inadequate because they fail to show the respect for science and the inherent optimism of heroic narratives usually expected in the genre. Readers of mainstream fiction, which either hews to social naturalism of the novel tradition or gets engaged in radical verbal experiment, are frequently not comfortable with excessive use of scientific language or with science as a foregrounded subject in span texts. These expectations make reading, appreciating, and even understanding middle ground texts difficult for readers who have different genre expectations. Some readers have the wrong set of expectations for such texts and this complicates their ability to grasp them and to appreciate their achievement. On the other hand, without sets of expectations, genre transgression would not be a possibility, and much of the originality of span fiction lies in the newness of its blended vision of what was formerly science fiction and mainstream fiction.

For writers, genre expectations outline their field of endeavor, but in establishing that frame they also open the possibility of creative transgression. Genres move, shift, and change and that creative jostling is immensely rewarding for writer and reader alike. But there comes a time where new genres are needed because certain kinds of transgression create bodies of texts in an identifiable new form. Then genre becomes an issue to be resolved in the identification of a new genre, a hybrid whose outlines will enhance the reading practice of such texts.

Without the frames provided by genre, the ability to analyze the text would be severely hampered. When, as in the case outlined in this book, the reading of new texts is hampered by wrong expectations based on understandings of existing genres, new genres emerge.

If span fiction is a new genre, a grouping of characteristics is necessary to provide a nexus or vision of what it ought to be, and some readings of its borders with the genres from which it has arisen will be needed to establish those borders and consider texts that are ambivalently placed on the fences of those borders. Examining a range of texts has been the purpose of chapters 2, 3, 4, and 5. I have sought to identify the detailed and always unique characteristics that make each text span. But the genre needs outlining in this conclusion, to recapitulate and abstract from the mass of detail.

Span fiction's most certain cornerstone is the presence of science in fiction as subject, attitude, metonymic language, or worldview. But the treatment of science varies immensely in these texts, and the key to the treatments is the inscription of doubt and questioning on what might have been taken as the positive truths of science. Pynchon's world is envisioned as a vast ballistic parabola in *Gravity's Rainbow*, a Newtonian clockwork infinitely extended into the minutiae of life, but there is no assertion that this is a good thing anymore than the laws of mechanics are a good thing. Science can, in fact, be the image and harbinger of horrifying and inexorable presents and futures in span.

The science fictional visions in span have undercut *novums* or even produced *novums* that turn out not to be at the center of the text in which they occur—pretexts rather than central texts. The associations of science with order, systematic development, and the heroic triumph of reason in linear narratives are subject to assaults from illogic, failures of closure, pessimistic outcomes, metafictive extravaganzas, pinwheeling of narrative voices, and the onslaughts of parody, pastiche, and satire. To partly believe in a *novum* or to partly believe in the naturalistic verisimilitude of a text are among the most salient characteristics of span fiction. Uncertainty and the myriad ways of generating it are central to the genre.

The possibilities opened by this new genre are myriad in nature. The reader can savor the feminist pastiche of *The Female Man* or the dangerous misapplications of science in *The Revolt of Aphrodite*. Readers of span must navigate new fictional territory and they must do so without referring to the old maps of the genres at the ends of this bridging genre. The genre is a challenge to the imaginations of readers, a place where the strange, re-visioned world of post–Hiroshima science and modern and postmodern literary experiment converge in strange and amazing ways.

My whole description of span, and the texts that comprise it, begs one central question: why is this bridging genre coming into existence at this point in time? I do not propose to answer this question so much as to ruminate upon the possibilities.

Mainstream writers who write such texts are fulfilling Wordsworth's prophecy that as science becomes part of the household of man, of our daily lives, it must become the subject matter or influence the language of their writing. Science has become a most equivocal part of our world, a boon and benefit in thousands of ways in our everyday lives, but a menace and challenge brought into focus by the horrors of modern warfare and the dangers of scientific error. The loss of faith in science impacted particularly on the genre of science fiction, where the romantic celebration of scientific possibility began to be undercut for some authors who sought to challenge the cold equations and dominance of reason that identified the genre.

Late twentieth-century Western culture accepted science and technology as an inevitable part of its horizons, but as the human values of the culture penetrate and challenge the paradigms of science a rigorous and varied literature has arisen to express these challenges. It its not surprising that this form should be in the "languages" that are current in the culture: modern and postmodern literary techniques with their psychological complexities and challenges to certainties of both science and the culture of which it is part. The spreading implications of Relativity and the Uncertainty Principle have opened science to forms of play that are both literary and ideological.

The hard and absolute rules of Newtonian science are giving way to the recognition that science is a way of describing the world, among other ways, and that, as Thomas Kuhn[1] first showed us, its knowledge is constructed within the moments of its culture. The genre of writing that is span fiction combines the overwhelming presence of science and technology in our lives with the consideration and critique of that presence in a variety of literary experiments. It is of our time and for our time.

Notes

Chapter 1

1. Samuel R. Delany prefers mundane: "The recent passage from 'mainstream' to 'mundane' as a term to designate that fiction which is neither science nor speculative strikes me as a happy gathering of generic self-confidence. (I first came across "mundane fiction" in a 1975 *Galaxy* essay by Roger Zelazny.)" *The Jewel-Hinged Jaw*. Elizabethtown, N.Y.: Dragon Press, 1977, p. 12.

2. See in particular Scott Bukatman. *Terminal Identity*. Durham: Duke University Press, 1993.; Strehle Susan. *Fiction in the Quantum Universe*. Chapel Hill: University of North Carolina Press, 1992.; Puschmann-Nalenz, Barbara. *Science Fiction and Postmodern Fiction*. New York: Peter Lang, 1992.; *Science Fiction Studies*. (Postmodernism Issue), vol. 18, pt. 3, #55 (November, 1991).; Ralph Cohen. "Do Postmodern Genres Exist." *Genre*. XX (Fall–Winter, 1988).

3. For a thorough summary see Roger Luckhurst. "Border Policing: Postmodernism and Science Fiction." *Science Fiction Studies*. (Postmodernism Issue), vol. 18, pt. 3, #55 (November, 1991), pp. 358–366. See also *Storming the Reality Studio: A Casebook of Cyberpunk and Postmodern Fiction*. ed. Larry McCaffrey. Durham and London: Duke UP, 1991.

4. Roger Luckhurst. "Border Policing: Postmodernism and Science Fiction." *Science Fiction Studies*. (Postmodernism Issue), vol. 18, pt. 3, #55 (November, 1991), p. 359.

5. For contrasting attitudes to this issue see David Dalgleish. "Naive Versus Postmodern Criticism: an Exchange." *Science Fiction Studies*. vol. 24, pt. 1, #71 (March, 1997), 79–92; and Istvan Csicsery-Ronay. "We're Not in Kansas Anymore: On Naivete in SF and Criticism." *Science Fiction Studies*. vol. 24, pt. 1, #71 (March, 1997), 93–108.

6. See Thomas Kent. *Interpretation and Genre*. Lewisburg: Bucknell University Press, 1986, 147–150.

7. Fredric Jameson. "Towards a New Awareness of Genre." *Science Fiction Studies*. vol. 9, pt. 3, #28 (Nov, 1982), 322.

8. *The Science Fiction Encyclopedia*. ed. Peter Nicholls. New York: Doubleday, 1979, p. 160.

9. Ms. Atwood stated her preference for the term speculative fiction when she visited an introductory class at the University of Guelph that was studying *The Handmaid's Tale* in November, 1990. This was told to me by the lecturer, Professor Constance Rooke of the English Department at the University of Guelph.

10. "Because many human beings experience a psychological need for narration—whether cultural or biological in origin—the literary system *must* include works which answer to that need." Robert Scholes. *Structural Fabulation*. Notre Dame, Ind.: Notre Dame UP, 1975. p. 39.

11. Ebert attributes it to: Zavarzadeh, M. *The Mythopoetic Reality: The Postwar American Nonfiction Novel*. Urbana and London: Illinois UP, 38.

12. Bruce Sterling. "Slipstream." *Science Fiction Eye*. vol. 1, issue 5, (July, 1989).

13. Due to an unfortunate accident of alphabet it is another SF, but the intention is that it be referred to as Span because it is not a substitute for genre SF. Nor, to deflect the punsters, is it spam.

14. "3. Of the rainbow, a bridge, etc.: To form an arch across or over (the sky, a river, etc.); to stretch or extend over in the form of an arch; to cross from side to side." *The Oxford English Dictionary*. Compact Edition. Oxford: OUP, 1971. vol. 2, p. 2938.

15. *The Oxford English Dictionary*. Compact Edition. Oxford: OUP, 1971. vol. 2, p. 2938.

16. *The Oxford English Dictionary*. Compact Edition. Oxford: OUP, 1971. vol. 2, p. 2938.

17. "When Adam delved and Eve span,/Who was then the gentleman?", John Ball (d. 1381). *The Oxford Dictionary of Quotations*. 2nd Edition. Oxford: OUP, 1953. p. 235.

18. Bruce Sterling. "Slipstream." *Science Fiction Eye*. vol. 1, issue 5 (July, 1989), p. 78.

19. Samuel R. Delany has written extensively on the semiotic specificity of genre SF in *The Jewel-Hinged Jaw* (1977) and elsewhere.

20. Emile Zola's *The Naturalist Novel* set out the parameters for this shift.

Chapter 2

1. Robert Scholes. *Structural Fabulation*. Notre Dame, Ind. : University of Notre Dame Press, 1975, p. 24.

2. See the "Author's Notes" at the close of *The Four-Gated City*.

3. Bildungsroman is variously defined as a novel of maturing into adulthood, a novel of the individual's rejection of collectives in order to achieve selfhood or in the following summation by G.B. Tennyson quoted in Betsy Draine's *Substance Under Pressure*. Madison: University of Wisconsin, 1983, 30–31. "(1) the idea of *Bildung*, or formation, cultivation, education, shaping of a single main character, normally a young man; (2) individualism, especially the emphasis on the uniqueness of the protagonist and the primacy of his private life and thoughts, although these are at the same time representative of an age and a

culture; (3) the biographical element, usually supplied from the author's own life in what Dilthey calls the "conscious and artistic presentation of what is typically human through the depiction of a particular individual life"; (4) the connection with psychology, especially the then-new psychology of development; and (5) the ideal of humanity, of the full realization of all human potential as the goal of life."

4. The science fiction work in the simile is probably Isaac Asimov's *Fantastic Voyage*. (1966).

5. "Yet this new and final installment does decline, I fear, into a reliance on a gimmick—the gimmick of the apocalyptic, or the science-fictional, which here takes the form of a not very specific "Catastrophe" resulting from the escape of nerve-gas from a research station and/or accidents involving nuclear devices." (Enright 22)

6. The authors are actually discussing *The Golden Notebook* at this point but the mention of science fiction indicates that they were looking towards the later works as well.

7. This principle of approach to Lessing's fiction is elegantly worked out by Betsy Draine in *Substance Under Pressure: Artisitc Coherence and Evolving Form in the Novels of Doris Lessing*. Madison: University of Wisconsin, 1983. pp. 143ff. See pp. 28–30 following for a discussion of Draine's difficulties with the Science fiction aspect of Lessing.

8. Listed in her footnote 8 to Ch. 8 of *Substance Under Pressure: Artistic Coherence and Evolving Form in the Novels of Doris Lessing*.

9. See Sandra Singer's review of Shadia S. Fahim's *Doris Lessing: Sufi Equilibrium and the form of the Novel. Doris Lessing Newsletter*. Vol 19 #1 (Winter, 1998).

Chapter 3

1. A contradictory view is expressed by David Cowart, who stresses that Pynchon is aware that "entropy can be applied to a society only by analogy." It seems to this writer that both positions are correct, for Pynchon is intent on the actual laws as well as their analogical implications.

2. "...but only Basher and his wingman saw it, droning across in front of the fiery leagues of face, the eyes, which went towering for miles, shifting to follow their flight, the irises red as embers fairing through yellow to white.... (151)

3. "...here's a Brocken-specter, someone's, something's shadow project from out here in the bright sun and dearkening sky...: (759)

4. Molly Hite describes it as "...the ontological equivalent of Gödel's theorem." (123)

5. This repeats Pirate Prentice's frightened speculation at the opening of the novel "What if it should hit *exactly*—ahh,no—for a split second you'd have to feel the very point, with the terrible mass above, strike the top of the skull...." (7)

Chapter 4

1. Portions of the section on John Fowles' *A Maggot* are extracted from a paper entitled "Maggots, Tropes, and Metafictional Challenge: John Fowles' *A Maggot*" which was read at the Science Fiction Research Association 1993 Convention at Reno, Nevada.
2. Quoted by David Porush in *The Soft Machine*. New York: Methuen, 1985. p. 113.
3. This theme has been a frequent one in science fiction, as, for example, in A.C. Clarke's *Childhood's End* (1953) and J. G. Ballard's "The Watch-towers" (1962).
4. Durrell is quoting from Petronius' great biting erotic satire, *The Satyricon*.
5. Including "Freeforall," *Toronto Star*, Sept. 20, 1986; "Homelanding," *The Norton Book of Science Fiction* ed. U. Le Guin and Brian Attebery, New York: Norton, 1990. p. 794–96.
6. Madge Piercy. *He, She and It*. New York: Ballantine, 1991. p. 431.
7. The neutron bomb has existed since the 1970s but this interpretation of its effects represents its supporters' view of the weapon's capability.

Chapter 5

1. Brian W. Aldiss. *The Billion Year Spree*. London: Weidenfeld & Nicholson, 1973, p. 284.
2. "In the dispute over the best definition of s.f., Heinlein casts his ballot for Reginald Bretnor's (paraphrased): '(Fiction) in which the author shows awareness of the nature and importance of the human activity known as the scientific method, shows equal awareness of the great body of human knowledge already collected through that activity, and takes into account in his stories the effects and possbile future effects on human beings of scientific method and scientific fact.'" ex. Damon Knight. *In Search of Wonder*. Chicago: Advent, 1956, p. 5: "A good science fiction story is a story with a human problem, and a human solution, which would not have happened at all without its science content." Theodore Sturgeon quoted in James Blish. "On Science Fiction Criticism." ex. Thomas Clareson. *SF: The Other Side of Realism*. Bowling Green: Bowling Green State University Popular Press, 1971, p. 167.
3. Kingsley Amis. *New Maps of Hell*. London: Four Square Books, 1961, pp. 110–111.
4. "It's wonderful to see Le Guin coming home to her sfnal roots, after wandering in the wilderness of Shobies, *Always Coming Home*, and other swelled-head literary foolishness. Let's keep Le Guin in the gutter where she belongs! 'Old Music' (1999) demonstrates—if there remain any doubters—that Le Guin is as good a story-teller as anyone working now, in or out of the gutter, er, *genre*. And a *whole* lot better than the lit'ry crowd she's wisely dumped." Peter D. Tillman. "'Old Music & the Slave Women' & Two stories by Ursula K. Le Guin:

35 years of Hainish future history." <tillman@aztec.asu.edu>, 1999. "The result is not a novel so much as a cult-in-a-box, and readers might well expect a board game and a rock video to be next on the Kesh agenda." Brian D. Johnson. "Artifacts from the End of the Rainbow." *Maclean's Magazine* vol. 98, no. 44 (Nov. 4, 1985), p. 72.

5. *Confessions of a Crap Artist*, 1975.

6. By date of writing: *Valis*, 1978: *The Divine Invasion*, 1980: *The Transmigration of Timothy Archer*, 1981.

7. Philip K. Dick. *Valis*. New York: Bantam, 1981, p. 156. "'Philip' means 'Horselover' in Greek, lover of horses. 'Fat' is the German translation of 'Dick.'"

8. "For me, science fiction is above all a prospective form of narrative fiction; it is concerned with seeing the present in terms of the immediate future rather than the past." ex. "A Conversation with George MacBeth." *The New Science Fiction*. London: Hutchinson, 1969, p. 46.

9. With David Pringle and James Goddard, "J.G. Ballard's SF for Today." James Goddard and David Pringle eds. *J.G. Ballard: The First Twenty Years*. Hayes, Middlesex: Bran's Head Books, 1976. p. 25. (reprints *Science Fiction Monthly* interview of Oct. 1975 pp. 9–11).

10. J.G. Ballard. "Which Way to Inner Space?" *New Worlds Science Fiction*, No. 118 (May, 1962), pp. 2–3, 116–118.

11. Joanna Russ. *To Write Like a Woman*. Bloomington: Indiana U.P., 1995.

Chapter 6

1. Thomas Kuhn. *The Structure of Scientific Revolutions*. Chicago: University of Chicago, 1962.

Bibliography

Ackroyd, Peter. *First Light*. London: Hamish Hamilton, 1989.
Adams, Henry. *The Education of Henry Adams*. With a New Introd. by D.W. Brogan. Boston: Houghton Mifflin, 1961, c. 1918.
Aldiss, Brian W. *The Billion Year Spree*. London: Weidenfield & Nicholson, 1973.
Amis, Kingsley. *The Alteration*. London: Cape, 1976.
_____. *The Anti-Death League*. London: Victor Gollancz, 1966.
_____. *New Maps of Hell*. London: Four Square Books, 1961.
Atwood, Margaret. *The Handmaid's Tale*. Toronto: McClelland and Stewart, 1985.
Barnes, Julian. *Staring at the Sun*. Toronto: Random House, 1987.
Baudrillard, Jean. "Two Essays." *Science Fiction Studies* 18, no. 3 (1991): 309–320. (translated Arthur B. Evans).
Beckett, Samuel. *Molloy, Malone Dies, The Unnamable*. London: Clader and Boyars, 1959.
Boyd, William. *Brazzaville Beach*. New York: Viking, 1990.
Bukatman, Scott. *Terminal Identity*. Durham: Duke University Press, 1993.
_____. "Postcards from the Posthuman Solar System." *Science Fiction Studies* 18, no. 3 (1991): 343–357.
Burgess, Anthony. *A Clockwork Orange*. New York: Norton, 1963.
_____. *The End of the World News*. London: Penguin, 1983.
Carey, Peter. *The Unusual Life of Tristan Smith*. Toronto: Vintage Canada, 1996.
Carter, Angela. *Heroes and Villains*. Harmondsworth: Penguin, 1969.
Clareson, Thomas, ed. *SF: The Other Side of Realism*. Bowling Green: Bowling Green State University Popular Press, 1971.
Cowart, David. *Thomas Pynchon: The Art of Allusion*. Carbondale: Southern Illinois University Press, 1980.
Crichton, Len. *The Andromeda Strain*. New York: Dell, 1969.
_____. *The Terminal Man*. New York: Bantam, 1973.
Csicsery-Ronay, Istvan. "Introduction: Postmodernism's SF/SF's Postmodernism." *Science Fiction Studies* 18, no. 3 (1991): 305–308.
_____. "The SF of Theory: Baudrillard and Haraway." *Science Fiction Studies* 18, no. 3 (1991): 387–404.

_____. "We're Not in Kansas Anymore: On Naivete in SF and Criticism." *Science Fiction Studies*. vol. 24, pt. 1, #71 (March, 1997), 93–108.
Dalgleish, David. "Naive Versus Postmodern Criticism: an Exchange." *Science Fiction Studies*. vol. 24, pt. 1, #71 (March, 1997), 79–92.
Delany, Samuel R. *The American Shore*. Elizabethtown, N.Y.: Dragon Press, 1978.
_____. *Dhalgren*. New York: Bantam, 1975.
_____. *The Jewel-Hinged Jaw*. Elizabethtown, N.Y.: Dragon Press, 1977.
_____. *The Terminal Man*. New York: Bantam, 1973.
DeLillo, Don. *White Noise*. New York: Penguin, 1985.
_____. *The Names*. New York: Vintage, 1989. (First published 1982 by Knopf, New York.)
_____. *Mao II*. New York: Viking, 1991.
_____. *Libra*. New York: Viking, 1988.
Dick, Philip K(indred). *Confessions of a Crap Artist*. New York: Timescape Books, 1975.
_____. *The Divine Invasion*. New York: Timescape Books, 1981.
_____. *The Transmigration of Timothy Archer*. New York: Timescape Books, 1982.
_____. *Valis*. New York: Bantam, 1981.
Draine, Betsy. *Substance Under Pressure: Artistic Coherence and Evolving Form in the Novels of Doris Lessing*. Madison: Univ. of Wisconsin. 1983.
Durrell, Lawrence. *The Revolt of Aphrodite*. London: Faber & Faber: 1974. (First published as *Tunc* [1968] and *Numquam* [1970]). Note that page numbers recommence at 11 in *Numquam*, the second volume in *The Revolt of Aphrodite*.
Ebert, Teresa L. "The Convergence of Postmodern Innovative Fiction and Science Fiction." *Poetics Today*. Vol 1:4 (Summer, 1980), 91–104.
The Encyclopedia of Science Fiction. ed. John Clute and Peter Nicholls. New York: St. Martin's Press, 1993.
Enright, D. J. "Shivery Games." *The New York Review of Books* (July 31, 1969). pp. 22–24.
Fowles, John. *A Maggot*. New York: Little, Brown, 1985.
_____. *The Magus*. New York: Dell, 1978.
Golding, William. *The Inheritors*. London: Faber & Faber, 1955.
Gordimer, Nadine. *A Sport of Nature*. New York: Penguin, 1988.
Hayles, N. Katherine et al. "In Response to Jean Baudrillard." *Science Fiction Studies* 18, no. 3 (1991): 321–329.
Heller, Joseph. *Catch-22*. New York: Dell, 1961.
Hite, Molly. *Ideas of Order in the Novels of Thomas Pynchon*. Columbus: Ohio State University Press, 1983.
Hoban, Russell. *Riddley Walker*. London: Cape, 1980.
Hume, Kathryn. *Pynchon's Mythography: An Approach to Gravity's Rainbow*. Carbondale: Southern Illinois University Press, 1987.
Huxley, Aldous. *Antic Hay*. London: Chatto & Windus, 1923.
_____. *Brave New World*. London: Chatto & Windus, 1932.
_____. *Point Counter Point*. London: Chatto & Windus, 1928.
James, P.D. *The Children of Men*. Harmondsworth: Penguin, 1992.
Jameson, Frederic. "Towards a New Awareness of Genre." *Science Fiction Studies*. vol. 9, pt. 3, #28 (Nov. 1982), 322–324.

Johnson, Brian D. "Artifacts from the End of the Rainbow." *Maclean's Magazine*. vol. 98, no. 44 (Nov. 4, 1985), p. 72.
Kent, Thomas. *Interpretation and Genre*. Lewisburg, PA: Bucknell University Press, 1986.
Knapp, Mona. *Doris Lessing*. New York: Ungar, 1984.
Knight. Damon. *In Search of Wonder*. Chicago: Advent, 1965.
LeGuin, Ursula K. *Always Coming Home*. New York: Harper, 1985.
_____. *The Beginning Place*. New York: Harper, 1982.
_____. *The Dispossessed*. New York: Avon, 1975.
_____. *The Left Hand Of Darkness*. New York: Ace Books, 1976.
_____. *Malefrena*. New York: Berkley, 1979.
_____. *Orsinian Tales*. New York: Bantam, 1977.
_____. *Searoad: Chronicles of Klatsand*. New York: Avon, 1993.
Lem, Stanislaw. *The Chain of Chance*. New York: Jove, 1979.
_____. *The Cyberiad*. New York: Avon, 1976.
_____. *The Investigation*. New York: Avon, 1976.
_____. *The Invincible*. New York: Ace, 1973.
_____. *Solaris*. London: Arrow, 1973.
Lessing, Doris. "An Ancient Way to a New Freedom." *The Elephant in the Dark*. Ed. Leonard Lewin. New York: Dutton, 1976.
_____. "Ant's Eye View: A Review of *The Soul of the White Ant*. by Eugène Marais." *New Statesman*. (Jan 29, 1971) as reprinted in *A Small Personal Voice*. ed. Paul Schlueter. New York: Knopf, 1974.
_____. *Briefing for a Descent into Hell*. London: Cape, 1971.
_____. *The Four-Gated City*. London: MacGibbon & Kee, 1969.
_____. *The Making of the Representative for Planet 8*. London: Cape, 1982.
_____. *The Marriages Between Zones Three, Four, and Five*. Cape, 1980.
_____. *The Memoirs of a Survivor*. London: Octagon, 1974.
_____. *A Proper Marriage*. St. Albans, England.: Panther, 1966.
_____. *Re: Colonised Planet 5, Shikasta*. London: Granada, 1980. (first published 1979).
_____. "Report on the Threatened City." *The Story of a Non-Marrying Man, and other stories*. London: Cape, 1972. (Originally published in *Playboy* (Nov. 1971), pp. 149–186.
_____. *The Sentimental Agents in the Voylen Empire*. London: Cape, 1983.
_____. *The Sirian Experiments*. London: Cape, 1981.
_____. *The Summer before the Dark*. London: Cape, 1973.
_____. "Vonnegut's Responsibility." *New York Times Book Review* (Feb. 4, 1973), reprinted in *A Small Personal Voice*. ed. Paul Schlueter. New York: Knopf, 1974.
_____. "Doris Lessing on Feminism, Communism and 'Space Fiction.'" Interviewed by Lesley Hazleton. *New York Times Magazine* 131 (July 25, 1982), pp. 20–21, 26–28.
_____, and Florence Howe. "A Conversation with Doris Lessing." (1966) reprinted in Pratt, Annis and I.S. Dembo. *Doris Lessing: Critical Studies*. Madison: University of Wisconsin, 1974. pp. 1–19.
_____, and Jonah Raskin. "Doris Lessing at Stony Brook: An Interview." *New American Review*. New York: New American Library, no. 8 (Jan. 1970), pp. 166–179.

Littler, Glenn, and Graham Littler, eds. *A Dictionary of Mathematics*. London: Harper, Row, 1984.
Luckhurst, Roger. "Border Policing: Postmodernism and SF." *Science Fiction Studies* vol. 18, pt. 3 #55 (1991): 358–366.
McCaffrey, Anne. *The Dragonriders of Pern*. Garden City, N.J.: Nelson, Doubleday, 1978.
_____. *The Ship Who Sang*. New York: Walker, 1969.
Malmgren, Carl D. *Worlds Apart*. Bloomington: Indiana UP, 1991.
Marlowe, Christopher. *The Tragical History of Doctor Faustus*. ex. *Christopher Marlowe: Five Plays*. ed. Havelock Ellis, New York: Mermaid, 1956.
McElroy, Joseph. *The Letter Left to Me*. New York: Knopf, 1988.
_____. *Plus*. New York: Knopf, 1977.
_____. *A Smuggler's Bible*. London: Deutsch, 1968.
_____. *Women and Men*. New York: Knopf, 1987.
Nadeau, Robert L. "Readings From the New Book of Nature: Physics and Pynchon's *Gravity's Rainbow*." *Studies in the Novel* vol. 11 no. 4 (Winter, 1979). pp. 454–471.
Oates, Carol. "Last Children of Violence," *Saturday Review of Literature* 52 (17 May 1969), p. 48.
The Oxford English Dictionary. Compact Edition. Oxford: OUP, 1971. vol. 2.
The Oxford Dictionary of Quotations. 2nd Edition. Oxford: OUP, 1953.
Percy, Walker. *Love in the Ruins*. New York: Ballantine, 1971.
_____. *The Thanatos Syndrome*. New York: Ballantine, 1987.
Piercy, Marge. *Dance the Eagle to Sleep*. New York: Fawcett, 1970.
_____. *He, She and It*. New York: Fawcett, 1991.
_____. *Woman on the Edge of Time*. New York: Fawcett, 1976.
Plater, William M. *The Grim Phoenix: Reconstructing Thomas Pynchon*. Bloomington: Indiana University Press, 1978.
Pratt, Annis, and I.S. Dembo, eds. *Doris Lessing: Critical Studies*. Madison: Univ. of Wisconsin, 1974.
Priest, Christopher. *The Affirmation*. London: VGSF Classic, 1988 (first published 1981).
_____. *A Dream of Wessex*. London: Abacus, 1987 (first published 1977).
_____. *The Glamour*. London: Cape, 1984.
Puschmann-Nalenz, Barbara. *Science Fiction and Postmodern Fiction*. New York: Peter Lang, 1992.
Pynchon, Thomas. *The Crying of Lot 49*. New York: Bantam, 1966.
_____. "Entropy." *Slow Learner*. Boston: Little, Brown, 1984 [first published *Kenyon Review*, Spring 1960].
_____. *Gravity's Rainbow*. New York: Viking, 1973.
_____. "Low-Lands." *Slow Learner*. Boston: Little, Brown, 1984 [first published in *New World Writing 16*, March 1960].
_____. *Mason & Dixon*. New York: Holt, 1997.
_____. "The Secret Integration." *Slow Learner*. Boston: Little, Brown, 1984 [first published in December, 1964].
_____. *V*. London: Cape, 1963.
_____. *Vineland*. New York: Little, Brown, 1990.

_____. "Under the Rose." *Slow Learner.* Boston: Little, Brown, 1984. [first published in The Noble Savage #3, May, 1961].
Russ, Joanna. *The Female Man.* Boston: Beacon Press, 1986 (first published 1975).
_____. *We Who Are About To....* Boston: Gregg Press, 1978 (first published 1975).
Scarry, Elaine. *The Body in Pain: The Making and Unmaking of the World.* Oxford: Oxford University Press, 1985.
Scholes, Robert. *Structural Fabulation.* Notre Dame, Ind.: Notre Dame UP, 1975.
The Science Fiction Encyclopedia. ed. Peter Nicholls. New York: Doubleday, 1979.
Seed, David. *The Fictional Labyrinths of Thomas Pynchon.* Iowa City: University of Iowa Press, 1988.
Simak, Clifford. *The Goblin Reservation.* New York: Berkley, 1968.
Sterling, Bruce. "Slipstream." *Science Fiction Eye* 1:5 (July, 1989): 77–80.
Strehle, Susan. *Fiction in the Quantum Universe.* Chapel Hill: University of North Carolina Press, 1992.
Suvin, Darko. *Metamorphoses of Science Fiction.* New Haven: Yale UP, 1979.
Tevis, Walter. *The Steps of the Sun.* Garden City, NJ: Doubleday, 1983.
Theroux, Paul. *O-Zone.* New York: Ballantine, 1986.
Tiger, Virginia. "Candid Shot: Lessing in New York City, April 1 and 2, 1984." *Doris Lessing Newsletter.* vol. 8, #2 (Fall, 1984), p 5–6.
_____, and Claire Sprague, eds. *Critical Essays on Doris Lessing.* Boston: G.K. Hall, 1986.
Todorov, Tzvetan. *The Fantastic: A Structural Approach to a Literary Genre.* Translated from the French by Richard Howard; with a foreword by Robert Scholes. Ithaca, N.Y: Cornell University Press, 1975.
Updike, John. *Toward the End of Time.* New York: Knopf, 1997.
Uvarov, E.B. and D.R. Chapman. *A Dictionary of Science.* Harmondsworth: Penguin, 1979.
Vonnegut, Kurt, Jr. *Breakfast of Champions.* New York: Delta, 1973.
_____. *Cat's Cradle.* New York: Dell, 1963.
_____. *Deadeye Dick.* New York: Dell, 1982.
_____. *Galapagos.* New York: Dell, 1985.
_____. *God Bless You, Mr. Rosewater.* New York: Dell, 1965.
_____. *Hocus Pocus.* New York: Berkley, 1990.
_____. *Jailbird.* New York: Delacorte, 1979.
_____. *Palm Sunday.* New York: Dell, 1981.
_____. *The Sirens of Titan,* New York: Dell, 1959.
_____. *Slapstick.* New York: Dell, 1976.
_____. *Slaughterhouse Five.* New York: Dell, 1969.
Wells, Herbert George. *The History of Mr. Polly.* London: Nelson, 1910.
_____. *The Island of Dr. Moreau.* London: W. Heinemann, 1896.
_____. *Tono-Bungay.* Dunfield: New York, 1909.
_____. *The War in the Air.* London: Nelson, 1908.
Wordsworth, William. "Preface to the Lyrical Ballads." (1800). *Anthology of Romanticism.* (3rd ed.) Ed. Ernest Bernbaum. New York: Ronald Press, 1948.
Zola, Emile. *The Naturalist Novel.* ed. Maxwell David Geismar. Montreal: Harvest House, 1964.

Index

Acker, Kathy: *Empire of the Senseless* 171
Ackroyd, Peter: *First Light* 116, 131–2
The Affirmation (Priest) 173–4
Aldiss, Brian 159, 172
aliens 81, 160; contact with 70, 108–9, 141–3, 146, 180; observations by 35–7, 115
allegory 42, 55, 174, 181
The Alteration (Amis) 164–8
Always Coming Home (LeGuin) 177–9
Amis, Kingsley 6, 128, 172; *The Alteration* 164–8; *The Anti-Death League* 116, 126–7, 164; *New Maps of Hell* 164
The Andromeda Strain (Crichton) 174
anthropology 100, 130, 176
The Anti-Death League (Amis) 116, 126–7, 164
apocalypse 40, 60, 61, 195n5; fear of 59, 148; nuclear 28; post- 100, 150–3, 158
archeology 131
archetype 51
Armageddon *see* apocalypse
Asimov, Isaac 46; *Fantastic Voyage* 195n4
astronomy 131–2
Atwood, Margaret 6, 9, 21, 194n9; *The Blind Assassin* 171; *The Handmaid's Tale* 134–40
author 106; intentions of 102, 111, 176; and narrative 68, 77, 173

Bacon, Francis 27–8
Ballard, J.G. 6, 20, 176, 186; *The Atrocity Exhibition* 182; *Concrete Island* 181; *Crash* 181; *The Crystal World* 181; *The Day of Creation* 181; *The Drought* 181; *The Drowned World* 181; *High-Rise* 181; *The Wind from Nowhere* 181
Barnes, Julian 6; *Staring at the Sun* 21, 100, 102–6, 115
Barthes, Roland 45
Beckett, Samuel 17, 58, 72, 159, 173, 175; *The Unnamable* 170
Benford, Gregory 15
Bentley, Eric 42
Bible, Judeo-Christian 138–9
Bildungsroman 30, 54–5, 169, 194n3
biology 72, 84, 117, 131, 150
Bishop, Michael 186
Blish, James 42, 196n2
borders, generic: as defining line 13–17, 23, 40–2, 189; and freedom 41, 52, 53, 99; overlap in 8, 19–20, 172, 185–6
Boyd, William: *Brazzaville Beach* 127–9
Boyle, T.C.: *A Friend of Earth* 171
Brave New World (Huxley) 18, 133, 142
Brazzaville Beach (Boyd) 127–9
Breakfast of Champions (Vonnegut) 162
Brecht, Bertolt 19, 42
Bretnor, Reginald 196n2
Briefing for a Descent into Hell (Lessing) 35, 37–8
Brin, David 15, 187
Brooke-Rose, Christine: *Amalgamemnon* 171; *Verbivore* 171; *Xorander* 171

Burgess, Anthony 6, 21; *A Clockwork Orange* 146–7; *Earthly Powers* 166; *The End of the World News* 100, 146, 147–9
Burroughs, William F. 6

Cadigan, Pat 187
calculus 67, 91–2; and differentiation 85–6, 87, 93; and integration 81, 85–6; and rocket 75–6, 95
Canopus in Argos: Archives (Lessing) 35, 40–2, 43, 52–3, 55–6; see also *Shikasta*
Carey, Peter: *The Unusual Life of Tristan Smith* 168–9
Carnell, Ted 9
Carter, Angela 6, 21; *Heroes and Villains* 150–3
A Case of Conscience (Blish) 42
Cat's Cradle (Vonnegut) 160–1
The Chain of Chance (Lem) 174–5
chaos 61, 65–7, 73–4, 78, 87–92, 129
Chardin, Teilhard de 152
Chaucer, Geoffrey 137
chemistry 69, 73, 97
Chesterton, G.K. 165
Childhood's End (Clarke) 42, 51
The Children of Men (James) 149–50
Children of Violence (Lessing) 26–8, 30, 55, 99; see also *The Four-Gated City*
Christ see religion
church see religion
Clarke, Arthur C. 110; *Childhood's End* 42, 51
A Clockwork Orange (Burgess) 146–7
closure 75, 136; lack of 112, 68, 174, 178; satisfaction of 10, 113–4
Clute, John 12
cognition 9, 19–21, 30, 31
colonialism 50–1, 168; see also imperialism
communication 151; and entropy 62–3, 91; theory 60, 70
Communism 28, 42, 48
computer 92, 100, 103–6, 118, 119, 131
Conquest, Robert 172
Conrad, Joseph 17, 175; *Heart of Darkness* 143
conspiracy theory 90, 92
control 95–6
cosmography 49, 56, 131

cosmology 20, 115
Cowart, David 58, 195n1
Crichton, Michael: *The Andromeda Strain* 174; *The Terminal Man* 174
Crispin, Edmund 175
The Crying of Lot 49 (Pynchon): entropy in 64–5, 90–1; language in 79, 82–3; search for meaning in 68, 74, 77–8; technology in 70, 73
Cyborg see robot

Dahlgren (Delany) 182–3
Dali, Salvador 84
Dance the Eagle to Sleep (Piercy) 153–4
Deadeye Dick (Vonnegut) 159, 162, 163
death 69, 90, 161–2, 179, 185; contemplation of 102–3, 132; inevitability of 64–5, 67, 122–6, 170; and meaning 75, 105, 126–7; technology of 84–5, 98
deconstruction 53, 59, 106, 152, 186, 187
Delany, Samuel R. 10, 176, 186, 193n1; *The American Shore* 182; *Dahlgren* 182–3; *The Jewel-Hinged Jaw* 182; *Starboard Wine* 182
DeLillo, Don 6, 127; *Ratner's Star* 171; *Mao II* 121; *The Names* 121; *White Noise* 116, 121–6
Derrida, Jacques 7, 8
Descartes, René 169
Dick, Philip K. 6, 20, 176, 186; *The Divine Invasion* 179, 180; *The Man in the High Castle* 164; *The Transmigration of Timothy Archer* 179; *Valis* 179–81
disorder see chaos
The Dispossessed (LeGuin) 176–7
distopia 100, 133–59, 178–9
The Divine Invasion (Dick) 179, 180
Dorsett, Richard 12
Dragonriders of Pern (McCaffrey) 19
Draine, Betsy 37, 41–3, 45, 194n3
The Drowned World (Ballard) 181
Durkheim, Emile 152
Durrell, Lawrence 6, 21, 121; *The Alexandria Quartet* 116; *The Revolt of Aphrodite* 116–21, 126, 190

Ebert, Teresa L. 10–11
Eco, Umberto: *Foucault's Pendulum* 171

Index

Effinger, George Alex 6, 176, 186
Einstein, Albert 22
electronics 70, 83–4; *see also* technology
Ellison, Harlan 176; *Dangerous Visions* 186
The Encyclopedia of Science Fiction 12–13, 183, 185
The End of the World News (Burgess) 100, 146, 147–9
Enright, D.J. 34
entropy 60–8, 74, 90–1, 195n1; *see also* physics, thermodynamics
"Entropy" (Pynchon) 60–3, 79–80
estrangement 19, 21, 31
ethnology 127
evolution 29–30, 33, 51, 54–6; *see also* Sufism
extra-text 6–7, 13, 15

fables 41, 48
Fabulation 12–13, 51
fairy tales 42
fantastic literature 43, 56, 97, 172, 177; and span 42, 151, 174; tradition of 41, 59, 124
Farmer, Philip José 46, 159, 186
Federman, Raymond: *The Twofold Vibration* 171
The Female Man (Russ) 183–4, 185, 190
feminism 28, 137, 152, 157, 183–4, 190
fetish 71, 90
Fiedler, Leslie: *Love and Death in the American Novel* 151
First Light (Ackroyd) 116, 131–2
Fleming, Ian 73, 165
folktales 177
formalism 5
The Four-Gated City (Lessing) 27, 31, 35, 99, 100; influence of 37, 38, 39, 40, 55; madness in 32–4, 43
Fowles, John 6; *Daniel Martin* 113; *The French Lieutenant's Woman* 113; *A Maggot* 21, 100, 106–14, 115; *The Magus* 17
Freud, Sigmund 28, 43, 119–20, 147–8, 149
frontier novel 143
future 30, 163, 169, 100; and distopia 114–15, 133–9, 143, 153–9, 178–9; projections 101–2, 171; truth in 25, 33, 103–6; *see also* novum: projective

Game Theory 128
Gass, Gunter: *The Tin Drum* 168
genre: crossover 10; definition of 9, 172, 193n1; detective fiction 5, 42, 149–50, 172, 175; expectations of 6–8, 16, 134, 186–9; integration of 106; study of 6, 23, 41–2, 149, 182, 188; western 5; *see also* Bildungsroman; borders, generic; mainstream fiction; science fiction; span fiction
geometry 90
Gibson, William 156, 187
The Glamour (Priest) 173–4
God *see* religion
Godard, Jean-Luc: *Alphaville* 151
Gödel, Kurt 67
Gödel's Theorem 67–8, 195n4
Golding, William: *The Inheritors* 100, 116, 129–31
Gordimer, Nadine: *A Sport of Nature* 100–2, 106, 115
Gothicism 151–2
gravity 67, 75, 93–4
Gravity's Rainbow (Pynchon) 15, 70, 97, 116; entropy in 64, 65–8; language in 83–5; rocket in 66–7, 69, 71–6, 83–4, 92–6; sciences in 60, 69–70, 72; search for meaning in 68, 78, 98; structure of 58, 74–6
The Grim Phoenix (Plater) 67, 76

hadrons 115
The Handmaid's Tale (Atwood) 134–40
He, She and It (Piercy) 155–7
Heinlein, Robert 9, 46, 175, 196n2
Heisenberg, Werner 22
Heller, Joseph, 17, 58; *Catch 22* 18
Herbert, Frank 10
hero 59, 93
Hirsch, E.D. 8
history 69, 137; alternate 164–5; as context 101–2, 106–7, 111; levels of 82, 88–9
Hite, Molly 60, 68, 73, 75, 195n4
Hoban, Russell: *Riddley Walker* 158–9
Hocus Pocus (Vonnegut) 159, 162
holocaust *see* apocalypse
Howe, Florence 30

humanism 74, 80, 176; and science 58, 82–3, 85–7, 121
humanity 56, 130; characteristics of 69, 75, 134, 160; and meaning 78, 105, 157, 130–1, 169–71; mechanization of 89–90, 98, 120–1; and science 93–5, 116–17, 119, 124–5, 128, 131–2
Hume, Catherine 59, 86–7
Huxley, Aldous 18; *After Many a Summer* 18; *Antic Hay* 18; *Brave New World* 18, 133, 142

identity 59, 77, 95
illusion 84
imagery 57, 80
imperialism 52, 54; see also colonialism
individuality 137, 144, 194n3
information theory 65, 80, 123–4; see also communication: theory
The Inheritors (Golding) 100, 116, 129–31
insanity see madness
Interpretation and Genre: The Role of Generic Perception in the Study of Narrative Texts (Kent) 6–7
intertextuality 137–9
The Investigation (Lem) 174–5
irony 8, 21, 99, 106, 139, 150, 164
Iser, Wolfgang 8

James, Henry 17, 175
James, P.D. 6; *The Children of Men* 149–50
Jameson, Frederic 8
Jauss, Hans Robert 8
Joyce, James 58, 59
Jung, Carl Gustav 17, 28, 43

Kent, Thomas 6–7, 8, 13
Kesey, Ken: *Sailor Song* 171
Keyes, Daniel 10
Knapp, Mona 42
Kornbluth, Cyril: *The Space Merchants* 134
Kress, Nancy 15, 187
Kubrick, Stanley: *2001* 169
Kuhn, Thomas 191

Laing, R.D. 28–30, 33, 38, 40, 43; see also madness

language, 57, 120, 173; and context 140, 158; and science 72, 79–85, 90–2, 129, 169–71, 189, 190; styles of 53, 97, 134–6, 177
Lawrence, D.H. 17
The Left Hand of Darkness (LeGuin) 21–2, 159, 176–7
legend 151
LeGuin, Ursula K. 6, 10, 20, 185, 186; *Always Coming Home* 177–9; *The Beginning Place* 177; *The Dispossessed* 176–7; *The Left Hand of Darkness* 21–2, 159, 176–7; *Malafrina* 177; "Old Music" 196n4; *The Orsinian Tales* 177; *Searoad: Chronicles of Klatsand* 177
Lem, Stanislaw 6, 21, 42, 134, 186; *The Chain of Chance* 174–5; *The Cyberiad* 174; *The Investigation* 174–5; *The Invincible* 174; *Solaris* 174
Lessing, Doris 6, 21, 23; "The Antheap" 31; *Briefing for a Descent into Hell* 35, 37–8; *Canopus in Argos: Archives* 35, 40–2, 43, 52–3, 55–6; *Children of Violence* 26–8, 30, 55, 99; *The Elephant in the Dark* 29; *The Fifth Child* 99; *The Golden Notebook* 26, 28; *The Good Terrorist* 99; *The Making of the Representative for Planet 8* 50–1, 54–5, 56; *The Marriages Between Zones Three, Four, and Five* 48–9, 51, 52, 54, 56; *The Memoirs of a Survivor* 35, 39–40; *A Proper Marriage* 26–7; "Report on the Threatened City" 35–7, 38, 40; *The Sentimental Agents in the Volyen Empire* 53–5; *Shikasta* 35, 39, 40, 44–8, 49, 51, 54–5; *The Sirian Experiments* 43–4, 46, 49–51, 52, 54; *The Summer Before the Dark* 35, 38–9; use of science fiction by 25, 33–5, 98–9; "Vonnegut's Responsibility" 30–1; writing style of 26–31, 40–7, 55–7; see also *The Four-Gated City*
Lévi Strauss, Claude 152
Lightman, Alan: *Einstein's Dreams* 171; *Good Benito* 171
love 93
Love in the Ruins (Percy) 157–8
Luckhurst, Roger 8

macrocosm 43

Index

madness 42, 43, 162, 179, 181; as alternate reality 28–9, 174; as different understanding 32–3, 38; understanding of 37, 154–5
A Maggot (Fowles) 21, 100, 106–14, 115
The Magus (Fowles) 17
mainstream fiction 12, 17, 154, 172; aspects of 20–1, 133, 157, 177; boundaries of 13–14, 40, 99, 171, 183; characterization in 140, 147; science fiction elements in 5, 6, 115, 187; writers of 179, 186–8
The Making of the Representative for Planet 8 (Lessing) 50–1, 54–5, 56
Maoism 46
Marais, Eugène Neilen 31
marketing 16
Marlowe, Christopher 137–8
The Marriages Between Zones Three, Four, and Five (Lessing) 48–9, 51, 52, 54, 56
Marxism 20, 26, 46, 148, 149, 153; and historical perspective 27, 28, 37, 43
"Mason & Dixon" (Pynchon) 96, 97–8, 99
mathematics 127–9
McCaffrey, Anne: *Dragonriders of Pern* 19; *The Ship Who Sang* 169
McElroy, Joseph: *The Letter Left to Me* 169; *Plus* 15, 169–71; *A Smuggler's Bible* 169; *Women and Men* 169
meaning 43, 74, 76; and humanity 78, 105, 157, 130–1, 169–71; search for 68, 69, 70, 180
medicine 69–70, 81, 85, 124–5, 154–5
The Memoirs of a Survivor (Lessing) 35, 39–40
Merill, Judith 9, 12
metafiction 136, 177–80; and narrative 56, 183–4; and novum 173, 185; and science fiction 11, 100, 106–8, 112–14, 148–9, 185
metaphor 70, 170, 177–8; science as 72, 82, 85–96, 126–7, 144
metaphysics 41, 42, 43, 56, 158; and death 123, 162, 179; *see also* religion, spirituality
metonymy 139, 144–6, 189
microcosm 43, 56
middle ground *see* span fiction
modernism 5, 17–18, 175

Moorcock, Michael 9; *Ecce Homo* 42
More, Sir Thomas 168; *Utopia* 133
Morris, William: *News from Nowhere* 106
mundane fiction 193n1
Murdoch, Iris 17, 58, 72, 175
Murphy's Law 68, 195n4
music 62–3, 72–3, 80
myth 19, 48, 55, 59, 150–2, 157

Nadeau, Robert 60, 73, 75
Nagata, Linda 15, 187
narrative 20, 46–50, 57, 164; and belief 111–12, 194n10; metafictional 56, 183–4; and structure 10, 74, 76, 106, 152–3; time in 128, 197n8; voice 76–9, 173; *see also* narrator
narrator 39, 44–5, 158; alien 35–7; ambiguous 102, 107, 185; author as 173, 179–81; first person 115, 134–6, 145, 147, 149, 162; multiple 177, 184; omniscient 27, 77, 78, 111, 128, 149, 164; and reader 52, 78–9, 114, 136, 147; *see also* narrative
naturalism 5, 56, 114, 168, 177, 185
nature 76, 92, 111, 178
New Wave 9
New Worlds 9
Niven, Larry 15
novum 26, 56, 100; believability of 175–6, 180, 184, 187, 190; projective 22, 101–2, 103–6, 115, 134, 137; in science fiction 19–20, 30, 33; in span fiction 21, 173, 174, 176, 185
Numquam see *The Revolt of Aphrodite* (Durrell)

O-Zone (Theroux) 140–3
Oates, Joyce Carol 27
objectivity 30–1, 42, 76; language of 35, 45, 54; and perspective 37, 38–9, 43, 48, 56
observation 76, 79
Oedipal complex *see* psychology: Freudian
Ondaatje, Michael: *Anil's Ghost* 171
Oppenheimer, Robert 161
order 92–3; *see also* chaos
Orwell, George: *1984* 133, 153
other 140

parables 20, 41, 150
paranoia 92, 95
parody 8, 20, 46–7; as narrative mode 21, 26, 99, 151; of science fiction 37–8, 160, 164, 173
particle theory 58
past 64, 106, 131
pastiche 8, 20, 173, 178, 190; postmodern 21, 148, 152
Percy, Walker: *Love in the Ruins* 157–8; *The Thanatos Syndrome* 157–8
perpetual motion 91
Persig, Robert: *Zen and the Art of Motorcycle Management* 171
"Persistence of Memory" (Dali) 84
philosophy 67
physics 60, 71–2, 83, 97, 115, 176; *see also* entropy, quantum mechanics, thermodynamics
Piercy, Marge 185; *Dance the Eagle to Sleep* 153–4; *He, She and It* 155–7; *Women on the Edge of Time* 129, 154–5, 157
Plater, William 60, 73, 77; *The Grim Phoenix* 67, 76
Player Piano (Vonnegut) 159
Plus (McElroy) 15, 169–71
poet 3, 6, 22
Pohl, Frederick: *The Space Merchants* 134
Point Counter Point (Huxley) 18
Poisson Distribution 73
postmodernism 6, 8, 150, 187; and pastiche 21, 148, 152
prefaces 7
present 25; *see also* future, past
preterition 59, 93, 95, 98
Priest, Christopher 6, 176, 186; *The Affirmation* 173–4; *A Dream of Wessex* 173; *The Glamour* 173–4
A Proper Marriage (Lessing) 26–7
psychology 97, 152, 173, 176, 181–2; Freudian 119–21, 145–6, 148, 175; operant conditioning 146–7; Pavlovian 66, 69, 71, 73, 96
psychotherapy 28
publishing 15–16, 25–6, 188
Pynchon, Thomas 6, 21, 23, 26, 126, 182, 195n1; "Entropy" 60–3, 79–80; "Low-Lands" 79; "Mason & Dixon" 96, 97–8, 99; "The Secret Integration" 80–1, 85–6; *Slow Learner* 57, 60; "The Small Rain" 72; structure of novels by 73–6, 86; "Under the Rose" 80; use of science by 57–9, 60–73, 98, 117, 125; *Vineland*, 57, 58, 63, 96–7, 99; writing style of 58–9, 68, 97, 99; *see also The Crying of Lot 49; Gravity's Rainbow; V*

quantum mechanics 76, 115; *see also* physics

Rand, Ayn: *Anthem* 133
Raskin, Jonah 30
rationalism 20
reader 37, 46, 100, 110; and communication 63–4, 85; connection with 27, 52, 77–9; and effect 102, 140, 170; and expectation 56, 65, 66, 68, 106, 134, 186–7; and genre 7, 16, 186–9; manipulation of 50, 55; and position 104, 111–12, 153, 161, 164, 168, 173, 176–7; role of 76, 81, 128, 179; and suspension of disbelief 21, 33, 112–13, 148, 159, 163, 173, 178–9; and uncertainty 109, 114, 130, 151–2
readerly text 45
realism 5, 26, 28, 41, 151; and modernism 17, 58, 169; objective 30–1; in span fiction 55–6, 148, 155; use of, 32–4, 37, 43, 160–1
reality 89, 179, 181; alternate 28–30, 37, 87, 130, 152, 173, 183; and fiction 26, 58, 59, 76, 136, 174; meaning of 43, 180; and metaphor 92, 169; and science 13, 72, 85, 129, 187; un– 106; understanding of 21–2, 34, 36, 38, 64, 68, 77, 151, 180
relativity 76, 79
religion 109–10, 111–12, 164–8, 179; *see also* metaphysics; spirituality
"Report on the Threatened City" (Lessing) 35–7, 38, 40
The Revolt of Aphrodite (Durrell) 116–21, 126, 190
Riddley Walker (Hoban) 158–9
Roberts, Keith: *Pavane* 165
Robinson, Kim Stanley 187
Robinson Crusoe (Defoe) 185
robot 70–1, 119, 120, 156–7, 162
romanticism 5, 152, 153–4, 190

Index

Rucker, Rudy 187
Russ, Joanna 176, 186; *The Female Man* 183–4, 185, 190; *We Who Are About To...* 183, 185
Russell, Mary Doria 42

Sartre, Jean-Paul 166
satire 162, 164, 183; of language 46, 53; and postmodernism 8; in science fiction 20, 173; as style 26, 96–7, 99, 158
Scarry, Elaine 27–8
Scholes, Robert 9–10, 13, 25
Schrödinger, Erwin 22
science 3, 132, 179; and humanity 93–5, 116–17, 119, 124–6, 128, 131–3; and language 57, 72, 79–85, 117, 123–4, 126, 129, 190; and metaphor 57, 59, 85–96, 126, 127; and rationality 20, 71; respect for 12, 13, 125, 163–4; and society 13, 58–9, 97–8, 113–14, 121, 167, 191; as subject in science fiction 11, 17–18, 45–6, 57, 60–73; as threat 166, 190; and truth 72, 190; and world view 5, 17–18, 22, 26, 57–60, 63, 68, 116, 174; *see also* technology
science fiction 5, 115, 153–4; believability in 106, 155, 161; characteristics of 19, 30–1, 36–7, 40–3, 56, 149, 182, 196n2, 197n8; characterization in 20, 28, 43, 100, 133–4, 163, 175–6; cyberpunk 8, 156, 187; epic 45–6, 56; and genre 5–6, 9–13, 23, 41–3, 53, 55, 151, 169, 171, 182, 186; and metafiction 11, 100, 106–8, 112–14, 148–9, 185; novum in 19–20, 30, 33; plots in 56, 162, 173, 178; readers of 112–13; relationship to span fiction 172, 175, 183
"The Secret Integration" (Pynchon) 80–1, 85–6
Seed, David 60, 63
selfhood 51
semiotics 7, 23
The Sentimental Agents in the Volyen Empire (Lessing) 53–5
Shah, Idries 29
Shakespeare, William 165–6
Shelley, Percy 166
Shikasta (Lessing) 35, 39, 40, 44–9, 51, 54–5

Simak, Clifford: *The Goblin Reservation* 19
The Sirens of Titan (Vonnegut) 160
The Sirian Experiments (Lessing) 43–4, 46, 49–51, 52, 54
Slaughterhouse-Five (Vonnegut) 161–2
slipstream 12
Slonczewsi, Joan 15, 185
sociobiology 135
sociology 152
Solaris (Lem) 42
solipsism 17, 72, 170
The Soul of the White Ant (Marais) 31
span fiction 39, 113, 117, 168; characteristics of 48, 150, 158–9; characterization in 95, 141–4, 147, 151–2, 175–6; complexity in 114–15, 121, 134, 169, 177, 180–1; as genre 13–17, 23–4, 171; humanity in 56, 157; novum in 21, 173, 174, 176, 190; relationship to mainstream writing 55, 58, 99–100, 140; relationship to science fiction 148, 164, 172–7, 189–90; writers of 20–2, 25–6, 41, 42, 99–100, 133–4, 171, 176, 181–2
The Sparrow (Russell) 42
speculative fiction 9, 12, 172, 175, 194n9; *see also* science fiction
spirituality 115; *see also* metaphysics; religion
A Sport of Nature (Gordimer) 100–2, 106, 115
Stapledon, Olaf 10; *First and Last Men* 41
Staring at the Sun (Barnes) 21, 100, 102–6, 115
step function 88–9
Stephenson, Neal 186
The Steps of the Sun (Tevis) 143–6
Sterling, Bruce 11–12, 187
Sterne, Laurence 59
stream of consciousness 20
Structural Fabulation (Scholes) 9–10
structuralism 182
structure 66, 73–6, 86, 93, 118, 162, 170
Sturgeon, Theodore 10, 162, 175, 196n2
subjectivity 42, 89, 90–1
Sufism 28–30, 33, 34, 37, 40, 43, 46, 50, 54–5
Sukenick, Ronald: *98.6* 171

The Summer Before the Dark (Lessing) 35, 38–9
surfiction 11
surrealism 26, 84, 181
Suvin, Darko 19–20, 21, 30, 31, 134
Swift, Graham: *First Light* 129
Swift, Jonathan 35–6, 163, 168
synaesthesia 80
systems 75, 80, 92; closed 67–8, 69–70, 76–9, 91

technology 5, 11, 110–11, 145; and art 17–18, 41; and culture 26, 72–3, 100, 125, 131–2, 143, 149, 168–9, 178, 191; dangers of 96–7, 142, 171; intrusive 116, 121–3, 154–5, 167; medical 85, 118, 174; and weapons 18, 49, 57, 98, 126–7, 156–7, 196n7; and worldview 57–8, 113; *see also* science
Tennyson, G.B. 194n3
The Terminal Man (Crighton) 174
Tevis, Walter: *The Man Who Fell to Earth* 146; *The Steps of the Sun* 143–6
The Thanatos Syndrome (Percy) 157–8
thermodynamics 60, 61, 67, 68, 71, 79, 91; *see also* entropy; physics
Theroux, Paul 6, 12; *The Mosquito Coast* 140; *O-Zone* 140–3
thought experiments 21–2, 23
time shifts 100, 136–7, 161–2, 164, 183; *see also* future; novum: projective; past
Todorov, Tzvetan 7, 41
transcendence 75, 115
transfiction 11
transgression 7, 23
The Transmigration of Timothy Archer (Dick) 179
truth 42, 64, 107, 111; and future 25, 33, 103–6; and history 33, 112; and science 72, 190
Tunc see *The Revolt of Aphrodite* (Durrell)
turbulence 128, 129

universe 60, 117–18; alternate 100, 164; death of 60, 61, 115; structure of 29, 65, 68, 74, 91

The Unusual Life of Tristan Smith (Carey) 168–9
Updike, John: *Toward the End of Time* 113, 114–15
utopia *see* distopia

V (Pynchon) 58, 73–4, 98; language in 79, 81–2, 87–90; science and technology in 63–4, 69–73; search for meaning in 68, 77
Valis (Dick) 179–81
Vineland (Pynchon) 57, 58, 63, 96–7, 99
Vonnegut, Kurt, Jr. 16, 21, 30–1, 46, 162–4; *Bluebeard* 159; *Breakfast of Champions* 162; *Cat's Cradle* 160–1; *Deadeye Dick* 159, 162, 163; *Galapagos* 162, 163; *God Bless You, Mr. Rosewater* 162; *Hocus Pocus* 159, 162; *Jailbird* 159, 162; *Mother Night* 159; *Player Piano* 159; *The Sirens of Titan* 160; *Slapstick* 162; *Slaughterhouse-Five* 161–2

Watson, Ian 6, 186
We Who Are About To... (Russ) 183, 185
Weber, Max 152
Weldon, Faye: *The Cloning of Joanna May* 171
Wells, H.G. 41; *The History of Mr. Polly* 18; *The Island of Dr. Moreau* 18; *The Time Machine* 133
White Noise (DeLillo) 116, 121–6
Wittgenstein, Ludwig 67; *Tractatus Logico-Philosophicus* 70
Woman on the Edge of Time (Piercy) 129, 154–5, 157
Woolf, Virginia 17, 58
Wordsworth, William: on science in literature 5, 58; on science in worldview 10, 13, 17, 20, 190; on writers 3, 6, 22, 132, 188
Wyndham, John 165

Yeats, W.B. 69

Zavarzadeh, Mas'ud 11
Zelazny, Roger 42

www.ingramcontent.com/pod-product-compliance
Lightning Source LLC
Chambersburg PA
CBHW032055300426
44116CB00007B/752